FOOTSTEPS TOWARD
PROFESSIONALISM

FOOTSTEPS TOWARD PROFESSIONALISM

THE DEVELOPMENT OF AN ADMINISTRATIVE
SERVICES PRACTICE OVER THE PAST
TWENTY-FIVE YEARS

Addresses and Articles by Joseph S. Glickauf

1948-1970

Library of Congress
Catalog Card No. 75-173085

This book contains addresses and articles by one of the leaders of the firm of Arthur Andersen & Co. A list of the volumes prepared in this manner follows:

Title	Author
Behind the Figures	Arthur Andersen
A Search for Fairness in Financial Reporting to the Public	Leonard Spacek
Footsteps Toward Professionalism	Joseph S. Glickauf

Foreword

THIS BOOK contains addresses and articles by Joseph S. Glickauf, which describe various phases of the work of Arthur Andersen & Co.'s Administrative Services Division over a period of some twenty-five years, as it traveled down the road toward professionalism.

During the early years of World War II, Mr. Arthur Andersen concluded that in the postwar years there would be an increasing demand for professional services in the field of management information systems, control procedures, and what is now generally called data processing. To this end, in 1942, the firm established its Administrative Services Division. J. A. Campbell was made responsible for its firm-wide development and kept that position through the formative years of the division, 1942-1951.

The growth of the division was slow during the war. By 1945 the total complement consisted of three managers and two staffmen. In 1946, upon their release from the U. S. Navy, the firm hired two men who were subsequently to be responsible for the division's greatest growth, John A. Higgins and Joseph S. Glickauf.

The scope of our administrative services practice in the late forties supplies an interesting backdrop for the problems of today. Then, we were involved with the impact of punched cards on our clients' accounting systems and on our auditing practices, just as the sixties have seen similar concern over the computer. Our management information work was beginning to seek out what sort of information management should have; our cost systems work usually aimed at producing something to substitute for the smaller entrepreneur's seat-of-the-pants approach. We grappled, too, with standard costs which often had not really been changed since the start of the war. As the division developed, our work embraced many other types of assignments.

During the late forties, the development of electronic computers for business purposes began to take shape. Joseph Glickauf was sent on an extended exploratory mission to study the first business-oriented computer, which was then in the prototype stage. From this survey grew the firm's deep involvement in electronic data processing. In this connection, Mr. Glickauf built a model computer to demonstrate its speed and operation potential; this is pictured on page 172.

In 1951 J. A. Campbell became Managing Partner of the Los Angeles office, and John Higgins took over firm-wide responsibility for Administrative Services. Under his direction, the division turned more and more to the growing impact of electronic equipment on the systems of large companies, and the division grew in size and sophistication. This period was highlighted by our installation of the first electronic computer to be used for business purposes and was also characterized by a number of important responsibility accounting engagements and by extensive development of our competence in the production control field.

In 1957 John Higgins assumed the office of Director of U. S. Operations for the firm as a whole, and the development of the Administrative Services Division was turned over to Joseph Glickauf, who presided over the destinies of the division for twelve years, the period of its greatest growth. To an increasing degree, the scope of our developing practice embraced highly sophisticated mechanized and electronic applications of the latest available equipment. Virtually all phases of accounting and data processing in industry came within its scope. Such old friends as production and inventory control, management information systems and accounting controls were by no means forgotten. The difference between this period and the development period of the forties lay in the far more complex hardware available and the correspondingly broader spectrum of potential uses.

During the twelve-year period of Mr. Glickauf's leadership, the Administrative Services Division of Arthur Andersen & Co. grew to an organization of 98 partners, 300 managers, and 756 staff, a total of 1,154. The division's 1969 gross accounted for roughly one-fourth of the firm's business, a fitting tribute to the men who joined the division, over the years, and to the leadership that made this growth possible.

PAUL D. WILLIAMS

Joseph S. Glickauf

About Joseph S. Glickauf

Mr. Glickauf is a native of Chicago. He attended Illinois Institute of Technology. After serving as an officer in the Research and Planning Division of the United States Navy, he joined the Administrative Services Division of Arthur Andersen & Co. in 1946.

He became a principal of the firm in 1953, and was given overall supervision of the division in 1957, a position which he held for twelve years. Mr. Glickauf's civic activities have included membership on the Chicago Crime Commission, the Board of Directors of the American Red Cross, Midwest Chapter, and the Board of Managers of the Florence Crittenton Anchorage.

Mr. Glickauf was one of the pioneers in the use of the computer in the business field. His deep involvement with its introduction and its development into a tremendous tool for serving management is discussed in the foreword and demonstrated throughout this book.

Contents

Selected Addresses and Articles by Joseph S. Glickauf

Modern trends in machine accounting

Before the Atlanta Chapter of the
National Association of Cost Accountants,
September 14, 1948

*We can be certain that business
needs will give rise to machine
developments to meet them.*

THE TOPIC on which I have been asked to talk tonight is one of those subjects which has the speaker at some disadvantage. I am quite sure that a group such as this is pretty thoroughly familiar with present-day mechanized accounting methods, and with the modern equipment which has made them possible. There would be little profit in my reviewing at any length the features of this equipment; you already know what they are. I intend instead to explore with you what we may expect in the way of future developments in the machine accounting field.

I must necessarily proceed without any certain knowledge of what is on the manufacturers' drafting tables; the accounting machine companies are understandably somewhat reticent on this subject. But the known developments of recent years afford some clues as to what may follow. We can also be quite certain that business needs and requirements will give rise to machine developments to meet them. This may not happen as quickly as the clothing industry follows women's styles, but it will come sooner or later. I think you'll all agree with me if I say that the word "competitive" is a mild understatement of the situation in the machine accounting field, and nobody in it can afford to ignore the needs of business.

Past developments, then, and what our own problems tell us ought to be developed are safe guides to what roads machine accounting will probably follow in the future. They are not conclusive, of course. It would be very fine to have a device which would permit all banks to be automatically self-balancing without help from human hands. This does not mean that such a device is to be forthwith expected. Nor does the existence of, say, a paper-handling volume problem mean that a mechanical solution is economically feasible. But the clues are interesting, and with your permission I would like to explore them.

In order to place some limits on a subject which, like any glance into the future, may seem boundless, I would like to make certain assumptions which the machine manufacturers, if not the users, will wholeheartedly endorse. Let us assume, at least for the time being, that all accounting machines are completely and unvaryingly accurate; that they are light and manageable, yet of long-lived, rugged construction on which maintenance is already at the irreducible minimum; that no changes in shape or appearance are necessary. I can then confine my remarks to the functions which they perform, and to the effectiveness with which they do or may perform them.

Speed

One feature in which I anticipate considerable future development is machine speed. I know that great strides have already been taken in this direction. Present-day calculators are a far cry from those available fifteen years ago. Electronics have been used in some types of equipment to increase their operating speed to the point where the theoretical limit is the top speed of the moving metal parts of the machine. Billing machines have long developed to the point where the question of speed rests on the operator, not the equipment. Yet accounting as an overall matter remains too slow to accomplish everything it should be able to accomplish as a management tool.

It may seem pointless on the face of it to speak of increasing the speed of any machine which has already surpassed even the peak speed of a theoretically perfect operator. Nevertheless, the time required to handle the details of a month's transactions typically results in late closings. Late closings mean delays in getting figures to management and subject both accounting and the accountant to criticism.

We thus have a real problem which, in my own experience, has not been getting any better in spite of past improvements in machine speeds. Many of its aspects have nothing to do with mechanization of accounting, and typical corrective measures customarily have their origins in areas far removed from accounting machines. A rearrangement of general ledger accounts to approximate more closely the order of monthly statement captions, and perhaps even outright changes in the chart of accounts to facilitate statement preparation, can often accomplish a great deal. So can earlier and insistently maintained cutoff dates for the closing of detail records involving considerable account distribution. Matters lying deep behind the reported results, such as inventory pricing, or shipment procedures may be delaying factors which can be speeded up only by changes, and possibly fundamental changes, in the system. Taking all such possibilities into consideration, the accounts seem never to be closed fast enough to suit everyone concerned with reported results. The problem of delayed closings may have been lessened, but it still remains with us as a problem.

The problem is of such substantial significance that I feel confident that machine speed improvements will play their part in helping solve it. I look for this development in three channels:

1. Further increases in speed of operating features such as transmission of key impulses, carriage movement and tape or form feed.

2. Increase in the speed with which an operator can work through changes, refinements and improvements in form-feeding arrangements and in location of keys, stops, etc. In such a simple operation as striking a subtotal on an adding machine, the differences in key placement and arrangement among half a dozen makes indicate pretty clearly that possibilities

along this line are far from exhausted.

3. Increase in the aggregate amount of work handled by an accounting machine operator by more efficient location of machines in relation to the source or result of the work. This is technically not a question of machine accounting, but it seems to me it is quite as important to the machine companies as the design of their product. We are too used to centralizing machine accounting functions in space selected because it is convenient to the area supervised by the chief accountant, or merely because it is not otherwise in demand. Wholly inadequate attention has been paid to the question of whether an accounting operation would be faster overall if it were handled in toto, machine applications included, in physical proximity to either the source of the data or its final disposition.

Two examples will help illustrate this last point. The typical savings bank has faced the problem squarely by placing an accounting machine at each window or group of windows; the teller handles the deposit or withdrawal and does all the bookkeeping at the same time and place. Again, I know of a large company which makes extensive use of punched-card accounting, and has two tabulating departments. One is extensively equipped with the tabulating company's full line, a veritable salesman's dream. The equipment in the other department consists of a single mechanical sorter. This sorter is used to sort prepunched cards received by mail from customers, and for that purpose alone. It is located in the department handling the customers' inquiries, where it rapidly does a job which used to take several full-time clerks.

I suppose that the optimum in speed would be a machine which would itself automatically sense the figures to be added, posted or distributed. Equipment is already available in the punched-card field which senses pencil markings in designated and rather exact locations on a card and translates them into punched holes. Wider use of such a principle outside the punched-card field should offer possibilities.

I can visualize a payroll machine which would automatically distribute the payroll charges to the correct account. A time card would, perhaps, be placed in a designated reading zone. While the machine operator entered other data on the keyboard, the machine would automatically sense the account distribution from printing, marking or other designation on the card, or even from the color of the card. Removal of the card would give the impulse to register the time charge in the appropriate distribution register. I am not a machine designer, or a patent attorney, or enough of an inventor to know whether such a device is feasible or economically practical. I only know that it would eliminate one operator's movement which is performed countless times each payroll period. As the optimum in gazing at this section of the crystal ball, think of a machine which would automatically print a columnar voucher distribution from carbon copies of vouchers passed through it at high speed!

Capacity

I recently attended an exhibition of road building equipment in Chicago. One of the most impressive things I saw was a thirty-five ton dump truck. No doubt this truck had a special hoist and countless other features. I had eyes for none of them; I simply stood and stared at the biggest dump truck I had ever seen, my attention entirely absorbed by sheer capacity. Capacity is something else that accounting machines could use more of.

Here again the machine companies have not been asleep; far from it. Several postwar models have a register capacity well in excess of that available a decade or so ago; one new large capacity machine has only recently been announced. Capacity, in one form or another, is a fundamental of machine accounting. The ability to make simultaneous machine postings on three forms is basically a matter of capacity, the machine completes three forms instead of one. The success of the electric typewriter in billing is a matter of capacity; the adjustable stroke makes it possible to make more copies, enough for many billing systems, at one typing. These are but a few of many similar illustrations.

Great as the progress has been, however, there is still much to do along capacity lines. One striking example is the question of the adaptability of an accounting machine to mail-order sales distribution.

In a mail-order operation, the order must be registered and distributed by merchandise departments or divisions; stock tickets must be prepared so that the order can be filled from the bins. The number of merchandise divisions frequently exceeds the number of registers in an accounting machine. Since the operation affects both sales and inventory, a complete and accurate distribution is essential. In the absence of machines with sufficient register capacity, manual methods are used instead, with an increase, both in the possibility of error and in the size and cost of the clerical force. Department stores are faced with a comparable problem in distributing sales by departments and sections; a similar situation exists in any large stock-pulling operation.

It seems to me that an accounting machine with an increased register capacity adequate to handle the average distribution problem would find a ready market. Existing machines can make up stock tickets and accomplish a certain amount of sales analysis; the solution would be in greater capacity rather than radical changes. The problem is widespread enough to justify a

solution, and I look for a machine to solve it in the not too distant future.

Punched-card accounting offers a solution to the sales distribution problem with a virtually limitless capacity for sales analysis. Whether or not it is the ideal solution in any given situation cannot be answered in generalities. In any event, the punched card itself is by no means a stranger to the problem of capacity. Present punched cards and punched-card accounting machines are limited to a fixed number of columns, varying with the make of equipment. None has sufficient columns to contain, in one card, enough punching for a customer's name and full address plus extensive dollar and statistical data such as that often required in public utility billing. The punched card companies have faced the problem squarely, and several alternate solutions are in use. One is an increase in the alphabetic capacity of the punched-card equipment by mechanical changes. Another is the coupling of punched cards with addressing equipment in such a way that the dollar and statistical data on the cards are mechanically combined with the correct address information. Both approaches are in satisfactory use, and offer interesting possibilities in many applications in addition to public utilities.

Nevertheless, an increase in the number of columns in the card, and consequent changes in the equipment to handle the larger card, are bound to come. One hears talk of an impending development of this character in punched card circles; it has a great deal to offer.

An increase in card column capacity would give an answer to the name, address and data question. It would present a new and admirable approach to standard cost records with adequate description of operations: it would increase the effectiveness of punched-card cash disbursement and voucher mechanics; it would result in more informative punched-card inventory records, just to mention a few advantages. Whether such a development has reached the blue-print stage or has gone beyond that point I do not know. But I trust that its advent on the market is not too distant.

Another specialized but very interesting answer to the capacity question is worth mentioning. All of you have stood impatiently in line at the railroad station while the ticket agent laboriously makes out coupon after coupon of an interline ticket for a prospective traveler. Within the past year or two, ticketing machines have made their appearance on an experimental basis, with the objective of cutting the time required in the ticketing operation, and improving the temper of the waiting line. One machine in the pilot model stage is essentially a capacity increase alteration in the ticket vending machine in use in practically every motion picture theatre in the country. This machine prints and ejects interline tickets with a number of coupons, prices the ticket and the various roads' shares, and accumulates the requisite sales statistics, all with a speed and dispatch which a present-day traveler would hardly believe possible.

Flexibility

All of you are fully aware of the vitally important place of costs in present-day economics. Cost is an equally significant consideration in any decision between a manual or mechanized accounting operation. In this area, the purchase cost of a machine may very well be controlling. One hears very widely that "machines do not pay if there are less than so many employees on the payroll," or "manual methods are cheaper with only so many customers." Such murmurings are not without justification. Perhaps there is no machine in the prospective user's price range which will handle several such functions with equal effectiveness. Any one machine should be adaptable to an increasingly large number of users; otherwise its contribution to the accounting effort will be limited to part time. Again, there are a number of common

problems of detail handling which have not yet been solved satisfactorily; flexibility in machine applications to meet these challenges would be welcomed.

Flexibility is no new concept in machine accounting, as evidenced by a number of current machine features such as the following:

1. The common alphabetic-numeric bookkeeping machine.

2. A multiplying device built into an accounting and posting machine.

3. The "two-speed carriage" permitting the same information to be posted simultaneously to two forms with different spacing.

4. Variable counters and registers, permitting the operator to change the patterns of subtotals and totals or the degree of analysis.

5. The mechancial sensing feature adapted to addressing equipment, as mentioned a few moments ago.

6. A changeable "control plate" or other device which permits the selection of various applications of the same machine.

7. Adaptability of the proof tape section of the machine as a straight adding machine.

8. Various features of punched-card tabulating equipment, beginning with the wiring panel itself.

These and comparable flexible features have in a large measure been responsible for some of machine accounting's greatest strides; they have made mechanization possible in many cases where it would otherwise have been impractical or perhaps uneconomical. For example, the use of a two-speed carriage makes it possible to prepare a stock ticket as a by-product of typing the order and invoice without involving any high-cost equipment. The punched-card field has an increasing number of special attachments to convert ordinary equipment to new uses.

What remains undone in the flexibility field? Well, several things. Here's one that is very familiar to all of you, the matter of payroll computation. The country is well filled with clerks extending hours times rate, usually on a calculating device because most accounting machines will not handle that function. Other clerks, in like numbers and for the same reason, busily extend material tickets by similar means. This question is obviously being worked on; if it weren't, we wouldn't have what multiplying features there are. But more work is needed before it can be said that flexibility has been combined with simplicity on a broad front.

Another gap is the little matter of telephone toll billing. Under the old-fashioned method presently in use, the toll operator writes up a ticket for each call; this ticket becomes the accounting medium. If preparation of the ticket could be automatic or even semiautomatic, and the result used in the rest of the accounting directly without transcription, a good many thousand hours would be saved every month or perhaps every day. Mechanical solutions to this problem are also in the development stage.

These illustrations include two extremely commonplace situations and one of very limited, highly specialized, application. There are others in between. All of us know that each prospective machine application which is at all out of the ordinary involves a search for the features most closely adapted, and perhaps a compromise between requirements and availability. On occasion the machine possibilities are dismissed after thorough investigation. I think we will see, in a few years, the day when compromises and unanswerables will be largely a thing of the past because of the all-purpose flexibility of accounting machines.

Remote control

There are two kinds of flexibility that deserve separate mention. One I will call remote control. This is not a feature which I expect will be built into all types of accounting machines. But it does have possibilities and existing uses which augur its greater application in the future.

Some of these existing uses are indicative of the possibilities of remote control machine accounting:

1. An eastern railroad is experimenting with a combined teletype and a key punch for freight and car accounting. An operator at one yard point can operate a punch which will produce punched cards at another yard which may be miles away, thus creating accounting media at a distance without waiting for the mails. Now the accounting and billing can catch up with, and perhaps beat, the fast freight, a matter of no little difficulty under other methods when car interchange points are close togther.

2. A mining company records orders on the teletype in the home office, thus simultaneously producing identical copies at the point of shipment and the point of billing.

3. Another wholly familiar task is the making of a plane or train reservation. Several machines have been developed which control reservations at a single central point, giving a mechanical answer in a matter of seconds as to whether the space requested is available. They also mechanically record reservations of available space. What information I have been able to gather on this type of equipment does not include its cost, but its appearance and performance are sufficiently impressive to suggest a discouragingly high price.

4. I understand that consideration is being given to a device which would make the meter reading and

billing activities of a public utility almost completely mechanical. Under this plan, the customer's meter would be fitted with a set of variable punches synchronized with consumption. The meter reader would insert a card in a slot and the punches would punch cumulative consumption in the card. Equipment already in use has completely mechanized the calculation and production of the customer's bill. This additional feature would limit the manual operations in the billing cycle to two, putting the card in the slot and taking it out again.

How extensive remote control possibilities may be is anybody's guess. At least there are chances for plenty of wishful thinking. Imagine to yourselves a factory timekeeping system providing for automatic registration, on a medium readily susceptible of analysis, of job hours and actual production by workers! Or picture a warehousing operation where a single clerk equipped with buttons could instruct the manual or automatic lumping of desired items on a belt or conveyor, and make the necessary accounting record at the same time. Things like these should be possible; how practical they may be is another matter. But there are enough indications of remote control features already in use to suggest the probability of further development in this fascinating field.

Mechanical devices for manual accounting

No discussion of flexibility can be complete without some mention of mechanical or semimechanical aids to manual accounting methods. As a title, this description is vague and probably misleading. What I have in mind is the whole field of devices which, without direct employment of machines as such, simplify the manual performance of the posting and distribution functions. This field includes reproduction processes to prepare copies of source documents for numerous purposes without extensive transcription. It includes pegboards and needle sorting. It includes various aligning devices for the accurate simultaneous posting of several records from a single longhand posting.

This last type of device has gained considerable popularity in the payroll field, particularly among smaller companies. It appears to be both economical and effective. The principle should be equally adaptable to other types of related records, such as sales, accounts receivable and customers' statements, or vouchers and account distribution. In fact, several devices embodying these extended applications are already on the market.

There are, and there probably always will be, companies whose officials do not consider accounting machines soundly adaptable to their situations. Semimechanical boosters to the time-honored manual methods of accounting offer real advantages to these companies. It seems entirely logical that there will be continued and new developments to serve this field.

Controls

One feature of machine accounting systems which will have to receive more attention and emphasis is the whole question of control. Accounting machine company representatives have not, taken as a whole, given this subject the attention it deserves, yet they know more about their equipment than their customers do. Control refinements are thus usually left to the user, who may be well versed in crosschecks but less so in machine technique. We have then, no general combination of the fullest understanding of both machine features and limitations, and of the elements of internal control, brought to bear together.

I do not by any means intend to imply that lack of internal control is rampant in machine accounting, or that there aren't many situations which have little room for improvement. I do say that I have seen enough weak spots to warrant repeating just one familiar thing. Despite the assumption made earlier in this discussion, no machine is so perfect that the chance of mechanical failure is completely eliminated. Neither can the possibility for human error be removed from an operator's work. The effective use of machine accounting dictates that adequate safeguards be established, independent of self-contained machine operations, to minimize the chance of any such errors carrying through into the accounting results. This is not a talk on internal crosschecks, and any excursion into the various control methods would be out of place, but it would be equally out of order to avoid mention of a principle which is so basic in successful mechanized accounting.

I said earlier that I was speaking without any certainty of what the machine manufacturers have in the development stage. It may very well be the case that much of my wishful thinking has been reality for some time. I hope it has; I shall feel no chagrin if something I look for in the future is already here. I know that many of the features I've been talking about will come, and on a large scale. The accounting machine companies have already proved that they are properly susceptible to the murmurs of the crowd, and have done a magnificent job in making their indispensable contribution toward the translation of our work from bookkeeping to accounting. I feel confident that their development work is marching steadily ahead, and that they will fill some of our more pressing needs long before they become so urgent as to necessitate substitute treatment.

Responsibility accounting for natural gas pipelines

Before the executives of Michigan-Wisconsin Pipeline Company, Detroit, April 25, 1951

Reporting by responsibility centers makes it possible for management to pinpoint variations from the budget and take prompt corrective action.

IN RECENT YEARS the subject of responsibility (or functional) accounting has been one of vital interest throughout the utility industry. Designed primarily for utility management rather than for regulatory commission purposes, this system of accounting has proven to be the most satisfactory method so far devised for obtaining information in a form best designed to promote the effective control of expenditures.

As with most new concepts, there have been many misconceptions of what functional accounting really is and how it works. The purpose of this presentation is to illustrate a functional system as applied to a typical natural gas pipeline and to answer some of the basic questions which usually arise in any discussion of this subject.

Stated simply, functional accounting is a system in which costs flow up the organizational lines and are accumulated and reported at the various levels of responsibility. Each supervisory area in the organization is charged only with the costs for which it is responsible.

The desirability of obtaining information detailed beyond the account classifications established by regulatory bodies and presented in a manner substantially different from the routine groupings of such accounts has been recognized by many natural gas pipeline companies for some time. Accounting techniques and operating reports attest to this fact. Until the advent of functional accounting, however, pipeline companies had only partially achieved the desired results.

Before proceeding further, one of the most important elements of functional accounting should be stressed. Under responsibility reporting the individual company's organization chart (Slide 1) indicates ex-

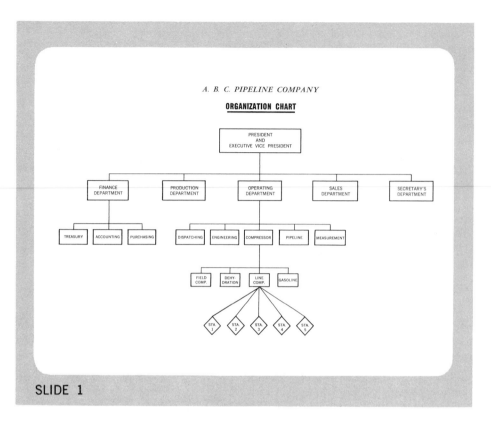

SLIDE 1

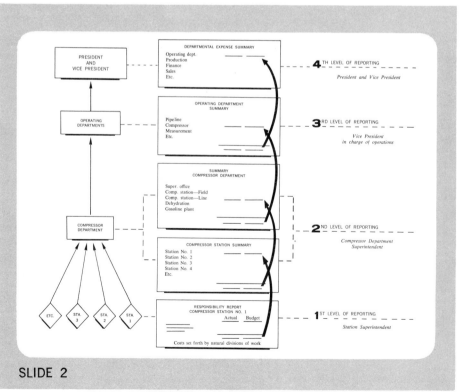

SLIDE 2

actly how the operating costs will be accumulated and reported. This means that every system of responsibility reporting is tailored to the requirements of a particular company. As no two utilities are identical, so no two functional systems are identical.

For illustrative purposes, therefore, it has been necessary to devise an organization chart of a mythical pipeline company. Below the top departmental level only the compressor department is shown in detail, since this is the department around which we have built a series of sample reports to illustrate how expenditures are reported and controlled from the lowest level of responsibility to the top management level, with final tie-in to the top income account.

Our starting point is compressor station number 1. From here we will progress upward through the various levels of the organization as illustrated by Slide 2. This chart will also serve as an anchor point in our illustrations of the various reports, so that we can constantly keep in mind the parallel relationship of the reports with the levels of responsibility within the organization.

The first statement we will discuss is the statement prepared for, and supplied to, the first level of supervision, the superintendent of main line station number 1 (Slide 3). The superintendents of each of the other main line stations, as well as the superintendents of the field stations and gasoline plants, will receive similar statements. This report consists of a listing by natural divisions of work of all costs for which the station superintendent is responsible.

These natural divisions of work are sometimes called functions and they are designed to meet the particular requirements of each department within the company. This is accomplished by having those individuals who are responsible for the operation of the department determine what they require in the way of uniform cost breakdowns for the most effective control of their operations. In addition, as you will observe, the work operations are described in terms that mean something to the operating people. This means that the operating man does not have to be an accountant, either to report the costs he incurs or to evaluate a report which describes the results of his operations.

This report is designed with one purpose in mind, to give the station superintendent a quick and concise overall picture of the station operations. It clearly sets out total maintenance and total operation and permits a ready tie-in with subsequent reports, as will be seen later.

Now if you will take note of the $15,673 grand total of the actual column we will refer back to our anchor chart (Slide 2) and from there proceed to the second level of reporting.

From Slide 4 we see that the totals for station number 1 are carried forward into a report which summarizes expenses for all main line compressor stations. You will observe that on the left of the organization chart it is indicated that the compressor department is composed of a series of main line stations. As a result, one of the reports prepared for the compressor superintendent summarizes the costs for all of the plants under his supervision.

You will note in this sample report that the amount of $15,673 which was the total actual cost of operating compressor station number 1 has been carried forward from the function report. Budget and variation

A. B. C. PIPELINE COMPANY

MAIN LINE COMPRESSOR STATION SUMMARY BY FUNCTION

FUNCTION DESCRIPTION	ACTUAL	BUDGET	VARIATION
OPERATION			
Direct supervision of station operation	$ 14,156	$ 13,043	$ 1,113
Operating compressor units	32,758	28,542	4,216
Operating water supply system	12,719	14,622	(1,903)
Operating auxiliary power supply system	7,760	6,514	1,246
Operating compressor cottage	1,182	1,356	(174)
General operating	2,560	2,665	(105)
Station maps and records	600	725	(125)
Fuel	51,256	47,525	3,731
Rents	750	750	—
	$ 123,741	$ 115,742	$ 7,999
MAINTENANCE			
Direct supervision of maintenance	$ 2,257	$ 2,750	$ (493)
Repair of station cottages	1,378	1,200	178
Repair of auxiliary power equipment	3,410	3,725	(315)
Repair of main engines	15,582	10,235	5,347
Repair of water supply system	3,426	1,550	1,876
Repair of circulating system	895	1,025	(130)
Repair of station piping and fittings	1,072	1,150	(78)
Repair of other station equipment	2,001	1,125	876
	$ 30,021	$ 22,760	$ 7,261
	$ 153,762	$ 138,502	$ 15,260

columns are also brought forward in comparative columns.

As you will recall from our original organization chart, the superintendent of the compressor department is not only responsible for the main line compressor stations but he is also responsible for the field compressor stations, the dehydration plants and the gasoline plants. Therefore, the costs of the superintendent's office are not included on this report. Had the organization of the A.B.C. Pipeline been such that a particular individual was held responsible for the overall operations of compressor stations, but was not held responsible for any of the other operations within the compressor department, this report would have been supplied to him and his own and his office costs would have been included in this report. Under the organization plan assumed here the stations are only a part of the super-

intendent's total responsibility and the amount of $153,762 represents only the total cost of operating the main line compressor stations.

The superintendent also receives a report which sets out by work operation the total cost of operating his stations without regard to station responsibility. You will note the grand total of $153,762 which appears in the actual column of Slide 5 is the same figure which appeared on the previous report.

This report tells the superintendent the total cost of each functional operation relating to main line compressor stations. In other words, it sets out the total costs of operating the main units, the auxiliary units, etc., and at the same time provides budget comparison and variation data. This report provides the means for studying the relationship of the various types of costs for the entire group of stations. It also provides the tie-in to the next report (Slide 6) which the superintendent receives. This tie-in will be recognized if you will remember the total operating figure of $123,741 and the total maintenance cost of $30,021.

The report above summarizes all of the operations which are a direct responsibility of the superintendent of the compressor department. You will observe that the cost for each of the four major types of stations are set out clearly and included in these figures are the $123,741 and $30,021 compressor station costs which we observed in the previous slide.

The functions which appear above the totals for the stations represent the costs of operating the superintendent's office; these costs are a direct responsibility of the superintendent. When these costs are combined with the total for each of the types of stations, we arrive at the amount of $206,058 which represents the total of operating the entire department. As with the other reports, budget and variation figures are shown.

Again referring to the anchor slide (Slide 2), we see that the third level of reporting is for the top administrative level of the operating department. In this report the total costs for each of the operating departments are summarized to obtain the total costs for the entire operating division of the business. This report is prepared primarily for the vice president in charge of operations whose responsibility it is to direct the operating department.

Let us now turn to a sample of the report for the operating department (Slide 7). The totals of the compressor department shown in this statement have been carried forward directly from the function report prepared

14

A. B. C. PIPELINE COMPANY
SUMMARY OF OPERATING DEPARTMENTS

DEPARTMENT	OPERATION			MAINTENANCE			INDIRECT EXPENSE			TOTAL
	ACTUAL	BUDGET	VARIATION	ACTUAL	BUDGET	VARIATION	ACTUAL	BUDGET	VARIATION	ACTUAL
Operation management	$	$	$	$	$	$	$ 4,250	$ 4,290	$(40)	$ 4,250
Engineering	18,275	18,305	(30)							18,275
Dispatching	3,250	3,200	50							3,250
Pipeline	85,746	76,264	9,482	49,400	45,150	4,250	4,750	4,725	25	139,896
Compressor	165,185	147,110	18,075	37,648	30,433	7,215	3,225	3,300	(75)	206,058
Measurement	21,172	21,372	(200)	6,500	6,475	25	3,500	3,550	(50)	31,172
	$293,628	$266,251	$27,377	$93,548	$82,058	$11,490	$15,725	$15,865	$(140)	$402,901
Supervision and general allocated	12,125	12,000	125	3,600	3,865	(265)	(15,725)	(15,865)	140	–0–
	$305,753	$278,251	$27,502	$97,148	$85,923	$11,225	–0–	–0–	–0–	$402,901

SLIDE 7

for the superintendent of that department. You will recognize the compressor department totals of $3,225 for indirect expense, $37,648 for maintenance, and $165,185 for operation. Up to this level of reporting, we have been controlling the indirect expenses on a total expenditure basis without regard to how the total expenditure would be allocated. At this level, and not until this level, we allocate indirect expense, so that we can obtain total operation and total maintenance figures, which will subsequently tie to the income statement.

In this type of reporting it is possible to see what the actual overhead expenses amounted to and what happened to them. In the particular example shown here it is indicated that all of the indirect expenses are allocated between operations and maintenance. On the A.B.C. Pipeline Company all construction charges are made direct.

Had the situation been such that certain of the indirect costs were related to construction, the necessary allocation would have been made at this point.

By adding the overhead allocation to direct operation and maintenance costs, we arrive at a total of operation and maintenance expense for the operating department. Total operation expense of $305,753 and total maintenance expense of $97,148 are carried forward to the next higher level of report.

Returning again to our anchor slide, we see that the fourth and top level report is a departmental expense summary prepared for the president and the vice presidents. You will observe that the tie-in of reports is here again established.

By referring to the exhibit of the departmental expense summary (Slide 8) we see

A. B. C. PIPELINE COMPANY

SUMMARY OF OPERATING EXPENSES

DEPARTMENT	OPERATION			MAINTENANCE		
	ACTUAL	BUDGET	VARIATION	ACTUAL	BUDGET	VARIATION
Operating	$305,753	$ 278,251	$ 27,502	$ 97,148	$ 85,923	$ 11,225
Secretary's	6,250	6,275	(25)			
Treasury	7,150	7,000	150			
Accounting	40,550	39,625	925			
Purchasing	11,272	9,980	1,292			
Sales	8,100	8,700	(600)			
Production	32,500	31,605	895			
General	53,500	52,700	800			
	$465,075	$ 434,136	$ 30,939	$ 97,148	$ 85,923	$ 11,225

that the total expenses are clearly indicated according to the department responsible for the expense. You will recall the $305,753 of operation expense and the $97,148 of maintenance expense from the functional report of the operating department.

Each vice president and the president of the company receives a copy of this statement. At a glance this statement gives a quick analysis of the total operating expenses by departments. Each department's performance in relation to the budget is also shown in the comparative columns. You can see that the side captions on the departmental expense summary relate directly to the departmental designations on the organization chart.

Totals for the financial and executive departments as shown in this statement will be supported by a detailed statement of expenditures by individual functions. Similarly the purchasing, sales, and production departments will each receive reports detailing expenditures by functions. The general section of this statement includes those activities which are not a direct responsibility of any particular department of the company. These include such expenditures as directors' fees, welfare activities, and other expenses of a general nature. These expenditures are the collective responsibility of top management. In addition to providing an analysis of expenses by departments, this statement also furnishes the final summary which supports the captions "Operations" and "Maintenance" in the top income statement.

If you will take particular note of the totals appearing in the actual column for operation and maintenance you will observe how they are carried forward. These figures of $465,075 and $97,148 will be seen opposite the appropriate captions in Slide 9. This is the top income account for the company and, as you have observed, it is directly supported by subsidiary reports of expenditures by departments and their subdivisions. It is the subsidiary functional reports which management uses in exercising control over the operations of the company.

Under responsibility (functional) accounting, statements prepared on the basis of regulatory commission accounts are prepared only for submission to the regulatory agencies. If responsibility reporting has been intelligently tailored to the organization, there should be absolutely no reason for any level of management to receive a report by regulatory commission accounts. We wish to emphasize, however, that under responsibility reporting, balances by regulatory commission accounts are available monthly if required.

Using Slide 10 let us examine briefly how variations from the budget can be traced from the top management's statements down through the various levels of responsibility in the organization to the lowest level. Starting with the statement of income and expenses, we see in the total that there is a variation of $30,939 in operations and $11,225 in maintenance. In order to determine the departments responsible for these variations, we examine the next statement below the income account.

The summary of operating expenses shows that the major portion of the variation of $30,939 occurred in the operating department. Therefore, we proceed to the summary of operating departments.

SLIDE 10

A. B. C. PIPELINE COMPANY
SUMMARY OF OPERATING EXPENSES

DEPARTMENT	OPERATION			MAINTENANCE		
	ACTUAL	BUDGET	VARIATION	ACTUAL	BUDGET	VARIATION
Operating	$ 305,753	$ 278,251	$ 27,502	$ 97,148	$ 85,923	$ 11,225
Secretary's	6,250	6,275	(25)			
Treasury	7,150	7,000	150			
Accounting	40,550	39,625	925			
Purchasing	11,272	9,980	1,292			
Sales	8,100	8,700	(600)			
Production	32,500	31,605	895			
General	53,500	52,700	800			
	$ 465,075	$ 434,136	$ 30,939	$ 97,148	$ 85,923	$ 11,225

SLIDE 11

A. B. C. PIPELINE COMPANY
SUMMARY OF OPERATING DEPARTMENTS

DEPARTMENT	OPERATION			MAINTENANCE			INDIRECT EXPENSE			TOTAL
	ACTUAL	BUDGET	VARIATION	ACTUAL	BUDGET	VARIATION	ACTUAL	BUDGET	VARIATION	ACTUAL
Operation management	$	$	$	$	$	$	$ 4,250	$ 4,290	$(40)	$ 4,250
Engineering	18,275	18,305	(30)							18,275
Dispatching	3,250	3,200	50							3,250
Pipeline	85,746	76,264	9,482	49,400	45,150	4,250	4,750	4,725	25	139,896
Compressor	165,185	147,110	18,075	37,648	30,433	7,215	3,225	3,300	(75)	206,058
Measurement	21,172	21,372	(200)	6,500	6,475	25	3,500	3,550	(50)	31,172
	$293,628	$266,251	$27,377	$93,548	$82,058	$11,490	$15,725	$15,865	$(140)	$402,901
Supervision and general allocated	12,125	12,000	125	3,600	3,865	(265)	(15,725)	(15,865)	140	–0–
	$305,753	$278,251	$27,502	$97,148	$85,923	$11,225	–0–	–0–	–0–	$402,901

18

A. B. C. PIPELINE COMPANY
COMPRESSOR DEPARTMENT SUMMARY

DESCRIPTION	ACTUAL	BUDGET	VARIATION
INDIRECT EXPENSE			
Superintendence	$ 1,950	$ 1,975	$(25)
Clerical service	925	1,000	(75)
Supplies and expenses	350	325	25
	$ 3,225	$ 3,300	$(75)
OPERATION			
Compressor stations—Field	$ 6,826	$ 3,215	$ 3,611
Compressor stations—Line	123,741	113,869	9,872
Dehydration stations	2,722	1,725	997
Gasoline plants	31,896	28,301	3,595
	$ 165,185	$ 147,110	$ 18,075
MAINTENANCE			
Compressor stations—Field	$ 1,256	$ 1,200	56
Compressor stations—Line	30,021	24,633	5,388
Dehydration stations	650	700	(50)
Gasoline plants	5,721	3,900	1,821
	$ 37,648	$ 30,433	$ 7,215
	$ 206,058	$ 180,843	$ 25,215

SLIDE 12

A. B. C. PIPELINE COMPANY
MAIN LINE COMPRESSOR STATION SUMMARY

DESCRIPTION	ACTUAL	BUDGET	VARIATION
Compressor station number 1	$ 15,673	$ 11,388	$ 4,285
Compressor station number 2	11,880	10,450	1,430
Compressor station number 3	16,726	17,250	(524)
Compressor station number 4	10,276	11,150	1,126
Compressor stations 5, 6, 7, etc.	—	—	—
	$ 153,762	$ 138,502	$ 15,260

SLIDE 13

19

A. B. C. PIPELINE COMPANY

RESPONSIBILITY REPORT

MAIN LINE COMPRESSOR STATION NO. 1

DESCRIPTION	ACTUAL	BUDGET	VARIATION
OPERATION			
Direct supervision of station operation	$ 750	$ 675	$ 75
Operating compressor units	2,950	3,250	(300)
Operating water supply system	1,125	928	197
Operating auxiliary power equipment	770	220	550
Operating compressor cottages	116	75	41
General operating	809	1,000	(191)
Station maps and records	72	50	22
Fuel	3,622	2,950	672
Rents	125	125	—
	$ 10,339	$ 9,273	$ 1,066
MAINTENANCE			
Direct supervision of station maintenance	$ 372	$ 275	$ 97
Repair of station cottages	67	75	(8)
Repair of auxiliary power equipment	388	375	13
Repair of main engines	3,980	750	3,230
Repair of water supply system	142	200	(58)
Repair of circulating system	126	50	76
Repair of station piping and fittings	68	90	(22)
Repair of other station equipment	191	300	(109)
	$ 5,334	$ 2,115	$ 3,219
	$ 15,673	$ 11,388	$ 4,285

SLIDE 14

A. B. C. PIPELINE COMPANY

DETAIL LEDGER

LINE COMPRESSOR STATION NO. 1 — REPAIR OF MAIN ENGINES

DESCRIPTION	REFERENCE NUMBER	LABOR	MATERIAL	OTHER	TOTAL
Balance brought forward		$ 1,150	$ 490	$ 125	$ 1,765
Labor	045126	270			
Labor	045127	310			
Transportation	045161			22	
Fittings	8642		8		
Pipe	1796		60		
Acme Supply Co	04511122			3,310	
Total charges for the month		$ 580	$ 68	$ 3,332	$ 3,980
Total charges to date		$ 1,730	$ 558	$ 3,457	$ 5,745

SLIDE 15

20

Upon examining Slide 11 we observe that the compressor division was responsible for the largest variation.

As the compressor department includes several types of stations, we turn to the compressor department summary (Slide 12). It is here indicated that a major budget variation occurred in the main line stations and therefore, we next examine the main line compressor station summary (Slide 13).

Here it is evident that the largest variation occurred at station number 1, so we proceed to the responsibility report for this plant (Slide 14).

This report indicates significant variations in two functions: "fuel" under operations was apparently considerably out of line for the month and "repair of main engines" indicates a variation worthy of further investigation.

To proceed further we carry our examination into the detail ledger (Slide 15). Here we see that the principal reason for the variation in this work operation is due to a large billing from the Acme Supply Company. Perhaps we have had an imprudent purchase of expensable material, but whatever the reason for the variance we have the tools to track it down.

Responsibility reporting has three major advantages. First, the cost reports prepared are simple, concise and easy to understand. A report is only valuable if it is used. Reports which are difficult to understand are only used by trained accountants and the individuals who control the company are not, for the most part, trained accountants. As a result they lose patience with any report which is full of accounting complications. If a company's operating reports are easy to understand and clearly define responsibilities, they will be used in the day-to-day operations by the operating people.

The second advantage is that responsibilities for costs are clearly indicated in all reports. Costs are matched with responsibilities at all levels.

The third advantage is that budgeting is simplified and budgetary control is improved. This is accomplished by segregating costs into natural divisions of work and by providing a direct method of fixing responsibility for budget variations.

I believe you will agree that the common sense method of building a budget is by estimating the expenditures for each element of work that must be done on the job.

For instance, in preparing a budget for the pipeline department you would estimate costs necessary to perform the natural divisions of work and would include such operations as lubricating, checking and cleaning valves, line walking, operating houses, etc. Most operating budgets start at this point, but if all these estimates are lumped and if the actual costs are recorded by the accounts provided in the uniform system, it becomes necessary to make a very extensive analysis to determine the causes for budget variations.

The installation of functional reporting involves four major steps. The initial step is to clarify the lines of responsibility within the organization and to clearly define the responsibilities of each department and executive in the company. As has been emphasized, the organization is the backbone of the system. Poorly defined lines of responsibility make it impossible to match costs with the persons responsible for those costs.

The second step is the development of a functional manual with instructions and descriptions of work operations. A standardized list of these field activities, described explicitly, is given to the field. The field organization is not burdened with any accounting instruction books, such as are issued by regulatory agencies.

The third step is to modernize all accounting methods and procedures. This generally means the installation of some form of mechanical accounting equipment and the streamlining of all accounting procedures and instructions. The sources of all accounting charges are relatively few and with properly designed mechanization of procedures this source data can be accumulated directly and automatically in monthly reports.

The fourth step is the revision of reports and a program for their distribution.

The organization and administration of a program for installing a functional system of control requires careful consideration. We believe the best way to organize such a program is to set up a procedure unit within the company. This unit can be provided with such outside assistance as may be required. If the company is in a position to staff the entire procedures group, assistance may be limited to consultation. Company participation is stressed as we have found that the employees are more inclined to actively support a new program if they have had a hand in its development. Further, they will be better prepared to operate the new system successfully if they have had an active part in developing it.

Electronics down to earth

An Article by John A. Higgins and
Joseph S. Glickauf, published in the
March-April, 1954, issue of the
Harvard Business Review

*Although the direct dollar savings are
important, the most significant
impact of the development of
electronics for business will be a
change from the emphasis
on historical reporting to one of
reporting in terms of the future and
providing data for forming
reliable management judgments and
effective management controls.*

IF YOU ARE an executive of a moderately large enterprise, you should be aware of the fact that electronics for business is not something that must wait to be developed in the future but that it is here now, today. No longer is the development of electronic equipment for business just an engineer's dream on a drawing board.

The year 1954 will see at least one and possibly several installations of large-scale digital computers for accounting and business operations. In January of this year a large-scale digital computer was delivered to the General Electric Company's Major Appliance Division in Louisville, Kentucky, for use in accounting and related operations. Several other companies have ordered such equipment and many more are in the process of studying the economic effects of utilizing such equipment in their operations.

Thus, at last, the machine which has probably had more advance publicity, which has been the subject of more speculation, and around which has grown as fancy a crop of misconceptions as has ever been seen or heard will make its opening bow on the American business scene.

Of what significance is this new development? Is not the electronic digital computer just another accounting machine? What distinguishes this piece of equipment from all prior forms of mechanization? What can this device provide in the way of more useful and timely control information for management? And what can electronics offer in the way of reduced clerical costs?

Our purpose in writing this article is to help you answer these questions and, at the same time, to attempt to dispel many of the fallacies which surround the subject.

Before proceeding further, it is important to define exactly what we mean by an electronic computing machine as something new and different on the business scene.

As used here, the term electronic computer is identified with a device which is capable of performing mathematical and logical operations entirely within itself, and which receives information into the system and delivers information out of the system by means of magnetic or paper tape.

It is important to differentiate this type of equipment from certain other devices which, while truly electronic in operation, are nevertheless extremely limited in their application and function and are used only in connection with, and as extensions of, present punched-card equipment. These devices, termed electronic calculators, have been on the market for a number of years, and they are serving well and faithfully to reduce clerical effort and save many dollars for management. The manufacturers of punched-card equipment are now marketing even larger and more impressive models of this type of equipment.

Irrespective of size and electronic operation, however, all of the equipment of this genre is still in the punched-card class, differing only in degree from its progenitors, and should not be confused with tape-operated equipment. The significance of this distinction is recognized even by the manufacturers of punched-card equipment, who are also bringing out electronic equipment operated by means of tape.

It it also important to distinguish between special-purpose and general-purpose electronic equipment. Special-purpose equipment is generally composed of one or more of the functional parts which comprise a large-scale computer. These devices are individually engineered for a special application. They are not flexible and, once designed to perform certain specific computing

or recording operations, they can be used only for this particular purpose. General-purpose equipment, on the other hand, is a completely flexible piece of apparatus and can be instructed to perform an unlimited variety of different operations. It is the general-purpose computer which is discussed here.

Operating characteristics

It is not within the scope of this paper to delineate the innumerable technical differences which distinguish the electronic computer from all prior types of mechanical office devices. Fortunately, most of these differences are of significance only to the engineer. From an operating standpoint, however, there are two prime characteristics of this equipment which are quite revolutionary.

Follow-through

The first and most important of these characteristics is the ability of an electronic computer to follow through a long series of sequential operations without human intervention. It is true that the sequential steps must at one time have been determined and set out in detail on magnetic tape in language that the machine can understand; but, once these instruction tapes have been fed into the machine at the start of an operation, the machine will follow through the steps automatically. No longer will the office machine require a human operator to take it through each step involved in a particular process or computation.

High speed

The second distinguishing characteristic of this equipment is its high speed of operation. Much has been written about this particular feature of electronic apparatus; and, while many of the speeds which have been quoted for a single mathematical operation are incredibly fast, it should be recognized that in performing an operation involving a complete function, the equipment operates at a slower, though still impressive, rate.

Thus, in spite of the fact that a slightly more conservative view must be taken of the machine's practical operating speed than has perhaps previously been indicated, it still remains, by a wide margin, the fastest automatic computing device ever developed. Many operations which manually have been measured in days or weeks can now be performed in a matter of minutes or hours.

Economic advantages

The adoption of electronic equipment by industry will bring about a profound change in what management will come to expect of its accounting and reporting systems, and the use of computers will also make possible substantial savings through a reduction in the total clerical effort. As direct dollar savings will presumably provide the impetus for many of the first installations of the new equipment, we shall first discuss this aspect.

Reducing operating steps

The automatic sequence-control feature of electronic computers eliminates the clerical labor that is normally involved in following through the successive steps of an office or accounting procedure.

Whenever any office or accounting procedure is analyzed in chart form, it is astounding to see the numerous steps or operations required to complete a procedure. Even when the procedure has been mechanized through the use of punched cards, which is the highest degree of mechanization that has previously been available, there still remain a number of steps, each one requiring a labor operation in order to follow through to the subsequent step. Hence, because the punched-card tabulating machines cannot perform a series of steps without some person to transfer the data from one operation to another, what has heretofore

been considered a very complete and high degree of mechanization, really involves a considerable amount of clerical labor.

Thus, the electronic computer, with its automatic sequencing of operations as previously worked out and translated onto instruction tapes, eliminates most of the so-called "operating labor" in present-day mechanized installations.

Routinizing exceptions

Another important reason why clerical savings accrue through the use of a computer is that practically all exceptions to a procedure can be routinized.

In any large mechanized operation, there are always certain procedures which do not adapt themselves to mechanized techniques. To force these irregular operations into the regular mechanized flow would in most cases impair the operation of the entire system. Therefore, in developing procedures it has heretofore been found expedient from both a time and a cost standpoint to handle these exceptions manually. These exceptions and complications in procedures have resulted in a periphery of manual operations around almost every mechanized operation, and it is this manual periphery that has so often dissipated the savings anticipated in a mechanization program.

The ability of electronic computers to follow through a set of complicated instructions at extremely high speeds makes it possible for the machine to handle most procedural exceptions heretofore requiring manual processing.

Handling new work

The third reason why computers can eliminate clerical labor stems from the ability of electronic equipment to handle work which has never before been susceptible of mechanization.

Before the advent of electronic computers, the mechanized areas in business were limited to those which did not involve judgment and logical decisions based on a review of a certain set of given facts. For example, in a payroll procedure there is much clerical effort expended in reviewing time sheets to determine eligibility for overtime, the amount of shift pay differential, and other factors involving a judgment decision after review of certain predetermined facts.

Because electronic computers in effect simulate human thinking when the proper factors to be considered in the decision have been previously given to the machine, they can now handle many of the clerical operations which require this type of logical decision. The possibilities for making inroads in this new area are tremendous.

There is only one limiting factor: man's ability to review a given problem analytically and then to translate that problem into language which the machine can understand. While new areas of mechanization are a rich potential for clerical savings, the difficulties of providing the machine with all the factors required to solve a particular problem should not be underestimated.

Summary of savings

In summary, then, a computer can provide direct dollar savings through the elimination of clerical labor because of its ability (a) to perform automatic sequential operations, (b) to handle most exceptions to regular procedures, and (c) to make inroads into clerical work areas never before mechanized.

It should be of interest to note that our studies, which have covered potential applications in a number of different industries, have in every case revealed clerical savings of very substantial proportions. Further, although we believe that our work represents too small a sample from which to draw concrete, across-the-board conclusions, there is strong evidence that an electronic computer can be economically justified as a direct replacement for many of the present large punched-card installations because of the savings accruing from automatic sequencing of operations and the routinizing of procedural irregularities.

As a matter of fact, a company which already has a punched-card system is in a particularly desirable situation. The installation of a computer to replace punched cards should materially simplify many of the conversion problems normally attendant on a systems change. And extension of the computer to handle new kinds of work, which is the more difficult move, can be effected at a later date when experience gained from actual operation of the equipment will materially facilitate the transition.

But it is perhaps well to note that, while we feel the conversion of a computer system from an established punched-card method has certain advantages, this does not mean that an operation which is not already on punched cards should be so mechanized as a prerequisite of computer operation.

Better management controls

Although the direct dollar savings just discussed are not to be dismissed lightly, we firmly believe that the most significant impact of the development of electronics for business is that it will bring about a profound change in what management will come to expect of its accounting and reporting systems.

In the past all of the emphasis on reports for management has revolved around the summarization of transactions that have already transpired; in other words, historical reporting. In a very real sense, management has been driving down the business highway using only the rear-vision mirror. Had the tools been available with which to prepare timely projections and forecasts as a guide for future operations, the business executive would have been in the position of looking through the windshield and using the rearview mirror of historical reporting only as a means of correcting any distortion in his forward look.

The inadequacy of such historical methods to meet the needs of a business enterprise operating in the milieu of a vigorous intrinsically complex economy has long been apparent. Actually, many techniques for the preparation of timely and adequate projections and forecasts have been developed. The big problem in implementing these techniques, however, has always been primarily one of mechanics. The forecasting and trending of business operations requires a tremendous amount of statistical manipulation which makes it simply impossible to produce such data economically or promptly enough to be of value under manual procedures or past methods of mechanization.

With the electronic computer's tremendous speed and facility for following through a series of complex operations, the only limitation on what can be done is human inability to define and develop the required formulas. As soon as we learn to define business problems in language (terms and formulas) that the computer can understand, there is practically no limit to what we can do with this new tool in the way of developing useful management control information.

So, let us look briefly at what this new forecasting tool, if properly used, can mean in relation to three of the major problems confronting business management: production control, projection of labor requirements, and sales forecasting.

Production control

With capital goods and tools of production showing constantly rising costs, it has become increasingly important that management use them in the most efficient manner. Consequently, during the past twenty years industry has been devoting more and more attention to the science of production control.

A good production control system utilizes the productive capacity of a plant in the most efficient manner. Here again the requirement for arithmetic juggling has impeded the progress of the art. The application of production control techniques requires a tremendous amount of clerical work. In addition to the disadvantage of extremely high cost, the staggering amount of work slows down the operation to a point where the information is presented so late that it loses much of its value to management.

The clerical problems presented by production control are not so pronounced during the development of the original production control schedule but arise when engineering modifications and changes in anticipated sales levels necessitate revisions in the original schedule. As a matter of fact, failure to revise the schedule to keep pace with these frequent changes often results in the production control operation deteriorating to a point where it consists of nothing more than a group of expediters meeting successive crises as they arise.

Electronic computing equipment opens the door to a degree of production control greater than heretofore possible under manual procedures or past methods of mechanization.

Projecting labor requirements

One of the problems confronting manufacturing companies is that of predicting labor requirements in the light of changes in the level or structure of operations. Further, as the labor relations situation becomes more acute, it behooves management to do everything it can to anticipate changes in its productive labor requirements.

The problem of projecting labor requirements is much the same, from the standpoint of control techniques, as that of projecting material requirements. As with a bill of materials, each item manufactured must be resolved into detailed labor factors (by type of labor) for each operation, so that it can be "exploded" into total labor requirements by type of labor and by period for the total items to be manufactured.

Here again, computers handle this tremendous task of clerical compilation with comparative ease. Under manual methods this type of "explosion" was almost prohibitive in cost, and under past methods of mechanization it was so untimely that it lost much of its value.

Sales analyses

More comprehensive and timely sales analyses and market forecasts afford another great potential application for electronic computers.

Preparing market forecasts involves the handling of complex multiple correlations in order that the projection will reflect the weighting of all variables in proportion to their significance. The statistical manipulation required to properly reflect the multiplicity of variables that must be considered for effective sales forecasting staggers the imagination. Because the amount of clerical work increases as factors for weighting are added to the formula, companies have generally limited the weighting factors to just a few major ones, with the result that the cumulative effect of the factors ignored often nullified the value of the entire forecast.

Many executives feel that the use of electronic computers in this application alone will have a profound effect on competition. Charles K. Rieger, the vice president and general manager of General Electric's Major Appliance Division, has stated that he believes the use of computers in this area will prove to be one of the most powerful competitive tools ever developed.

Summary of control advantages

Although the advantages that will accrue to management through the use of computers are manifold, there is little doubt that the most significant impact of this whole new development is that the emphasis on accounting and reporting for business will change from one of historical reporting to one of reporting in terms of the future, and hence, of providing data for the formulation of reliable management judgments and effective management controls.

Evaluation of potential use

It has been our experience that after presenting to an executive only a brief explanation of the possible applications of an electronic computer, he quickly grasps the significance of office automation and immediately visualizes the possible advantages of an installation within his own organization. Almost as quickly, however, he is drawn up sharply by the sound question of cost, and his first question usually is: "What determines if a company can economically use this type of equipment?"

Obviously, without a detailed study of a particular organization the question can be answered only in generalities; and here, as in most situations, generalities can be extremely misleading.

The fact that a major installation such as that made by GE can run into a million or more dollars is not in itself determining. For one thing, the cost is likely to be reduced in time. For another, it is possible to use the computer on a lease basis. Whatever the cost, either the amortization charges over a period of time or the rental fees must be matched against the values to be secured. Thus the elimination of 100 clerks might save $250,000 in salaries per year, and would amortize a million-dollar investment in four years.

Criteria of applicability

It might at first appear that a determination of applicability could be made on the basis of the number of employees on the payroll, or on the dollar volume of business, or perhaps on the basis of some other generally accepted criterion of size or volume. Unfortunately, we have found no such common denominator of applicability. (It is true, of course, that at least for the present, electronic computers will not be economically useful for the very small business enterprise, but even identification by elimination is hazardous.)

A case in point

We were recently asked to undertake a study for an organization which has approximately 5,000 employees. Certainly, at first glance, a company of this size appears far too small to consider the installation of an electronic computer. Yet, upon investigation, we found that this organization had such a tremendously complex payroll procedure that approximately 150 clerks were required to handle this single phase of their operations.

In this particular instance a computer might well have been economically justified. However, it was our suggestion that, before giving serious consideration to an installation, the management make a detailed study to see whether the contractual obligations and organizational policies that were the primary factors complicating the payroll could not be simplified; and that a computer be considered only if the situation could not be alleviated by such a simplification.

While it is doubtful whether this particular company will install a computer within the next few years, we can perhaps glean from this study one factor which bears directly upon the applicability of a computer in a particular situation, namely, the complexity of the reporting or accounting problem.

As many of the first computer installations will undoubtedly replace present punched-card operations, the rental and clerical costs of the latter can often be matched against the rental of a computer to obtain a quick comparative check. However, it is well to remember that, as discussed previously, this type of comparison may be most deceptive, inasmuch as substantial clerical cost relating directly to the punched-card operation may be buried in a periphery of separate departmental operations which, while far removed from the machine room, would be completely absorbed by a computer operation.

In general, it might be stated that if a computer can replace 125 to 150 clerks or the equivalent of their salaries in machine rentals, depreciation, and so on, the equipment's cost will be economically justified. It is, however, difficult to generalize about the characteristics of the companies in which such a situation is likely to prevail.

Misconceptions

As in most new fields, the early reports of overenthusiastic individuals have vied strongly for ascendancy with those of the confirmed pessimists; and, as usual, this situation has given rise to innumerable misconceptions concerning the desirability, the adequacy, and the accuracy of tape-operated electronic equipment. These erroneous concepts have ranged from such obviously mistaken assertions as that present equipment and techniques provide the answer to all management and office problems to equally exaggerated doubts of the value of any electronic automation until all facets of the problem, including the direct translation of source data into a form acceptable for electronic processing, have been mechanized to the nth degree.

Size of computers

One of the more specific fallacies is related to the popular belief that today's computers are too large, that they are too powerful, and that at their present stage of development they are designed only for the super-size organization whose clerical operations are centralized in one grandiose office comprising untold hundreds of clerks surrounded by banks of automatic and semi-automatic calculating devices. Smaller computers for smaller businesses is the battle cry of the protagonist of this misconception.

On the surface it would appear reasonable that there should be a direct correlation between office and computer dimensions, of such exactitude that most of the present potential users of electronic equipment would be best advised to defer any further consideration of this equipment until technology and manufacturing had scaled the devices down to a range of appropriate sizes that could be matched to the particular organization's requirements. But such a conclusion reflects a basic misunderstanding of a computer's operation and its application.

To refute this misconception in detail would require a technical discussion which is beyond the scope of this paper. Suffice it to say that the inherent capabilities of such equipment are more nearly measured by the size of the equipment's memory than by any other criterion and, in particular, that application of the equipment to those peculiar business and accounting problems which heretofore have never been successfully mechanized can only now be handled because of the additional facility provided by this internal memory.

As a practical matter, while there is a relatively large element of fixed cost in a computer installation, the break-even point, in terms of the size of the organization which can afford such equipment, is not as great as is generally believed. Moreover, the future developments which will scale down the break-even point so that computers will be economically feasible for even smaller organizations, may be expected to be more along the lines of generally less expensive equipment rather than computers of smaller capacity.

Fast printing

Another misconception concerning tape-operated equipment, which got started early, has become so ingrained in the thinking of engineer and consultant alike that alone it has materially slowed the development and utilization of electronic equipment in the commercial field. This misconception concerns the printing of information emerging from the system. The output data or computational results emitted from the computer proper are recorded on tape in the form of magnetic spots. This is very similar to the recording of voice or music on conventional wire or tape recorders. Information in this form is precise and permanent, but it cannot be directly observed and read. It is required, therefore, that output tapes be placed on some type of device which can read the magnetically coded data on the tape, translate the code, and then print the results in Arabic numerals and English alphabetical characters on the conventional forms and reports generally used in business.

It has been generally held that this output mechanism must be capable of printing the computational results of an electronic computer at speeds ranging from four to twenty times faster than any printing devices heretofore operated. Indeed, it has been vigorously asserted that until such printing speeds are attained or exceeded, the use of electronic computers will not prove practicable for commercial or business applications.

This premise has gained such wide acceptance that not only are the immediate manufacturers of computing equipment engaged in extensive and expensive programs of research designed to produce printers of such fantastically high speeds, but even manufacturers not concerned with the production of computers proper have become active in the development of high-speed printing equipment.

This preoccupation with high-speed printing devices appears entirely unwarranted. In a series of intensive and detailed studies which we have made in a number of representative industries there has been only one situation where the requirements for output printing were of such proportions as to indicate the desirability for providing a device that would operate at speeds in excess of those presently attained by electromechanical devices in general use today. Even in this one instance the requirement for a high-speed printing device was not considered mandatory; it merely simplified certain other problems involved in the automation of the overall operation.

It is possible that the requirement for high-speed printing devices has assumed exaggerated proportions because many of the earliest studies that were aimed at evaluating the desirability and applicability of electronic equipment for commercial use involved specialized situations, where creating a printed output was a significant part of the problem.

This was undoubtedly true in the insurance industry where progressive management, quickly recognizing the tremendous potential for economies and competitive advantages that electronic equipment could provide, inaugurated extensive programs to investigate this new scientific development. Many of these studies were devoted to the problem of premium billing and, of course, in this particular area printing presents a serious problem. But obviously, premium billing is a highly specialized situation and should not be considered typical of the average commercial or industrial problem.

Changes in routines

One other misconception which is important to refute, relates to the general impression that extensive changes in underlying business routines and methods are required before a computer can be installed. Ironically, this belief is diametrically opposed to the facts, and precisely because a computer can handle extremely complex transactions with ease, we are fearful that there may be a tendency to apply this equipment to a problem without regard to the efficiency of the basic system being mechanized. This can only result in the use of the equipment to perform a poor job more rapidly.

Future trends

As might be expected, many executives have questioned whether it might not be desirable to defer investigation into the computer field pending further development of the art. In particular, their concern has revolved around the possible rapid obsolescence of equipment presently available.

It is our opinion that the business risk may well be greater on the side of waiting rather than on the side of too rapid an approach. Our belief rests on the basis that machines can be rented, thereby minimizing the obsolescence factor, and that the ultimate use of the equipment as a management control tool can be reached only through experience and this experience cannot be obtained from a policy of watchful waiting.

The progress of electronics for business is going to be one of evolution as much as revolution, thinking not of how rapidly it will find its way into the majority of companies in our country, but primarily of how extensively it will be applied by these companies as a useful management tool.

The initial use of computers will be limited to the more prosaic functions such as general and cost accounting, the simpler sales and market analyses, and many other of the routine operations which over the past decade have been handled by less efficient and slower machines. As in any complex piece of new equipment, a period of time will be required for a company to become adept in the actual operation of an electronic computer and to develop applications for its more extensive and spectacular use. Fortunately, the routine business functions will provide the background for this education.

Thus it can be expected that management will look upon the initial period of a computer's installation as a period of training and development, a period of testing and trying, a period of experimentation and education, all of which will be subsidized by the savings to be realized through mechanization of the more routine office operations.

The more spectacular use of the equipment will only emerge as each individual organization capitalizes on the firsthand experience gained in direct use of the computer; and this experience can only be derived from a proper organizational setup which will, during the early period of installation, place constant emphasis on the integration of all management control problems to the end that they may be tested against and matched with the abilities of the computer. Only by this means can an organization develop the competence, the insight, and the ability to transform a chassis of wires, tubes, resistors, and condensers into an effective implement of management control.

It is this coming use of the computer as a management control medium which explains and underlines the real significance of electronics in business.

Background of electronics and its application to business

An article written for the firm in March, 1955

The electronic computer will not be limited to performing routine accounting functions. With its tremendous and unexplored potential it is destined to become a powerful force in shaping the destinies of the business world.

FOR CENTURIES man has used all of his ingenuity to develop new and improved mechanisms which would add strength to his arms and lend wings to his feet. But only within the past few years has he turned his attention to the development of machines which would relieve him of many of the more onerous forms of mental drudgery.

Thus it is that today we are in the very act of stepping across the threshold of a great new development in technology, a technology dedicated to automation but not concerned with the foundry, the mill, or the factory, and not designed to operate machines, to speed up production, or to control power. Rather, this new technology is concerned with the store and with the office and its ultimate purpose is to automatize those vast areas of clerical work which heretofore have remained outside the province of the simpler forms of mechanization.

Considering the tremendous advances which have been made in all fields of scientific endeavor during the past fifty years, it appears strange that the business office is only now beginning to feel the impact of this automation, while the factory and the production line have benefited from it for many years. Unreasoned as this situation may appear on the surface, there is no great mystery involved and no scientific or technical knowledge is required to understand this apparent discrepancy.

The devices used in the factory to automatically operate machines and to mechanize the adjacent supply lines are built from gears, cams, wheels, slides and other such components all assembled together and motorized to provide a recurring cycle of movement. Until just recently the same type of parts, only on a smaller scale, served as the operating mechanism in all

33

the usual forms of office machines. In the factory these mechanical mechanisms have performed eminently well, and particularly important is the fact that in many instances they have been capable of mechanizing an operation in its entirety.

Mechanical office equipment has also served satisfactorily, but always with the serious limitation that it could be used to perform only a part of the total job. Consequently, in a typical mechanized office routine it will be found that the mechanical operations are always interspersed with one or more functions or steps requiring a clerical skill or a considered decision, which functions or steps are beyond the ability of any of the usual mechanical devices to handle.

As a result, even in those instances where mechanization has been carried to the extreme, as with punched cards, it will be found that there is still a very substantial volume of work which must be handled by clerical employees. So long as the wheel and other related mechanical units remained as the basic medium for building office equipment, the mechanization of the business office has been limited.

But today all this is changed. With the advent of the electronic computer, the routines of the business office have been unshackled from the binding limitations of mechanical units, and with the replacement of gears, wheels, and cams by electron tubes and associated parts, we have, in truth, not an improved model of an old machine but a new device, a new mechanism, an entirely new tool for use in solving the many problems of American business.

The development of the electronic art as applied to business devices is a direct outgrowth of the tremendous impetus given all electronic research during World War II, and this new field has continued to grow and expand so rapidly that three distinct areas have evolved.

The areas of development are:

1. General purpose computers,

2. Fixed program or special purpose computers, and

3. Auxiliary electronic devices.

The major area of development has been and probably will continue to be the general purpose digital computer. This is the device which is capable of performing automatically and completely within itself an almost unlimited series of sequential steps involving both logical and mathematical operations. So extensive are the capabilities of this class of device that there has been a very decided tendency to attribute human qualities to the machines. This tendency to personify computers is understandable when you consider that many of them have electric eyes which see, sensing mechanisms which feel, and memory that recalls. In addition they have logic sections which, under certain conditions, can make decisions and in an elementary way they can learn from past experience.

Within this category of equipment there are two sizes of machines. There is the so-called large-scale computer which, perhaps, has been given its name because of its tremendously large capacity, its ability to handle a gigantic load of office routines, and its not insignificant cost. It is this particular piece of equipment which has received the most attention from the business world during the past five years, and it is this type of device which will be discussed in more detail in a few moments.

In the general purpose computer category there is also the small computer. This computer is very similar to the large-scale machine but it is smaller in size, capacity and productivity and, of course, lower in cost.

It is important to realize that electronic techniques are not confined to the supersize organizations. Technological developments are making this equipment available for various size organizations and for a multitude of uses.

Our second classification of equipment has been designated as fixed program machines. This equipment operates electronically and in many cases makes use of the same components as are used in the general purpose computers. Fixed program machines are inflexible in that they are designed to perform a particular job and, generally speaking, cannot be used for any other purpose.

An example of this type of machine is the Distributron. This is a device which was built for John Plain & Company, a Chicago mail-order house, and it is used to tally sales by items for the purpose of furnishing buyers with current information on sales trends. The Distributron is not a large-scale computer, but rather it is an adding machine with a magnetic memory. The capacity of this particular model is 39,000 items consisting of a merchandise code and a quantity figure.

Another excellent example of a fixed program machine is the Reservisor, which is a device installed by American Airlines in New York. The purpose of the Reservisor is to maintain an inventory of all space on flights departing from the New York area for a period of ten days. Sales offices located around the metropolitan area can quiz the memory of the device to see whether seats are available for a certain number of passengers on a specific flight. An average of 35,000 interrogations a day indicates the usefulness of this machine.

This, then is the second classification of equipment, electronic devices designed for a particular purpose and capable of performing only the specific functions for which they were designed. We now have covered two of the developed areas, the general purpose computer, which is a completely flexible information handling system and the special purpose device which is a good but an inflexible information handling system.

Third and last, there has been the development of electronic techniques to improve or speed up what are essentially mechanical devices. In this area we find a great deal of developmental work being done to devise high-speed paper handling machines. Commercial banks, for instance, are in dire need of some sort of device to sort, post, and otherwise process their commercial customers' checks and this is one of the fields in which there is a great deal of research being done.

This particular area of electronic development might be described as the harnessing of muscles and it is quite similar to the use of electronics in the factory, as in both cases the problem is one of moving physical objects.

This has been a very condensed coverage of the areas in which electronics are being developed, but even with this brief glimpse of the field it should be evident that electronic techniques and electronic devices are being designed to give a lift to practically all the functions which are found in the large and in the small business office.

All of the developmental areas mentioned could be discussed profitably at great length, but this discussion will be limited to the large-scale computer. This particular piece of equipment has been selected because:

1. It is the most significant technological development which has been made in the electronics field.

2. Being an extremely flexible general purpose machine, this device fits most commercial applications. As a result, industry generally has studied this device more thoroughly than other electronic apparatus and more of this type of equipment is being installed.

3. The operation of a large-scale computer is basic to the operation of all types of electronic equipment. Consequently, an understanding of

35

the computer affords an insight into all other forms of electronic devices.

The discussion of a computer naturally divides itself into three major topics:

1. What distinguishes computers from all other forms of mechanization?

2. What is the basic principle of their operation?

3. What does industry expect from this new technology?

The comments and illustrations which follow will reflect the electronics picture as it is presently seen on a wide horizon. This extended viewpoint is being given to provide a bench mark against which anyone can measure the present accomplishments and the future potential of electronics in his own type of business.

It has already been mentioned that historically the wheel has been the basic device which accomplishes mathematical operations in all types of calculating equipment. The simple comptometer, the complex adding machine, the desk calculator and even the punched-card tabulator all use the wheel as the means of performing additions, subtractions, and other mathematical calculations. However, the wheel can revolve only a limited number of times per minute and still add with any degree of accuracy. Friction and inertia are the principal problems in this respect. As long as the wheel remained the basic unit for calculation, speed was limited.

The release from the wheel is the focal point which differentiates the computer from all other devices which are bogged down and held back by the physical properties of friction and inertia. With the replacement of the wheel by the electronic tube comes speed, . . . speed of such magnitude as has never been dreamed of before.

For example, the wheel as used in a standard piece of tabulating equipment can add a column of 150 figures, each with 10 digits, in 1 minute. In the same length of time the electronic computer can add over 100,000 similar numbers.

Another unique feature of computers is their ability to perform, within the sphere of a single piece or system of equipment, more than just mathematical computations. Computers can sort and arrange items, collate data, compare values, make decisions and, in effect, perform all the functions involved in a routine clerical operation, all within what is essentially one piece of equipment.

Speed is dramatic, and certainly important. Multiple operation is very significant, but perhaps of greatest importance is automation. The large-scale computer is a completely flexible machine which will follow an almost unlimited number of sequential steps, automatically and without human intervention. But it can do absolutely nothing without first being told exactly what to do.

How do you tell a machine what to do? The underlying key or device which motivates the computer and causes it to perform in orderly sequence the desired routines is instructions.

The process of developing a set of instructions is called programming. Programming is the very core of computer operation and as such it is an art. To understand what is involved in programming, imagine what would be involved if you were to attempt to give oral instructions to a group of wholly uninformed individuals so that they would be able to process each step of your payroll or be able to perform all of the operations required in a complete sales audit. Each detailed step would have to be described simply, directly, and explicitly.

Programming is giving the same type of instructions to a computer in a language or code which the computer can comprehend and follow. There is one significant difference, however, between these two types of instructions. In manual clerical procedures all of the elementary decisions are left up to clerks' discretion and common sense. Obviously the computer has no innate intelligence and everything must be spelled out to the last detail. This is particularly true whenever there are decisions to be made in the course of the routine. In such instances the computer must be provided with all of the possible situations and with all of the possible choices to be made.

To use a computer to perform a particular operation you must first study the operation in detail, next determine each minute step in the process and, finally, translate each operation or step into a code or an instruction which the computer can understand. Reaching the point of actually using the computer, the first operation then is to place the predetermined instructions into the machine. This is just like feeding a computer an instruction manual. These instructions are stored internally within the machine and are used to guide the computer step by step through the process.

The time required to study and develop a set of computer instructions is not negligible. Further, because of the variations found in procedures and policies, even between companies in the same business, it does not appear that there will be any royal road to obtaining programs which someone else has worked out and paid for. It can be expected that those who start in the field first will finish first. And many businessmen confidently believe that this is an area where it is better to be a leader than a follower.

To summarize, computers differ from all prior forms of mechanization in three important respects:

1. They are tremendously fast.
2. They perform multiple functions.
3. They operate automatically.

Generally speaking, the medium for transferring instructions into a computer is magnetic tape. However, it should not be deduced that magnetic tape is the only medium for communicating with a computer. Actually, the electronic computer is an extremely versatile linguist and it can be built so that it can comprehend many different types of input forms.

For instance, it would be possible to design a computer which could accommodate, in addition to magnetic tape, punched garment tags and punched paper tape. It could also have one or more manual keyboards for entering data directly into the machine.

It can be seen, then, that electronic apparatus can be built to almost any specifications required, because the medium permits the maximum of flexibility. And this flexibility often has far-reaching advantages. For instance, by means of the various types of input and output mediums, communication is possible between different pieces of electronic equipment situated at varying distances apart, whether they be in the same room, the same building, or miles apart.

For example, let us assume that within the computer room it is necessary to transfer an output tape from the computer to a printing device in order to produce checks, reports, lists or other types of output in the conventional printed form. In some types of systems it is necessary to physically carry the tape from one machine to the other. In more advanced systems the tapes are switched electrically from machine to machine.

Often communication is desired between the computer and some form of input recorder or register. This input device may be located within the store or the office but it may be at some distance from the computer. In this situation communication can be effected either by direct electrical connection between the device recording the original transaction and the computer or the original recording device can prepare magnetic or punched paper tape, which tape can then be physically transported to the computer for processing.

Still a third type of communication which may be required in a computer system involves the transmission of data from one physical location to another. Here again, of course, tapes could be prepared and mailed or otherwise physically transported between the two locations. But within the past few years there have been important improvements made in tape operated wire transmission and today a number of the larger decentralized companies are installing apparatus to use this new facility.

From all this it can be seen that electronic equipment is powerful, flexible, and versatile and already all manner of applications are being studied by the important industrial, commercial and utility companies, both in this country and abroad.

Among the companies whose computers are already installed are General Electric, U. S. Steel, Westinghouse, Monsanto Chemical, Metropolitan Life Insurance Co., and E. I. du Pont. Some of the early applications have included payroll, material control, sales analysis, order service, departmental cost statements and forecasts.

The du Pont company has ordered two computers and has an established program designed to research their use in many different fields. This program has initially been budgeted to cover several years of work and provides for using up to 200 programmers on the project.

Other companies with computers to be delivered by the end of this year include:

Sylvania Electric
Chesapeake & Ohio Railroad
Commonwealth Edison Company
Consolidated Vultee Aircraft Corp.
Lockheed Aircraft
Franklin Life Insurance Co.
Pacific Mutual Life Insurance Co.
Prudential Life Insurance Company
Pratt & Whitney
Eastman Kodak
Esso Standard Oil
Chrysler Corporation
Ford Motor Company
Bank of America
International Harvester

There are, of course, many others scheduled for delivery during 1956, and others scheduled into 1957.

Thus it can be seen that the electronic computer is no visionary's dream to be realized some time in the future. Already it has been accepted as a practical and useful machine which is well-suited to processing the complex accounting routines found everywhere in modern business. And with this acceptance has also come the recognition that the computer will not be limited to performing these prosaic functions, but with its tremendous and unexplored potential it is inevitably destined to become a powerful force in shaping the future destinies of the business world.

Electronic computers in the utility industry

Before the public utility partners and managers of Arthur Andersen & Co., Chicago, June, 1956

Perhaps the most important use of the electronic computer will be in assisting management to plan for future operations.

SOME YEARS AGO electronics was the art which dealt with circuitry, centering around the operations of the electron tube. This is still true today, but only in part. Today electronics and electronic circuitry include solid-state units, such as the transistor and other similar crystalline devices. But it does not stop there, for the term, electronics, today also encompasses the field of magnetics in many different forms.

This extended concept of electronics is particularly far-reaching when it is applied to the device identified as the electronic computer. For this broad class of devices may make use of vacuum tubes, transistors, diodes, and other circuit elements, including magnetic cores and magnetic drums. It may even make use of such unromantic devices as old-fashioned electric relays.

The history of the electronic computer is a curious one; it is an anachronism. This history literally runs backward. But before we discuss the computer itself, it would be well to trace briefly the background of mechanized processes in the accounting and record keeping area of many public utilities.

Mechanization, beyond the elementary bookkeeping or manually operated posting machine, dates back to the early 1900's, when the first punched-card installations were made. About 1920, the Los Angeles Department of Water and Power was the first utility to install punched-card equipment for customers' accounting, followed soon after by Buffalo Gas and Electric Company. With improvements in equipment and the development of additional and more versatile machines, the applications were extended to include practically all of the routine accounting operations.

These original machines were rather simple devices. They were electro-mechanical in nature and consisted for the most part of relays, cams, wheels, and gears. It is not their method of operation, however, which is important to understand, but rather that these were simple machines, each capable of performing only a very limited number of different operations and these operations at a constant, but relatively slow speed. Consequently, in order to prepare a payroll or to handle the store's records, it was necessary to have a battery of machines, each performing its own individual function, the sum of which comprised the total operation. Thus there was a machine to sort, a machine to multiply, a machine to interfile, and a machine to add the list.

This type of mechanization, crude as it was, was not without its advantages. First, because the machines were simple, their application and operation were also relatively simple. Second, because of their limited ability, the areas which could be mechanized were sharply defined. This, coupled with the constant speed of the machines, permitted reasonably accurate determination of the economics involved in the installation of the equipment. And third, because the equipment was moderate in price and the number of pieces used in a particular situation could be scaled with reasonable accuracy to the size or volume of the operation, the machines were adaptable to utilities which varied widely in size and in organization or physical setup.

In 1948 a new device appeared on the horizon. This machine was called the electronic calculator. Basically, this machine was just another of the unitized punched-card devices, but it possessed three distinctive features which foreshadowed things to come. First, this machine performed operations at speeds many times faster than had any previous piece of equipment. Second, it was extremely versatile and was capable of performing quite a number of different operations. And third, the machine was considerably more expensive than any of its predecessors.

It is significant that in spite of its relatively high price, the machine was rapidly integrated by many utilities into their mechanical operations, particularly into their billing functions.

In 1949, there was heard the first faint whisper about a new and most unusual machine which could process accounting and business-type data. Because the machine itself was not in evidence, nor would be for several years, the story of its capabilities, its speed, and its overall effect upon accounting and clerical processes became more exaggerated with each telling. Unfortunately, this exaggerated aura of superability which surrounded the yet unveiled machine, was carried over to the first actual electronic computer which was built for business purposes.

Computers have had a very brief history. The first machines developed during and immediately following World War II were scientific devices designed to solve lengthy and involved mathematical problems. And, indeed, there are many people who still believe that the equipment available today is limited to this type of operation.

The first machines, however, differed from present equipment in two very important aspects. Because they were designed solely for mathematical processes, no provision was made for the handling of alphabetic characters, and this feature separates all early scientific computers from later business models. Further, the scientific machines required little in the way of equipment to handle the input and output of data and as a result, the input-output mechanisms were crude in comparison to the computer proper.

A business computer is not a machine but a system. Included in the system there must be input devices capable of handling the extremely large volumes of source data which is generally associated with business operations, and there must be a means of output which is capable of preparing the numerous accounting and business records and reports.

Following the initial use of computers for purely scientific research purposes, there was an intermediate period when the device was put to work to solve more practical engineering problems and to handle statistical computations.

The first complete computer system for business purposes was marketed in 1953 and General Electric was the first manufacturing organization to place an order. Since that date, several other systems have become available. In 1954, the so-called small computer was first placed on the market, and additional systems became available in 1955. In 1956 we will see a continuation of development with improved small machines and more powerful larger ones.

You will notice a most unusual situation here. Most inventions start on a simple basis and become increasingly more complex as time goes on. The automobile, for instance, with its wagon-like body and hand-cranked motor gradually developed into the high-powered, luxury machine of today.

The computer on the other hand, emerged as a mammoth device, highly mechanized, extremely complex in operation, and above all, very costly in price. Following the initial group of machines, however, there has been a scaling down in size, a decrease in speed and complexity, and most important, a decrease in cost. This is a complete reversal of practically all inventions. But this backward direction means a broadening of the market for computers and considerable simplification in their installation.

Before proceeding further, it might be well to give a brief explanation of the basic difference between the various sizes of electronic machines.

We have already mentioned the punched-card calculator. This is an electronic ma-

chine which serves primarily to substantially enhance the scope of a punched-card installation, but it is still only a single unit which is an integral part of a complete installation. In terms of capacity, capability and versatility, the punched-card calculator ranks lowest on the list of electronic machines. In terms of cost and simplicity of installation and operation, it ranks first. The calculator has been included in this discussion primarily because its exceptional operation did much to pave the way for larger equipment by demonstrating the dependability and high degree of accuracy provided by electronic equipment.

The next larger group of machines has been designated as small computers. In this class of equipment, the input is generally by means of punched cards and the output is also by means of cards. On the output side, the resulting cards are converted to printed output by placing the cards in a conventional punched-card tabulator-printer. Obviously a system of this type is limited in speed to the speed of processing punched cards.

A number of variations of this system are available or will be shortly. For instance, some computers provide for direct input from one or more keyboard devices; some also provide for input by means of punched-paper tape. Output may be accomplished by connecting a regular punched-card printer directly to the computer and printing out.

It is important to understand that this type of system is capable of performing all of the operations that can be processed by the largest devices built, the only difference being in the speed of operation. This speed limitation is imposed by two conditions: the input and output speed is limited to punched-card feed speeds, and second, the processing is limited to the internal speed of the computer.

Broadly speaking, a fast computer will process data five to ten times as rapidly as a slow machine. Electronic input and output methods, however, are fifteen to one hundred times as fast as punched-card methods. To increase the speed of this type of system, magnetic tape files have been added. These files may contain reference tables, account balances or any other data involved in or resulting from the processing.

This type of equipment can be used in customer billing and revenue accounting operations and a few utilities are experimenting in this area. These intermediate-size machines are expensive as compared to punched-card equipment. They are relatively difficult to install, but not too difficult to operate.

This brings us to the third group of machines, the largest type of equipment, the large-scale computer. Here we have, not a machine, but a system, which will include input and output devices all operated electronically. Input to the computer is by means of magnetic tape. To place source data onto the tape, the original information is generally punched into cards, and then by means of a card-to-tape converter the information on the cards is transferred to tape.

Many public utilities have eliminated meter books and have their meter readers mark the meter readings directly on tabulating cards. The cards are then automatically punched and are ready for further processing. This particular method of originating source data fits directly into a tape processing system.

With the large computer, the output is also tape. Any printed records which are required are obtained by transferring the tapes to tape printers. These printers spew out printed results at speeds ranging from 150 to 1000 lines of printing per minute.

An important feature is the multiple inputs and the multiple outputs attached to the system. Up to the present time, this particular characteristic has been found only on equipment of this class. And it is this multiple input-output feature which adds great versatility and speed to the operations of the machine.

This third class of equipment, then, is the fastest and the most versatile. On the other hand, it is also the most difficult to install and the most expensive to rent or purchase.

Let's get more specific and examine this situation more closely. During the past twenty years, an increasing number of public utilities have installed punched-card equipment. The primary reason for mechanization has been economic: to reduce costs or at least to hold the line on costs. It is true that some installations have been made to improve management reporting, as in the case of utilities which have mechanized as a consequence of installing responsibility accounting. But even in this situation, the underlying reason is economic.

It can be expected that the installation of electronic computers by utilities will have to be justified on the same basis. Or to put it more bluntly, if computers can't reduce expenses, utilities won't use them. And here we come to grips with the nub of the problem. A large computer costs from $300,000 to $500,000 a year to operate. Obviously, it must offset at least that much expense. This immediately identifies the machine with a very few of the largest utilities, specifically, those which have accounting and clerical costs of comparable proportions.

As a matter of fact, at the present state of the art, the marketable area for the large computer is probably even more severely limited. This comes about because of the difficulties involved in the installation of a computer, and the length of time and the costs attendant thereto.

The installation of any mechanized system starts with a detailed review of the manual procedures which are in use. This is followed by the development of procedures for the machines. Generally, methods of reporting source data and related forms must be revised, as greater accuracy is required in their preparation and more rigid time limits must be imposed on their submission. New and more effective preaudit procedures must be developed to minimize erroneous data being fed into the machine, and finally an efficient control procedure must be set up to verify the accuracy of the mechanical processing.

With punched cards, the machine and related procedures required to effect an installation might take from six to eight months to complete for a single function such as payroll or material control. To mechanize customer billing and accounting might take a year or longer.

An electronic computer system is many times more difficult to install than a punched-card system and there is every evidence that the installation is correspondingly lengthened. This brings about a severe problem in the economics of installing the equipment which, for the immediate future, at least will probably severely limit the number of installations to be made.

Some comprehension of this problem can be gained when it is recognized that with the limited experience developed so far, it takes between one and two years to develop the procedures necessary to place a single complex function on the computer. From this it can be appreciated that labor costs for this work would run many thousands of dollars.

It follows that if four, five, or six functions must be mechanized to displace costs equivalent to the costs of the computer, the costs to develop the procedures alone could run exceedingly high, and presuming, which is most likely, that neither the supervision or manpower would be available to develop the procedures in less than two or three years, there would be the additional cost of the unabsorbed time of the computer.

This is, of course, a dark picture and is heavily weighted by the fact that the field is still very new. In time it can be expected that improved techniques and increased experience will substantially reduce the installation time, and thereby substantially change the economic picture.

Even at best, however, it does not seem likely that any except the large utilities will install the present large-scale computer. It is more reasonable to expect that the greatest number of utilities will look to the medium or small computer as the next step in their mechanization program, and that this step may well be a wedding between electronic equipment and punched cards.

But large-scale or small computers in all electronic or combined equipment, there are many problems other than cost which must be solved. With many utilities, the problem of centralization will have to be solved before any mass processing device can be installed. This will be particularly true in the area of customer billing and revenue accounting. Here many of the larger utilities now operate on a completely decentralized basis, with numerous policy and operational deficiencies which are minor individually, but in the aggregate, add up to a problem of substantial magnitude. Where this situation exists, there is a great deal to recommend the installation or extension of a punched-card system to accomplish this centralization. As a matter of fact, we have made such a recommendation to one of our large utility clients.

You may wonder at the advice to install a punched-card system and then to turn around and completely change over to a different form of mechanization. In many cases such a procedure would be ridiculous. However, the centralization and mechanization of the billing and revenue accounting procedures of a large utility is a gigantic job. In fact, either job alone is sufficiently difficult to stretch the abilities of any group to do the job well in a reasonable period of time. Consequently, it is better to centralize and then to mechanize, using equipment which is familiar, rather than to burden the job by adding to all the problems of centralization, the problems related to new equipment, on which few if any individuals would have had any depth of experience.

Closely akin to centralization, and perhaps so closely involved as to require only mentioning, is the problem of communications. For the most part, high-speed mass processing will have little to offer unless the source data flows into the processing location and the produced results flow out to the required areas on a timely basis. This problem again, like that of centralization, can probably be solved by using punched cards, which can thereby set the stage for electronic processing operations.

Any form of mechanization, and in particular computers, tends to lead into the production of more and more summary records. This trend naturally follows and becomes more pronounced as advancement is made in the development of automatic processing. For the more automatic the process, the less printing out there is as an operational step. Nor can this situation be reversed, for either you minimize the automation, or you slow it down by a printing requirement, and any degree of slowdown for printing can very quickly make this type of mechanization more costly than some simpler form.

Actually, summary records in and of themselves are not bad. On the contrary, it is probable that in today's systems there is a great deal being printed which is superfluous. The nature of the equipment itself produces printed output which then becomes a requirement. Much of what is printed in the average system today is used only occasionally, and there would be little loss if, on those occasions, some additional work would be required to fill in the detail. Any high-speed, automatic system will force changes. Education is the solution to the problem.

It should be understood that there is a sharp difference between producing summary results and records behind which the detail does not exist, and producing summary records behind which there is complete detail, which may not be prepared in printed form prior to the preparation of the summary results. The former was a situation which prevailed in the early days of punched cards and did much to discredit this method of mechanization. The preparation of summary results, with detail to be printed later or upon request, will be part of the overall systems change involved in greater automation.

There is another point which probably should not be overlooked when discussing the extension of mechanization in the utility industry. This point has to do with the actual realization of the possible savings attained. Effectively, a machine, no matter how fast it runs or how efficiently it operates, can only produce cost savings by the removal of personnel from the payroll.

In most utilities this is no small problem as there seems to be a general policy in the industry not to discharge employees but to achieve diminution of personnel by attrition. For small changes in personnel this type of corrective policy is adequate and satisfactory. However, an electronic computer is apt to affect from one hundred to two hundred or more positions and the displacement of the related personnel is not likely to be solved satisfactorily by natural attrition.

It can be seen, then, that the installation of an electronic computer, particularly a large one, is no small undertaking. In addition to the difficult problems inherent in developing the procedures and applying the machine to the accounting operations of the utility, there are problems of centralization, organization, policy, and education which have to be solved.

Naturally, these problems are not going to stop the use of this type of equipment. Already there are three utilities in the process of installing the equipment, Commonwealth Edison, Detroit Edison, and Consolidated Edison. There will be more to follow.

On the other hand it is likely that many utilities will not see fit to leap into the large computer, but will move forward at a more leisurely pace by installing smaller equipment. Perhaps a machine for payroll and material and supplies, another machine for general accounting, and perhaps two or more machines for customer billing and accounting. It is even possible that this approach might prove out in the end to be the more economical.

No discussion of utilities and computers would be complete without mentioning the analog computer.

The computer which we have been discussing up to this point has been the digital computer. This is a computer which operates with discrete numbers (digits) just like adding machines, calculators, etc.; obviously, this is required when dealing with most accounting matters, particularly cash.

An analog computer is something else. It does not deal with digits or discrete figures; rather it deals with continuous variables. A familiar example of the mechanical type of analog computers is the slide rule, which functions by making lengths on a stick analogous to numbers.

The electronic direct analog computer includes a device called a network analyzer. It is the network analyzer which will be of increasing interest to the public utilities. With this device an exact model of the utilities' systems can be set up:

1. To allocate generation among a large number of generators so as to minimize the cost of power.

2. To study the effect of changes on the system.

3. To assist in planning for future operations.

As used in connection with dispatching operations, the computer must be supplied with:

1. Cost of fuel at each location (including incremental maintenance cost and ash handling expense).

2. Generation of each generator.

3. Power flow over each interconnection.

4. Transmission loss constant for each line.

5. Etc. . . . .

Based upon the system requirements, the computer will determine the load for each generator for minimum cost of power.

Another use of the analog computer is to study the effects of changes upon the system. For this purpose the computer would be supplied with an analyzer board which would permit the engineers to duplicate the system under such conditions as would be encountered if a power failure occurred during a thunderstorm.

And last, but perhaps most important, is the use of both the analog and the digital computer to assist in planning for future operations. Here the computer would answer such questions as: where should new plants be located; how big should they be; will new transmission lines be economical, etc.

All in all the electronic computer will undoubtedly prove to be a most important device in the growth and economical operation of the public utility.

Introductory address

Before the Data Processing Conference,
at the University of Florida,
Gainesville, April 28, 1960

The release from the wheel and the substitution of the electronic circuit was the focal point which differentiated computers from all devices which were bogged down and held back by the physical properties of friction and inertia.

I AM PLEASED to have this opportunity to give the introductory address to you this morning.

The use of electronic impulses as a means of handling information and data is not new anymore. And any group which gathers to study and discuss the subject today is almost bound to be composed of individuals with a rather wide range of interests and backgrounds. Almost certainly, there will be some among you who have already had a substantial amount of experience in the field and are particularly knowledgeable with respect to the mechanics of the equipment. It is equally probable that there are some of you who have had only a minimum of exposure to the subject and who are particularly anxious to become better grounded in the more basic aspects of the subject.

What then to cover in the introductory phase of this meeting? I concluded that it might be profitable to use the time allotted to me to cover two broad points: first, a brief discussion reviewing with you the development of business equipment; second, a discussion covering certain fundamental axioms which should always be kept in mind when dealing in the vast and complex field of electronic data processing.

First, then, a brief review. Without in any way minimizing the profound and important effects which the great religions have had upon the world, it can probably be truthfully said that the history of tools is the history of civilization. When man developed a language, he forever separated the species from the beasts. When he developed an alphabet, recorded history began. When he invented the wheel, he took the first step toward relieving himself of his physical burdens, and ultimately this same device relieved him of the tedium of many mental calculations.

The printing press started mass thinking. The steam engine developed the power for the industrial revolution. The Wright Brothers at Kitty Hawk broke the gravitational chain which bound man to the earth, and forever ended any assured security afforded by geographical location. Albert Einstein, at the Institute for Advanced Study at Princeton, developed his famous equation for energy, the ultimate effect of which is not yet fully known.

As the problems of science and business became more complex, the need for tools and equipment to handle these problems became more apparent. Necessity, it is said, is the mother of invention. Certainly this statement has never been more true than in the development of machines to handle scientific and business problems.

In 1885, Dr. Herman Hollerith, a distinguished statistician employed by the United States Government to assist in the completion of the 10th census, was wrestling in Washington, D. C. with a problem involving the expeditious handling of business facts. The information Dr. Hollerith was dealing with was collected in 1880 and 1881, but five years later there was still a struggle to compile it. The tenth census was completed in 1887, but it was evident that, at the rate the country was growing, one census would not be published before the next one was taken.

Dr. Hollerith set to work to find a way by which all recording, tabulating, and analyzing of facts could be performed by machinery. The results of his efforts were truly the foundation of the equipment you will study today.

Dr. Hollerith's system was fundamentally simple. It consisted essentially of a method of recording facts in any given situation by punching holes according to a definite pattern in a piece of paper. The original plan used strips of paper, but Dr. Hollerith later found it better to use a separate card of standard size and shape for each "unit — item."

It is interesting to note that Dr. Hollerith started with strips of paper which were encoded, and that today the cycle is complete, with many of the larger computer systems using this basic principle.

The original equipment was composed of three units: a punch, a sorter, and a tabulator. The tabulator had mechanical counters, with visible dials for the reading of totals. On this initial effort improvements were continuously made.

The development of the printing tabulator was one of the early major accomplishments in the new field. This piece of equipment emerged in 1919. Improvements and additional developments continued throughout the 1920's and 30's, and they were needed to meet the ever-expanding requirements for faster and more powerful tools.

In spite of this continuing development, the clerical labor force in this country was growing at a faster rate than all other classes of employment. In 1940 the ratio of clerical workers to productive workers was one to five. In 1958 the ratio had fallen to one to three. It is evident that even today we are struggling with the same problem that plagued Dr. Hollerith in 1885, how to handle an increasingly larger volume of office work faster and more economically.

It is interesting to note that an important reason for the disproportionate growth of the clerical force during the 1940's was that scientific research, which substantially increased the productive capacity of the plant, did not meet the same challenge in the office.

For over one hundred years the wheel has been the basic tool which has been used in all types of computing equipment. The simple comptometer, the more complex desk calculator, and even the most advanced electro-mechanical punched-card calculator all use the wheel as a means of performing addition, subtraction and other types of mathematical calculations.

However, the wheel operates on a shaft and as a result it can only turn a certain number of revolutions a minute and still perform with any degree of accuracy. Friction and inertia are the principal problems in this respect, and as long as the wheel remained the basic tool for calculations, speed was bound to be limited.

In the search for release from the wheel it was natural that engineers began to experiment with electronic impulses as a medium for recording figures, because electronic impulses do not have the limitation of friction or inertia. It was easily conceivable that you could have one electronic impulse to represent the digit 1, just like throwing a light switch on one time, two impulses to represent the figure 2, throwing the light switch on twice, etc. But the problem was how to set up a device that could record and accumulate these electrical impulses much like the wheel operated.

It is not surprising that the first development was by a bright engineer who hit upon the idea of taking the wheel and, in effect, opening it up and substituting an electronic tube for each of the numerical values on the wheel. In other words, a row of electronic tubes was substituted for the wheel. Thus, when one electronic impulse hit the row of tubes, the first tube conducted representing the digit 1. If three more impulses were impressed on the circuit the fourth tube conducted, indicating the value 4. This type of circuit was known as the cascade circuit and it was the first step in the development of electronic computation.

With the wheel, the fastest practical speed of adding was approximately 1500 digits per minute. With the first cascade counter, speeds of 3,000,000 digits per minute were achieved.

The release from the wheel was the focal point which differentiated computers from all devices which were bogged down and held back by the physical properties of friction and inertia. And time may well prove that the substitution of an electronic circuit for the wheel was a historical breakthrough of the same magnitude as those epochal events which were mentioned earlier.

The first electronic calculators were hardly more than high speed counters, although they did include one operating element which might well be characterized as the most important functional element of the equipment. This feature is the ability to follow automatically through a long series of successive steps or operations without human intervention. This was the key to minimizing labor, and represented a long step forward in the development of a truly automated operation.

Since the historic day when the first crude electronic calculator was assembled, there has been an almost continuous flow of these devices from the laboratory. Large and small equipment, specialized devices and general purpose machines have become available. But it is not my purpose to discuss with you the modern machines. You will hear this firsthand this afternoon from the manufacturers' representatives, themselves. Rather, I would now like to address myself to identifying a few fundamental axioms which are undoubtedly relevant to many situations, but which I feel are particularly worthy of stress in connection with computers.

When studying or analyzing any field, an essential prerequisite is objectivity. An unfortunate aspect in the early years of development of any new field is that there can be only a relatively few people who have been exposed to a sufficiently broad experience to be able to objectively evaluate its numerous aspects, its problems and potentialities.

The computer field is no exception to this generalization, and thus we find that today the field is rife with claims, rumors, denials, as well as sharp differences of opinions between both users and experts. Furthermore, the entire situation is accentuated by strong, although certainly healthy, competition between manufacturers of equipment. It is little wonder then that those who seek a depth of knowledge in this field, whether expert or novitiate, find themselves at times confused.

And so it is that we are confronted with our first axiom which might be stated, read and study but don't believe everything you see or hear. Let me hasten to say that this includes your speaker. I would be the first to admit that many of my own ideas and convictions of say five, six, seven, or eight years ago have changed considerably!

I do not mean to imply that we should not absorb the mass of material which is characteristic of the field, for there is some value in everything. The important point is to recognize that we all have our own viewpoints and our own reasons for giving expression to our ideas and thoughts. Think for yourself is a byline for cigarette advertising. It might perhaps be even more importantly applied to a field such as computers.

Many surveys have been published which attempt to tell us where we stand with respect to the computer art. For instance, one group of surveys has been made to obtain a consensus regarding the results of computer utilization. One recent survey indicates that a substantial percentage of users are less than satisfied. These surveys imply that there is a norm by which we can anticipate the success of a future effort. But having fixed a norm for one company or one industry can we expect that all other companies will be normal? Perhaps there is even an advantage in being unique.

This brings us to our second axiom which, although a cliché, is still pertinent. What is good for one company may not be good for another.

Take two companies, A and B, both in the same industry and highly competitive. Company A became a "pioneer" in the electronics field and made an early installation. The management of Company B, feeling it had to be "competitive," also installed a computer and followed the same general trail blazed by Company A. Each company installed identical computers for the same application, which in this case was billing.

Some weeks after the start of the installation we find the net cost of running the billing system has substantially increased. There is, of course, a proper and valid reason for this. Neither company felt that it could disband the old system until the new one was completely proven. The obvious result, then, was a duplication of costs. At this point, however, neither company was particularly concerned, since the situation was exactly as expected. The costs began to recede as the former system was gradually abandoned, and efficiency picked up under the new procedures.

Although the two companies were in the same industry and were highly competitive, their methods of billing were far from identical. Company A had approximately one-third more personnel involved in the billing function than Company B, and was a much more likely candidate for a computer, since the potential for savings was considerably larger than in Company B. The resulting savings were satisfactory to Company A but not to Company B.

Unfortunately, the fact that Company A used more people than Company B to perform the same function was not considered by Company B when its management decided it should install a computer "to be competitive."

This case study may appear to be extreme, but it does point up the danger of attempting to set up a norm or of relying heavily on what someone else has done. It is not intended that this example should imply that Company B could not or should not use a computer. It is only intended to demonstrate that it should not have considered Company A's use of this device for billing as a substantive reason for its own installation.

Axiom number three is simple, obvious, and too often completely disregarded. Don't expect a computer to solve all your problems.

Prior to the advent of the electronic computer the average individual in management held a "show me" attitude with respect to all mechanization procedures relating to the office, if he was interested in these problems at all. This has all changed with the computer. Even the very top levels of management, which a few years ago probably had no idea how their paperwork was handled or how their reports were prepared, suddenly became intensely concerned with the subject.

The decision for mechanization has even been found on the agenda of board of directors' meetings. Why this metamorphosis? The underlying cause for this transformation can probably be traced back to the atomic explosion at Hiroshima. The startling realization that man had solved the mysteries of the atom triggered a feeling of awe for science and scientific developments.

This feeling of awe developed an aura around all things atomic or electronic. A general belief was built up that almost anything could be accomplished if electronics had anything to do with the process. While this type of thinking is gradually fading, it is still far from dead, particularly at the management level.

Obviously the computer is not in itself a solution to all of the problems which beset a business, and, as a practical matter, the device can propagate all kinds of trouble on its own. And that leads directly into my fourth axiom, which will be the last one for today. A prerequisite of a good computer system is to have people who know computers.

Again, we have a seemingly obvious axiom, which is too often overlooked or ignored. It is certain that any business would insist on having trained architects and contractors build their new plant, that they would use professional engineers and scientists in their research laboratories, that the responsibility for production would be assigned to an individual trained in production. Yet any number of these same businesses have had no compunction about jumping into the installation of a computer without any attempt to develop the necessary degree of competence within their organization for this technical project, something which they demand in other technical fields.

This has probably been fostered by the numerous discussions which insist that the only proper way to use a computer is as a management tool, not to duplicate present procedures but to apply computers to the basic problems of operating a business. This is without question the most effective use of this powerful tool. Further, it will certainly require individuals of top management skills to develop the pattern. But never forget that it will still take the technical man to make it work properly.

Undoubtedly the computer is going to have a tremendous effect upon accounting and management reporting. In the past all the emphasis on reporting for management has revolved around the summarization of transactions that have already taken place; in other words, historical reporting. In a very real sense management has been driving down the business highway using only the rearview mirror. Had the tools been available with which to prepare timely projections and forecasts as a guide for future operations, the business executive would have been in the position of looking through the windshield and using the rearview mirror of historical reporting only as a means of correcting any distortion in his forward look.

The computer does open up new horizons for the future. This forward look may require new concepts of reporting, new media for recording transactions, new methods of operation, and even changes in basic policy. It may be many years before the goal is realized.

In the meantime there is certainly nothing wrong in duplicating present procedures at a reduction in cost, and there is no reason to apologize if a computer is not used to run a company. In fact, there is nothing at all wrong with just saving money.

In closing, let me say that, whatever your interest in the computer field may be, I hope that this conference will be stimulating, interesting, and helpful to you.

Electronic computers, their changing dimensions

Before the Louisville Chapter of the National Machine Accountants Association, at University College, University of Louisville (Kentucky), December 5, 1961

In the future it is probable that the manufacturer will offer a single basic computer unit to which pluggable segments may be added to provide any size machine with any specialized characteristics that would be desired by the customer.

I HAVE ALWAYS been intrigued with that old story of the ancient Eastern potentate who, on a particular occasion, called his wise men together and asked them to develop a single philosophy which would hold true for all situations and for all time to come.

You may remember how the wise men stumbled away after receiving this almost impossible request, and did not return for many months. Finally they asked for an audience with the king and upon being received the king immediately inquired if they had developed the required philosophy.

"We have, Excellency, we have," the oldest one replied. "Well, let me have it," the king demanded. The reply has become historic. "This too shall pass away," the ancient one replied.

Traveling as we do down the unceasing stream of time, change is constant and the scene on the shore of today recedes and vanishes almost before it is observed or fully comprehended.

Perhaps the only thing that is really important about this rather obvious statement is the fact that during the past fifty years our rate of progress has been constantly accelerating, particularly in the fields of science and engineering. Today, technological developments are following each other with such rapidity that it is to the credit of businessmen and managers everywhere that they are not completely bewildered and befuddled by the resulting operating and financial problems.

Perhaps nowhere has this accelerated development been more evident than in the field of automation and data processing. And the electronic computer, which should and will be of primary assistance in helping to solve many of the problems of the present period has itself been beset with such developmental complications that at times this important device has probably caused more problems than it has solved.

To appreciate the rapidity of developments in this particular field, think back only to the early 1940's. It could truly be said of many of that period's theories, concepts, and practices, both in the factory and in the office, "This too shall pass away." And it has; these concepts and practices have practically disappeared.

So it is desirable occasionally for those of us who work in the field of automation to step back, as it were, to try to obtain a broader view of our endeavors, to scan the past, to review the present, and to squint through the haze at the future in order that we may address ourselves more objectively, not only to our current but also to our future problems.

Looking backward, it is somewhat revealing to note that the sequence of events in the technical development of the electronic computer was quite the reverse of normal technological developments. With rare exception, everything in our physical world progresses from the small, the frail, and the highly imperfect to the improved, the strong, and the more practical state. Take the automobile of thirty or forty years ago; it was small, uncomfortable, unreliable and generally impractical. With the passing of the years has come the large, comfortable, and reliable limousine of today.

Earlier forms of data processing equipment proceeded along this same evolutionary line of development, from the simple hand-operated punches of the twenties to the streamlined equipment today. Not so with computers; they emerged in full bloom, enormous in size and tremendously complex in operation. From the date that the first machine was installed to process a business application in 1954 there was a steady decline in the size of the equipment marketed. It took about four years before this trend

was reversed and larger units were again developed.

The problems resulting from this unprecedented direction of development were immediate and devastating, and some of them are still with us. Initial users floundered on such rocky reefs as overembellished applications and underestimated machine processing time, inadequate and improper controls, programming and debugging problems, to name only a few.

At the same time, the manufacturers faced a competitive situation never before imagined, and they plunged headlong and, in many cases, blindly into the battle. The cost of those early years is impossible to measure, but to users and suppliers alike it was tremendous.

Where are we today? In comparison with the situation of only five years ago considerable improvement is evident, but we are still faced with equipment that is highly complex, relatively costly, and generally not completely system-serviced by the supplier at the time it is first delivered to the field.

However, during recent years notable improvements have been made in electronic circuitry and in the electronic components of computers. Diodes and transistors have replaced vacuum tubes, printed circuits have eliminated hand-wired units and the basic circuits have been redesigned for greater speed and reliability. These advancements are commendable in every respect and represent great strides forward in technology. They are certainly graphic illustrations of the accelerated rate of technical development which was mentioned previously. The industry generally refers to the new machines as "solid-state" equipment and frequent reference is made to the stability and reliability of this type of system.

By comparison with previous elements used to control and store electronic pulses, the newer components have less variation in operating characteristics and have longer life if they are not exposed to high temperatures or to excessive currents. In some respects, crystalline substitutes for tubes and other components of electronic circuits are more fragile than the parts they replace, but, on balance, there should be a greater degree of reliability with this type of device and construction.

At this point it would be well, however, to insert a word of caution. In spite of the heavy emphasis on reliability, it is important not to become oversold on this consideration. Computer systems are not infallible and it is prudent not to relax required controls with the thought that the ultimate in accuracy has been achieved. It should be noted that any type of electronic computer, whether it be controlled by redundancy checks or by means of dual circuitry, can still sustain major errors if the main frequency oscillator intermittently fails to operate properly. This means that potentially an item can be miscalculated or improperly transferred or handled within a computer without evidence of such a situation being exposed by the system. In other words, where intermediate checks are made during a processing operation, an incorrect total could check to an incorrect control generated internally.

Perhaps an even more likely point of error is in output printing. Not all of the printing equipment now available has the same degree of built-in control exercised over the actual printing as had certain types of punched printers which incorporated a so-called "echo check" as a means of checking type of selection. This means that a system could be tightly controlled right up to the end of the processing operation and then, just as the end product is produced, the controls may be permitted to fly out the window.

I make no pretense of being able to evaluate the technical considerations involved in the various types of printers used in electronic systems nor can I give you the statistical probability of error related to each of them. I do make this point: various methods are available to exercise control in any given situation and each particular operation or function that is handled by the computer system must be carefully studied to determine the best and most economical means to accomplish the purpose.

Returning to our evaluation of the computer proper, it is rather evident that although substantial improvements have been made in the electronics of the equipment, no such improvements have appeared with respect to the operating characteristics. In particular, there has been a notable lack of simplification from the point of view of ability to use the equipment.

One reason for this has been the emphasis on flexibility. Unfortunately, increased flexibility has meant increased complexity and increased complexity has meant increased installation costs.

To attempt to solve this problem, all manner of automatic programming systems have been developed. Today, there are well over one hundred of these in existence and they are called by such bizarre names as, *CAGE, MYSTIC, PRINT, FAST, SOAP, QUICK, BIOR, SIMPLE, UGLIAG, FLIP, MAGIC AND JAZ.*

I think it is appropriate to raise a question as to the reasonableness of the manufacturers' spending millions of dollars to develop a tremendously powerful machine, a machine with a language all of its own, and then finding it necessary to spend another million dollars to develop a second language so that it is possible to communicate with the machine in its own original language. Why spend enormous sums to design a machine and then more money so as to be able to use it? Perhaps the answer is that the basic equipment is too powerful, too flexible. Thus, secondary languages, or programming systems, are required to offset some of this flexibility and to make the machines more utilitarian. In view of this situation there is certainly a question whether or not there has been adequate communication between the designers and the users of the equipment.

As previously mentioned, after the initial introduction of electronic computers to the business world, there was a steady decline in the size of equipment produced, and this reduction in size was accompanied by comparable reductions in rental cost. The reduced rentals have substantially enlarged the potential market for electronic data processing equipment. But this has also brought into sharp focus the total system cost, which, I am sure you all know, is comprised not only of the sum of equipment rental but also the amortized installation costs.

Although equipment rentals have decreased, there has been little evidence that installation costs have dropped. As a practical matter, the installation costs for the small or medium-sized users may well be greater than the installation cost of more expensive equipment for the larger organization. This is due to the fact that where the larger company can fully utilize the equipment on one or two applications, many of the smaller companies are required to convert a number of different applications in order to offset cost and utilize time available.

I am sure that I am well within the mark when I say that today there would be hundreds of additional electronic computer installations, either in process or installed, if the cost of installation had been reduced over the past few years. The need for today, as well as the need for the future, is increased emphasis on providing the means and the methods to help reduce installation costs and to assist in better utilization of the equipment. This is a matter solely for the suppliers.

How can this be accomplished? In general, services must be provided in two broad areas: first, programs to assist the user in the details of converting his particular application to the equipment in the most simple and effective manner, and second, by providing generalized application programs which require a minimum of effort to tailor to a particular company's system. It is rather a sad commentary on the industry, but it is doubtful if any manufacturer has had these services available at the time he first released a particular machine to the field.

It is said that coming events cast their shadows before, and it would be appropriate to digress briefly and discuss a rather specialized area of automation, because it is certainly a pertinent subject today and concerns events and considerations which are transpiring at this very moment, and because it is a good lead into any discussion of the future.

One of the most important developments in the area of automation during the past few years has been the device which automatically handles documents, and is capable of character recognition. Undoubtedly this equipment will ultimately be perfected to the point where it will be capable of reading and interpreting any reasonably legible type of information. At the present time it has, of course, found its broadest acceptance in the banking field where it is used in the area known as deposit accounting. Essentially, deposit accounting covers the function of recording and maintaining the balances of customers' checking accounts.

Deposits, which may include cash, checks or items for collection, are presented to the bank accompanied by a deposit slip. In an automated system, this slip is normally one that is supplied to the customer by the bank along with his checks. Both the deposit slip and the check are pre-encoded with magnetic ink digits which identify the customer account number and the transit number. The transit number is composed of the Federal Reserve routing and a code which identifies the bank.

After receipt of the cash and proof that the items total to the amount on the deposit slip, the slip is processed through a machine which encodes on the form with magnetic ink digits the total amount of the deposit in dollars.

Checks received for customers of the bank may come from several sources. The most simple situation exists when they are presented as part of a deposit of some other customer of the same bank. The checks, like the deposit slips, are identified by account number but not by amount. Accordingly, the dollar figure must be encoded on the check before further processing. Where blank counter checks or deposit slips are used it is necessary, of course, to encode both account number and amount. Controls are established over all of the input data, both by item count and by amount. Checks and deposit slips are then sorted by account number and the amounts are posted to the individual account.

Daily transaction records are prepared in this process and any checks which are in excess of the amount in a particular account are noted. These are, of course, N.S.F. checks. There are some other routines which occur, and then, finally, the documents are filed. The deposit slips to be retained by the bank and the checks to be returned with a statement at the end of the period.

If the description sounds confusing, it can be summarized by saying that checks and deposits are received by the bank with the source document pre-encoded with the customer account number. The dollar amounts are entered by the bank and controls are established. Then all items are sorted to account number. Amounts are posted by account and new balances are determined.

That is the basic function which is performed and I am sure you will agree that it is of only modest complexity. As a matter of fact, it is amazing that such an uncomplicated situation could turn into such a "Pandora" box of trouble.

We have heard a great deal about control. An incident is being discussed currently which has spotlighted the need for a complete rethinking on this subject and which, in addition, has opened up a whole new area of interest and consideration that has never before been of major importance in connection with computers, or for that matter, data processing equipment.

Recently an individual, who shall remain nameless, apparently had an urgent need for additional funds. Now, I appreciate that there is nothing unusual about this situation; in fact it is almost universal. What was unusual was that this particular person had an account in a bank that had recently installed a highly automated system and he recognized that the means to obtain the necessary funds lay close at hand.

Gathering up a handful of deposit slips, which were magnetically printed with his own account number, he paid a visit to the lobby of his bank and left these deposit slips conveniently located in the customary places where bank customers who wish to make deposits normally look for deposit slips. The inevitable took place and a number of depositors entered their deposits on these precoded deposit slips. Then, all unsuspectingly, they took their deposits to the teller windows. Automation then took over.

The credit for all of the deposits went directly and automatically to the perpetrator's account. Then this individual withdrew his balance and quietly disappeared before the error came to light. About the best thing you can say regarding this whole affair is that procedurally everything went well and the equipment functioned perfectly.

Several not too difficult solutions to this particular problem are suggested. The most simple solution would be to print the individual's name, as well as account number, on deposit slips. Another possibility would be to review all deposit slips before entering them in to the system. In addition, any account with more than one deposit daily could be printed out and a double check made of the transactions.

This, however, is the answer to only the first problem. As you can see, a whole new field of interesting possibilities is opened up. For instance, checks could be fraudulently encoded with someone else's account number and thereby charged to that account. Necessarily, the checking of signatures, called by banks the signature paying operation, must be extremely strong to detect and eliminate this type of fraud. While such checks would eventually be detected by the customer when he receives his statement, the exposure risk to the bank in the interim would be very great.

There is a possibility of trouble from still another angle. Due to the fact that the main file records in deposit accounting represent an inventory of cash, all computer runs will have to be very closely controlled, guarded might be a better word. In particular, instruction tapes, main file records and other such items cannot be handled in the usual manner, but must be protected from any possible tampering. The best way to do this is still a moot question.

There are a number of other interesting possibilities. How should program changes be made? An individual with larceny in his heart could have a field day here.

In one automated bank there is a lock on the computer console. Any instructions, changes or other entries manually entered into the computer from the console are typed out, digit by digit, on the typewriter/printer. Paper fed into the typewriter is serially prenumbered by page. Every page must be accounted for daily and each morning the auditor collects the sheets from the prior day. Sounds fairly foolproof doesn't it? The bank thinks so. I have often wondered what would happen if a blank sheet of paper were placed in front of the preprinted pages on the typewriter and an illicit entry was made into the system. Someday we will find the answer to that question.

Now, before you lose interest in what I am saying because you feel that this is a specialized problem in a specialized field, let me connect it all up with the basic point I am trying to make. I am convinced that we are rapidly approaching the point where major or radical improvements in computers will not be forthcoming each year. I will explain my reasoning on this shortly. Meanwhile, assuming that this is true, it becomes reasonable to expect that the manufacturers of computers will turn their research in other directions. All signs point to the development of automated data recording and pickup devices, that is, electronic sensing mechanisms, which will be connected to every conceivable type of machine or device from time clock to screw machine and from office machine to orifice meter. These sensing mechanisms will then be directly connected with a computer. As a result, source data in the form of externally and manually prepared pieces of paper and cards will disappear and data will be fed directly from point of source into the computer.

More and more you are going to hear the term, "Data Collection," being used and discussed. In fact, I will forecast that if these annual conferences are continued, and I hope that they will be, data collection will become an important subject on the agenda before too many years have elapsed.

Perhaps the first step in data collection will be the development of a mechanism which will be connected to a punch press or some other typical machine tool. Production quantities and all forms of time will automatically be reported directly to a computer for processing information related to production control, inventory, cost accounting and payroll.

Just how this data collection science will develop is not important here. What is important is to realize that, as we found in the banking industry, when you get away from a tight little package of equipment and procedures which are confined to the four walls of a machine room, a whole new series of problems develop. Problems that can be strangely different from those previously encountered in the data processing field. This will inevitably be true in the case of data collection and I am sure that these new areas of exploration will open up avenues of interest and challenge equal to and perhaps beyond anything we have experienced to date. In the interest of preparing for the future, I suggest you follow closely the developments in the banking industry. There is much to be learned from the work in this pioneering effort.

You may recall that I said that the advent of document handling equipment not only would require a complete rethinking on the subject of control but that it opened up a whole new area of interest and consideration which had never before been of major importance in connection with computers or data processing equipment. To explore this subject let me give you an interesting "for instance" which was cited in the February 23, 1961, issue of *The American Banker*.

A check, in passing through the bank processes, is encoded for an amount in excess of the figure for which the depositor wrote it. Now suppose that this excess encoding results in all but depleting the customer's account or even causes an overdraft which is allowed. Then suppose that the next check that comes in is for the customer's insurance premium and is "bounced" for insufficient funds. Because the insurance premium check has come back marked N.S.F., the customer's $500,000 life insurance policy lapses and before any other action can be taken the depositor dies. It is not unlikely that this horrible situation has, itself, caused him to have a heart attack!

Nevertheless, the $500,000 insurance policy is in jeopardy and, if it is not paid in full, someone is going to sue somebody. The question is, who will do what to whom and what will the courts say?

So far we have kept our situation rather simple in that we have only considered the case where the depositor's own bank handled the check. A more complex situation was discussed at a forum in Washington, D. C., last month, sponsored by a Joint Committee on Continuing Legal Education of the American Law Institute and the American Bar Association.

In the instance described, the check is first presented for deposit at a bank other than the depositor's own bank. The check thus becomes a transit item and goes to the Federal Reserve Bank for processing, and returns to the bank on which drawn. Since Federal Reserve Banks will shortly begin encoding and automatic processing of checks, our incorrectly encoded check has now become a problem of national proportions. And, who does what to whom *now?* Well, we have apparently made a Federal case out of it. As you can appreciate, lawyers have been looking into the legal aspects of this problem and it is generally agreed that a new body of laws will be forthcoming to answer the many technical legal questions involved.

I think there is a rather interesting corollary to this problem. The automated equipment in the ABC Bank has been giving trouble and the manufacturer's engineers have been working on the problem diligently. Presuming the machine is repaired, they return the equipment to the bank employee so that the current day's transactions can be processed.

Now, the 13th check in the 13th batch to be processed on this day, which by coincidence happens to be the 13th of the month, represents the payment by a Mr. Rich But Slow on his mortgage on the International Steel and Iron Building. Mr. RBS was fortunate, he just got his check delivered in the nick of time or he would have been foreclosed and lost his total equity in the fictitious skyscraper. He feels comfortable now that he has met his payment and paid off the mortgage.

Paid off, that is, until our automatic equipment in processing his check breaks down with a repetition of the same problem that was plaguing the manufacturer's engineers some hours ago, and Mr. RBS's check, to use the vernacular, "bounces." No need to relate the rest of the story. We might have another heart attack victim. But now, who is apt to be sued? The bank? Perhaps, but then again, perhaps not. Perhaps this time the manufacturer may be involved.

Necessarily, we must leave these problems to the legal profession, but it is significant that new equipment, new applications and new procedures bring up problems and take us into areas where we have never been before.

In a sense we have already taken quite a good look at the future, at least from the standpoint of some of the problems which may be met. Now, let us look a little more closely at some other items of interest.

During the past ten years data processing equipment has advanced from the use of relays, to the use of tubes, to the use of transistors as the medium for adding and controlling information. As a result, computing speeds have increased approximately 10,000 times. Increased speeds are still possible and proportionately these increases can be substantial, but a formidable barrier now faces the research engineer in the laboratory. This barrier is the speed of electricity. Unbelievable as this may sound, the speed of electricity, which incidentally, is the same as the speed of light or 186,000 miles per second, is the great barrier to be faced.

Now, you may well ask on what premise do I make such a drastic statement. Because,

obviously, if it is the speed of electricity that has become the barrier toward further development, then it may well be said that we can foresee the end of what might be referred to as major developments in the main frame of electronic computers. This, in itself, would mark the end of an era!

Further, we could then deduce that future developments would be along other lines. Such a conclusion, therefore, while perhaps negative in one sense, could be of profound importance in future planning. It could also give direction to the current and near future training and development of individuals who will be responsible for future automated programs.

With that preamble, let me take you through my own thinking on the matter. During the last six months I have seen at least a dozen articles on the subject of memory devices. These articles have ranged from highly technical papers in engineering publications to nontechnical information releases prepared for the businessman.

Basically, all of these reports state in essence that one of the latest and most significant developments in computer memory devices is the thin film memory. A thin film memory consists of tiny dots of magnetic material, several millionths of an inch thick, deposited on a thin glass plate. One dot represents one bit just as one magnetic core represents one bit in a core memory. Information can be stored in and retrieved from magnetic thin film memory at speeds hitherto impossible. The speed of magnetic core memory is measured in millionths of a second, but the speed of thin film memory may be measured in billionths of a second. Other advantages of the thin film memory are its small size, lower power requirements, and economical production cost.

Let me repeat the most important statement in this description, the speed of thin film memory may be measured in billionths of a second. Memory is, of course, a vital unit in computers. But what about the pulse generator and counting and switching gear? One major manufacturer in the computer field has already experimented with devices that are 100 times as fast as transistors in switching, and they have concluded that devices for this purpose are possible and that they would be compatible with magnetic film memory.

Pulse generators, operating at almost unimaginable speed, have also been designed and Dr. Esaki, an inventor and consultant in the electronic computer field who has already demonstrated an oscillator which operates at frequencies of over four billion cycles per second, has stated that the ultimate frequency could be over one hundred billion cycles per second. So it would appear that basic computer units could be designed which will operate at multibillion cycles per second.

Consider the electronic pulse itself. Electricity travels at the rate of 186,000 miles per second. Multiplying this figure by 5,280, we get the rate in feet per second; and dividing this answer into 1, we obtain the length of time it takes a pulse to travel 1 foot. The answer is approximately one billionth of a second! This is, of course, much slower than the operating elements themselves and thus it is the speed of electricity which becomes the limiting factor.

The way to minimize this problem, up to a point, is to move the various elements closer together. And this is being done. Subminiature electronic components are being developed. These elements will be perhaps 1/1000th of an inch in length and thus can be spaced no more than a hair's breadth apart. Once this is accomplished, and remember it is still in research, the end of the line in this area of development will probably have been reached.

What other developments are likely in the computer of the future? I envision that a manufacturer, instead of offering a line of data processing equipment to meet the need for various-sized requirements, will offer a single basic unit to which pluggable segments or units may be added to provide any size machine with any specialized characteristics that would be desired by the customer.

The new small-in-size but enormously large-in-capacity memory units which were just mentioned would fall into this category of pluggable units and I can conceive that these pluggable memory units will replace tape drives, reels of tape, and other associated equipment for such items as programs, master records, etc. Carried to its logical conclusion, this could well mean that the computer of the future will have only one or two tape drive units and these will probably only be used to transfer information to tape for storage elsewhere than within the electronic system.

There is more that could be envisioned about the computer of the future. For instance, we have said nothing about the concept of Cryogenics, which is that area of electronic research which derives its name from the Greek word Cryoton, meaning creation of icy cold. There are undoubtedly tremendous possibilities for development of radically new elements in that subpolar region of absolute zero where all forms of matter behave differently than they do in the more normal temperatures to which we are accustomed.

We have not mentioned terminal equipment for use in multiplexing nor the related communication lines and equipment which would be required to connect a computer to the various mechanisms which will be attached to production equipment. And nothing has been said about voice translation and the almost "Arabian Nights" possibilities of two-way verbal communication between man and machine. All this will have to await another opportunity for exploration as time does not permit any further discussion of the central processor of the future.

Before closing, I would like to cover briefly the systems and applications areas of the future.

There is little doubt that there will be a continued expansion of the so-called "integrated data processing" approach and the "total systems concept." In fact, we have been moving inch by inch and step by step toward this goal ever since the first punched card tabulating machine was installed. In most situations, however, this is truly a long-range goal and equipment itself is not the only barrier in the way of actual accomplishment.

We are only starting today to develop the techniques and skills which are required to gather and evaluate data which is concerned with certain of the more difficult operations of a business, and it appears to me that, until we have advanced substantially farther into those still somewhat nebulous areas of game theory, business strategy, and mathematical model building of total business processes, it is probably premature, in most instances, to be too concerned about total systems concepts.

I do not want to leave you with the idea that nothing has been done toward the development of scientific techniques for assisting management. Nothing could be farther from the truth. Amazing progress has been made in this direction during the past ten years. Again, I wish there were time to talk about the solution to problems such as one that was solved for a candy and confectionary manufacturer involving the forecasting of demand for purposes of production scheduling and the setting of inventory levels. Or the development of a method for controlling the material and supplies inventory in ten warehouses to meet service requirements at a minimum cost for an electric utility. Or even the procedural requirements of crew scheduling for a passenger airline.

These and many more examples which could be cited, including the use of electronic computers to simulate business situations in a program usually called a "management game"; these represent important steps which have been taken in developing techniques which are, and will be, useful to management.

In closing then, let me take you into the imaginary office of the Inter-Nation Manufacturing Corporation at some time in the future. Mr. Jones, the president, has just pushed back his usual morning coffee from the edge of the desk and has suggested to his secretary that she call in his Division Managers from Melbourne, Paris, Mexico City, Tokyo and Buenos Aires. Within minutes they are there around the edge of his desk. Not literally there, of course, but their images are in the inset screens all around the edge. The discussion runs to alternate production schedules for the next three months in the light of an impending price change in the Asian markets by their major competitor. It is agreed to develop the consequences of a dozen alternate production and pricing strategies, based on information to be fed into the central computer by the various local subcomputers by 9:30 that morning. "We should have the answer by 10:00," Jones advises. "See you then. In the meantime, I'll see what intercorporate sales can do."

Closing down his audio-visual circuit he calls his sales manager and suggests that they go to the game room. "I've already asked them to set it up for a day-by-day play against all competition for the next three months. Let's see what we can do."

Closing the door marked "Intercorporate Game Room, Authorized Personnel Only," they look up at the map displayed in front of them. In each sector of the map data is displayed showing customer distribution, sales activity and profitability, with information current right up to yesterday morning. Competitive activity, production and inventory data are also shown.

A half-hour later Jones and the sales vice president are back at the president's desk with a set of summary results of the sales campaign they have finally agreed on in competition with the computer.

"All that remains now," Jones said as he sat down, "is to get the detailed instructions out to the district salesmen and the plants. We should have that accomplished by noon using our new tape transmission facilities. Let's meet again day after tomorrow to review progress and look over the first results. I'll have to break this off now, I've got to see some fellow who wants to talk to me about a better computer."

Is this fantasy or is this the future? Is this a dream or is it a coming reality? I will leave the answer up to you.

New dimensions in management decision-making

Keynote Speaker Address before Arizona State University, Annual Business Day, Tempe, Arizona, April 18, 1962

Procedures which involve the use of advanced mathematics, statistics, and electronic computers are becoming increasingly useful in the area of management decision-making.

AUTOMATION HAS BEEN a vital force in the development of American industry, and its contribution to the elimination of physically burdensome tasks and to the continued improvement in productivity is well-known. Equally well-appreciated, and receiving the most serious attention of leaders in business and government, are the attendant problems of labor displacement and the obsolescence of manual skills.

It is a curious and significant fact, however, that while management has been earnestly considering these problems as they relate to its employees, the same technology in a quiet and subtle way has started to embrace management and supervisory areas which hitherto have been considered far outside the province of crude machines. As a matter of fact, already today scientific procedures which involve the use of advanced mathematics, statistics and the modern electronic computers, are having an important effect on one of the executive's most important functions, that of decision-making.

Based upon the evidence displayed as a result of automation in the factory and in the clerical areas of the office, it is not too far-fetched to say that if an adequate understanding of this new science is not developed by present and future executives, it has the potential to obsolete them with the same impersonal thoroughness that the sewing machine obsoleted the seamstress and the motor car the horse.

In order to better project the ultimate potential of this new development, consider this comparison. Scholars tell us that man's first industrial activities date back over 3,000 years when, apart from the manufacture of tools and weapons, he developed the two industries of pottery making and weaving. In order to satisfy both domestic needs and burial requirements, the handmade pot-

65

tery was fashioned in many shapes and sizes and decorated with geometric designs which were either incised or painted on the clay.

In spite of crude processing methods and limited production it is likely that these first industrialists still had to make certain business decisions. These must have been concerned with size, color and perhaps even price, and when the potter was not producing against a specific order he undoubtedly had to decide whether he wanted to produce for inventory or go fishing.

The use of scientific techniques in conjunction with electronics in the area of business decision-making has had no such extended history. As a matter of fact, electronic computers for business were only first discussed in the late 1940's and the first computer to be used for business purposes was installed in 1954. And thus, measured against the history of business decisions which span a period in time of some 3,000 years, the age of the computer, which still numbers less than 3,000 days, is brief indeed.

Types of decisions

In discussing the role of this new science as it applies to decision-making, it is desirable to distinguish between the types of decisions that are made by management personnel. I wish to point out that the method of classification which follows is not intended to connote a relationship with any particular level of management or any particular type of organization, and none should be assumed.

For our purpose a distinction might well be made between management decisions and operating decisions. Management decisions would involve such situations as determining whether or not a company should become vertically integrated, should introduce a new product line, or should expand into foreign operations. On the other hand, operating decisions might include the determination of weekly production schedules,

salary payment to sick or injured employees, the volume of inventory to stock at various distribution points, etc.

The operating system which generates the need for an operating decision is generally analogous to mechanical and electrical systems, and such terms as feedback, networks, maximum, minimum, and optimum are particularly relevant.

Management planning and control systems are quite different. Mechanical and electrical analogies are usually not suitable methods for these systems and unlike many operating systems which can be viewed as a thermostat which turns the furnace on or off according to its perception of changes in temperature, management controls and management systems are not readily automated.

In his book, *The New Science of Management Decisions,* Herbert Simon, of Carnegie Institute, categorizes management decisions in a manner particularly useful for this discussion. Professor Simon identifies two major types of decisions which he calls programmed decisions and nonprogrammed decisions, as follows: "Decisions are programmed to the extent that they are repetitive and routine and to the extent that a definite procedure has been worked out for handling them so that they do not have to be treated anew each time they occur. Decisions are nonprogrammed to the extent that they are novel, unstructured and consequential. There is no cut-and-dried method for handling the problem because it has not arisen before, or because its precise nature and structure are elusive or complex, or because it is so important it deserves a custom-tailored treatment."

In summary then, management or nonprogrammed decisions are unusual and nonrepetitive in nature. There are no definite or established procedures to be followed in solving the problem and the decision itself must be reached through what are termed general problem solving techniques. This means that the executive reaches his decision through the use of judgment, experience, intuition and creativity.

Conversely, operating or programmed decisions are repetitive and relatively routine, and definite procedures have been or can be worked out to develop the information which is required so that the decision can be made. This is the type of operation which can be expressed in the written form of a manual or in the form of a model with mathematical symbols. Decisions of this type can often be made more accurately, more rapidly, and more efficiently when an electronic computer is used to develop the necessary data and to show the effects of possible alternate strategies.

Specific areas of application

Having now broadly identified the areas where the new and advanced techniques are most likely to be associated with the business decision-making process, let us now look more closely at certain specific areas where they have already been used and where their peculiar abilities have been particularly useful.

To date the most fruitful and extensive field for using electronic equipment to develop information for business decisions has been in the area of inventory management, in the solution to so-called blending and mixing problems, in which category are also included certain types of allocation problems, and in the evaluation of possible strategies as disclosed by using what is known as the critical path method.

Inventory management

Most business decisions arise by reason of competitive considerations and these considerations vary sharply between different types of businesses. For instance, some businesses, by reason of their nature, do not have a problem of inventory management. For example, in a service business or in a business with a very fast stock turnover and frequent merchandise receipts, or in one in which the merchandise can be modified to suit the customer, or in a business in which mistakes in inventory management can be easily overcome (such as in the small restaurant business where yesterday's New England boiled dinner is today's stew), inventory problems are generally not too critical. These businesses have other problems.

On the other hand a business probably has significant inventory management problems when in its operations one or more of the following situations prevail: when market demand displays a significant seasonal fluctuation; when relatively long lead times are required; when merchandise shipments are received relatively infrequently; when the product has a long service life; when the merchandise spoils or becomes obsolete; or when people want what they want when they want it. It is in situations such as these that the application of scientific methods and the use of an electronic computer are often very useful in solving the problems of inventory management.

Reduced to its simplest form, the objectives of inventory management are to have the right merchandise (or material) in the right place, in the right quantities, at the right time. Stated another way, inventory policies and procedures should be established so that the principal costs relating to inventory, those of procurement, possession, and shortage, are maintained at a minimum.

Procurement and possession costs are generally susceptible to determination through recognized accounting routines. On the other hand, the cost of a piece of material or an item of merchandise which is out of stock when it is desired is not so easily calculated. To circumvent this problem, procedures have been developed which are directed toward minimizing the cost of procurement and possession while maintaining a specified level of service. This level of service is identified as a percentage of the time that a particular item is called for and is available. For example: management may say that during the next month item A must be available at least 95% of the time that it is called for.

Basically, management must make two decisions for each item of inventory at each location where it is stocked. These decisions can be stated simply; how much should be ordered and when. In technical jargon they are referred to as reorder point and reorder quantity. In some situations, inventory is ordered on a periodic basis but we are not concerned with this system here.

There is one standard formula that has been developed and is in wide use for determining the economic quantity to order. The mathematical computation is concerned with procurement costs, unit cost for the item, a possession cost factor, and annual usage. If the usage of a particular item or group of items exhibits a strong seasonal pattern, it becomes necessary to replace the annual usage factor, which implicitly presumes a relatively constant use throughout the year, with a factor which is appropriate for the conditions which actually prevail. Once the formula has been properly established, an electronic computer can handle the computations easily and rapidly. It is perhaps redundant to point out that the everchanging pattern of business requires a constant check on the variables used in the formula, and adjustments must be made in the various factors as indicated. The blind use of the computer to control inventories without appropriate external controls by management could lead to nothing but disaster.

The other item, reorder point, is considerably more complicated. In determining the reorder point the factors of lead time, management's level of service requirement, and sales or usage demand are all involved. Lead time can be identified with reasonable accuracy and management can set the level of service rather arbitrarily, but the problem of anticipating the demand requirement is not so easily handled. The anticipated demand, whether for raw material parts,

assemblies or finished goods, is inherently predicated upon a sales forecast and thus this item becomes the pedestal upon which the entire inventory system stands or falls.

Throughout this discussion reference has been made to the use of scientific methods and procedures. This methodology has been termed by some "operations research" and by others "management science." Whatever the name, however, the individuals working in the field have made significant contributions to business. One such contribution has been in this area of sales forecasting, where historically demand was sensed rather than measured and trends were felt rather than plotted.

Today, procedures have been developed to derive information that can assist management in setting its sales forecasts. These procedures use running records of historical sales data, together with perpetual inventory information. The system extracts seasonal and trend information from past years' data and applies this to recent experience in order to project the probable future demands.

As previously stated, the sales forecast is a crucial segment of the information required for successful inventory management and it can be the most difficult to obtain. This activity can be substantially assisted by the use of procedures scientifically developed and electronically processed. Nevertheless, it is an activity that requires the use of all available market information and the full exercise of management's acumen and judgment.

In summary, then, it can be said that in a complex business where inventory management is a critical problem, scientific methods can provide management with the information necessary to anticipate demand, to recognize when to reorder, and to determine the most economical quantities to be obtained. These are the areas where management decisions must be made with regard to inventories and these new techniques can be of great assistance in making the decisions.

Blending and mixing problems

A second major area where mathematics and the electronic computer are working together to provide a useful service to management is in situations where decisions regarding blending and mixing can have an important effect upon the profitability of an enterprise.

Reducing this type of problem to its simplest form, consider the following example which depicts a basic business situation which confronts a fictitious firm which we will call "Nutty Nuts Inc." NNI is a packaging and distributing firm which purchases cashews, hazels, almonds, and peanuts in bulk. These are, in turn, mixed and packaged into four products called: Top Mix, Regular Mix, Special Mix and just plain Mix.

Although the price of the bulk nuts constantly fluctuates, experience has indicated to the management that in spite of variations in their cost, the selling price of the products must remain relatively constant. As NNI is in business to make money, and naturally wants to make as much money as possible on each package of mix, it follows that the percentage of each type of nut must be changed in each of the four products as the wholesale bulk price of the nuts changes.

Of course, if there should be a protracted period of rising prices for all nuts it could be expected that in a short time all four of the packaged products would end up full of nothing but peanuts. But as this makes the problem too easy, and in addition, would probably reduce the sales of NNI to almost zero, management has seen fit to set certain specifications on the four mixes. In general there must be at least a minimum volume of cashews in each mix, and conversely the volume of peanuts must be limited so that it does not exceed a certain maximum percentage of the total.

Now the simple act of mixing four kinds of nuts together has become a problem of substantial proportions and what at first appeared to be a relatively simple business now turns out to be an enterprise which requires management decisions of a significant order.

Restated formally the question becomes, for any possible combination of input nut prices, what mix formulation will maximize profits?

Answers to this problem can be generated "by hand" but at some point the cost of these calculations could have a marked effect upon profit. As a practical matter, so much time might be spent in determining the quantities to mix that the nuts themselves would never get mixed. What then does NNI do? The answer lies in the use of a mathematical technique known as linear programming.

The underlying difficulty in our nutty problem, which is also the difficulty in the typical blend or mix problem, can be identified if we express the problem in mathematical terms. Stated mathematically, this particular situation requires eight simultaneous equations and would involve sixteen variables or unknowns. As you may remember, when the number of unknowns is equal to the number of simultaneous equations which can be written, the solutions can be derived algebraically. But when the number of unknowns exceeds the number of equations, there are an infinite number of solutions to the problem. Linear programming is an efficient procedure which gives consideration to all restrictions and, in our example, would move rapidly to select the pattern which meets the profit maximization objective.

The problem of mix is seen in many different industries. Here are a few examples with which you are familiar:

Luncheon meats and sausage are made using five or more types of meat, all varying in cost and in lean and fat content. Again we have the problem of producing a product within specified limits at the lowest possible cost.

Cattle feeds are mixtures of a number of grain products. The objective in this situation is to make a mixture at the lowest possible price which still meets rigid standards of nutrition. This may require some quantity of all the grains involved.

On a larger scale, every major oil company uses linear programming techniques in its refinery operations to solve the problems posed by constant changes, both in the volumes and compositions of crude oils available for processing and in the customer demand for the various end products.

Critical path scheduling

In addition to inventory management and blending and mixing problems, the third major area where scientific methods are proving extremely useful in assisting management to make more rapid, more informed, and consequently more accurate decisions is in connection with a relatively new technique which is called critical path scheduling.

This technique, which is the successful application of network theory to scheduling problems, has initially found its broadest use in the construction industry where there is a strong monetary incentive associated with on-time completion of projects. Its usefulness, however, is not restricted to a single industry and it will undoubtedly find wide application in maintenance work, engineering and other similar areas which require project control of a very high order.

The estimating of cost and time in construction work is still to some degree an art. It is something of a paradox that even though the individual tasks or jobs which constitute the projects can often be enumerated and estimated with reasonably good reliability, the project as a whole may seriously overrun time and cost. The reason for this seeming inconsistency can be explained by the fact that the most complex aspect of such projects lies in the difficulties which surround the planning and control of the sequence in which individual tasks are carried out. Foundation forms cannot be placed until excavation has been completed, and in turn must be finished before concrete can be poured. This certainly seems obvious enough, but on a large project the multiplicity of such interrelationships introduces such complexities that the job defies simple analysis.

In the past, the problem has been left to the construction superintendent to cope with as best he can. Today, the critical path method provides a powerful tool in dealing with this situation. In practice, it is necessary to break the total effort down into specific steps. Then for each step, the manhours, equipment and elapsed time required must be specified.

Next, the information is set up in a prescribed form, after which it can be processed by a computer using appropriate critical path programs. As a result of using the critical path technique, the computer not only determines the sequence which yields the shortest overall completion time, but further highlights those jobs which are critical to completing the project in the least amount of time. These constitute the "critical path." Typically, only ten to fifteen percent of the individual steps will be critical in the sense that a delay in the completion of any one means a comparable delay in the ultimate completion of the project. Obviously, this type of identification permits the concentration of supervisory effort on the critical areas of the project and provides a basis for the most economical scheduling of the trades on the job.

Stated simply, the critical path method is a new way to improve scheduling in a complex operation. Improved scheduling gives better cost control and better cost control is the key to cost reductions.

The future

These, then, are the broad areas where the electronic computer has touched upon the management-decision areas. It is true that these areas are still limited in scope, but then the computer is still a very new addition to the business office.

In opening this discussion, reference was made to the two general types of decisions made by management. These were identified as programmed and nonprogrammed. We then briefly discussed how computers have been successfully applied in the programmed area.

No doubt it has occurred to many of you that a majority of management decisions cannot be so easily compartmentized and do not fall neatly into the two rigid classifications which were given. Rather, they are a combination of the two types described. This is certainly true, and it can be expected that in the course of time, scientific techniques used in conjunction with the computer will make larger and larger inroads into these less discrete areas of decision-making and thus will become an even more useful tool for business management.

Inescapably, the direction of this discussion must eventually lead to the delicate question, "Does this mean the ultimate displacement of management?" I think not.

We will not see the removal of the need for the executive, neither will we see an easing of the problems with which he is faced. Rather, we will see that the type of problems to be solved will be different and far more difficult. The executive will be concerned with the fundamental concepts of his operation and he will also be faced with problems of morality and ethics. The accounting profession is illustrative of this point. During the past fifty years, the accountant has moved from the consideration of bookkeeping problems to the deep examination of the underlying principles of his profession. So far as the manager or executive of the future is concerned, he will have to be brighter, more intelligent and more reflective than his counterpart of today.

Kepler, who with Newton, was the father of astronomy and celestial navigation, made a very profound remark about quantitative thinking. He said, "Just as the ear is tuned to sound, just as the eye is attuned to color, so is the mind attuned to number and quantity. When the mind is denied number and quantity it wanders lost in the darkness."

Quantitative thinking is becoming increasingly important in the area of management decision-making.

Machine accounting in Europe

Before the Education Seminar of the National Machine Accountants Association Southeastern Regional Conference, Atlanta, Georgia, April 20, 1962

As one of the results of establishing the common market, Europe will not continue to lag so far behind this country in accounting methods and procedures.

IF I HAD TO summarize the machine accounting situation in Europe today in two or three sentences, I would say that in general machine accounting in Europe is about 25 years behind that in the United States or roughly about where this country was about 1935. I would have to add, however, that there are some exceptions, and in these exceptional situations Europe is on a par with us or perhaps even ahead of developments in this country.

To have a clear understanding of machine accounting in Europe, you must have some insight into the historical, cultural, and economic situation in Europe and it helps to have some understanding of the European businessman.

I talk as though there was a compound individual who represented the typical European who is in business. There isn't, of course; there obviously isn't even a representative English businessman, French businessman, German businessman, or Italian businessman. But I do think we can point out some rather broad characteristics which are reasonably common to certain large groups of European businessmen, and which have had and will have an effect on machine accounting in Europe.

Before I proceed let me limit my subject. When I use the word, Europe, I am, of course, talking about Western Europe.. I don't know anything about Russia or the so-called satellite countries which are under Communist control. Further, my first-hand knowledge is limited to the countries of England, France, Italy, Switzerland, The Netherlands, Luxembourg, Belgium, and Germany.

When I use the term, machine accounting, I am using it in a restricted sense. My remarks will be confined to punched-card equipment and to various types and sizes of electronic devices. This eliminates bookkeeping machines, duplicating devices of various kinds, and many other smaller machines and devices. I believe, however, that I am covering the area in which you are particularly interested.

I opened my discussion by stating that generally the situation in Europe with respect to machine accounting was about 25 years behind that in the United States. Now what did I mean by that? I did not mean that available equipment was comparable to that offered in the United States 25 years ago. Primarily, I had reference to the acceptance or perhaps the lack of acceptance of larger forms of mechanization and to the category of present users.

Let us start at the bottom of the map and see how this applies in Italy. Italy has been one of the more fortunate countries in Europe and since the war it has achieved a sound fiscal policy, accompanied by hard currency, a steadily improving economic situation and, barring unforeseen political problems, it has every expectation of continued improvement and prosperity. It would perhaps be well to point out that Northern Italy, particularly around Milan, is the primary industrial area, and the economic situation is the healthiest in that part of the country.

But in spite of an expanding economy and the excellent prospects for the future, mechanization of the office is still in its infancy in Italy. Why is this so? To answer this question, two other questions must be asked and answered. Who are the present users? And why are users so limited in number? A third question naturally follows. What are the prospects for the future?

Let us take these questions in order; first, who are the present users? Essentially they break down into two large groups. One group is composed of subsidiaries of American corporations. The other group consists of the various departments of the Italian government. In addition, of course, there are some privately-owned industrial users, but the number of such companies is relatively small.

There is, however, a little quirk here. As many of you know, a number of the important industries in Italy have been nationalized, including shipbuilding, transportation (buses and railroads), iron and steel, and large sections of the petroleum industry. As there has been some use of punched cards in these areas, as well as in the more obvious fiscal and record-keeping departments of the government, the coverage is not quite so restricted as it might appear on the surface. Yet compared to the extensive use of this type of equipment in this country, it is extremely small.

The second question, then, why are the number of users so limited? The first and most obvious reason is economic.

What is the primary reason why the American businessman has installed mechanization in the factory and in the office? To save money, of course. This implies that machines can do the job cheaper.

It is probable that back in 1935, in this country there were only a relatively few jobs which could be performed more economically by machine than by hand, because at that time office labor was relatively cheap. In the intervening years, and particularly since 1945, there has been a sharp upturn in clerical costs, and this, coupled with a relatively fixed cost for office equipment (particularly fixed rentals) has provided a tremendous impetus for mechanization.

As you might suspect from the parallel which I am drawing, clerical costs in Italy today are low as compared to comparable costs in the United States, and at first blush it might appear that the use of any form of office equipment would be completely unwarranted. This is particularly true if only the direct labor costs are considered, as the average office clerk in Italy earns only about

74

40% of his or her counterpart in the United States. To be more specific, a job paying $3600 here would pay about $1500 in Milan.

The picture is not quite so clear cut, however. In Italy, as in many European countries, the employer pays a large social charge that is something like our social security. There are some major differences but they are not important to this discussion. What is important is that these social charges may run 40% or more of the base pay of the employee and are, therefore, extremely significant. In other words our $1500 employee actually costs $2100 or more per year to the employer.

This figure, while still low, is approaching the point where the economics of using machines can become favorable. However, as you can appreciate, at this level of labor cost the interest in the use of machines for processing accounting data is hardly red hot.

Another avowed though somewhat less distinct reason for using mechanized accounting is to provide additional data, particularly cost data, which would not otherwise be available. This reason falls completely flat in Italy. It may interest you to know that cost accounting is still in its infancy in Italy.

What about the future? Well, the future of machine accounting in Italy is so wrapped up with the overall problems of Europe that I'm going to defer answering that question for a few moments.

Turning now to France, we find a somewhat different situation. Where Italy has been one of the most prosperous countries since the war, France has not been so fortunate. The currency in France has been anything but hard and only recently the DeGaulle government has found it necessary to again devalue it.

The effects of this unfavorable fiscal situation are reflected in many ways, and undoubtedly it is the individual who is on the bottom rung of the income ladder who is hurt the worst by it. But businesses, too, are severely affected and this type of fiscal climate does little to engender growth or expansion.

In spite of this gloomy background, there is probably a greater use of punched cards and small electronic computers in France than in Italy. Why this disparity? I can only rationalize it by the fact that one of the major equipment manufacturers, Bull, is located in France and has been in business for many years. Bull machines are quite similar to IBM machines and they have a line of equipment which includes some items not found on this side of the Atlantic Ocean.

It is rather interesting that even though Bull equipment is generally very close to IBM in physical operation, their management affiliations are with Remington Rand. I gathered that there was some sort of informal arrangement between the two companies in Europe, and I have heard that Remington is now introducing a Bull computer, the GAMMA I, into this country. Again I must point out, however, that there is no extensive use of such equipment in France.

France and Italy have had one thing in common which may have had an adverse effect upon mechanized accounting. In both of these countries tax practices have been, shall we say, unusual. Federal taxes, both on personal and business incomes, have been assessed not on the basis of audited records but on the basis of negotiation. This negotiation has been conducted as an individual matter between the taxpayer and the tax collector.

Under this system it has been common practice for businesses, and I am referring to reputable businesses, to maintain two complete sets of books, one set for tax purposes, one for management. This situation is hardly conducive to the use of an automated system, unless it were some high-powered computer which could be programmed to examine each item and determine whether or not it was to be entered and, if so, into which set of books.

I might say that this situation is not hearsay. I ran into it myself two years ago and I think I will digress from my subject for a moment, as the case was interesting. At that time our firm was just establishing its systems department in Italy and we were asked by a very large, locally-owned pharmaceutical house to review their inventory procedures and make suggestions for improvement.

If any of you are familiar with the multitude of items found in the inventory of a large pharmaceutical manufacturer, such as Lilly or Squibb, you know it is a good candidate for the use of cards. Accordingly, when we finished our study and made our report, this was one of our suggestions.

After our report was delivered and read we met with the owner. (It is still not unusual in Europe for single individuals or families to own or control enormous enterprises.) So we met with the owner, his factory manager, and other responsible individuals to discuss the problems of installation. One of the first steps, we pointed out, was to develop a stock catalog and to give each item a stock number. We were informed that this would be a rather simple job as the company could use its present stock record cards for the basic data. Accordingly, the owner immediately appointed a qualified group to start the work.

Without going into too much detail, let me tell you that apparently all was going along well until about two weeks later, when we were called up and told bluntly that we were fired! No reason was given and we were afforded no opportunity to inquire.

We heard no more for about two months. Then we received a call from the controller. He was very apologetic. They had been most rude in firing us out-of-hand, but the company had received a great shock.

It developed that as soon as work was started on the stock catalog a catastrophe was discovered. This company, like most Italian companies, kept a number of separate records, particularly with respect to inventories. When the stock catalog project was started it quickly became evident that in its attempt to develop a confusing record, the company had completely confused itself. As a result, they had lost control of their inventory, and even worse, they now had quantities of obsolete or useless stock on hand. The controller explained that our program would be revitalized when the company had their stock situation under control again.

As time is short, let us say farewell to Italy and France and steam across the channel to England.

You sense, rather than see, the pressure of technological influence in England. Certainly there is no widespread use or acceptance of mechanization for office or clerical detail in the sense that we know it. But neither is there any aversion to its use. England, after all, is the home of the Powers-Samas tabulating machine and, although this company did not make a successful entry into the market in the United States, it is relatively successful in Britain. British Tabulating is also a successful company there.

But there are other signs. IBM is expanding in Britain, and is rapidly becoming a force to be reckoned with. Their line of products includes both conventional punched-card machines and their larger electronic devices. It is interesting to note that they have transplanted their idea of the "applied science department" across the Atlantic and this group will undoubtedly develop business for their Service Bureau.

One point is of particular interest because it will give you a good perspective on the relative development of mechanization. All of the men who are assigned to the applied science department, and there are representatives in all of the major sales offices throughout the United Kingdom, are required to have a detailed knowledge of the functions and operations of all equipment which is sold. They must also be acquainted with the more technical phases of Operations Research, linear programming, and the development of mathematical models.

Undoubtedly the requirement for detailed knowledge of punched-card techniques and operations arises in part because there is at the present time in Great Britain an insufficient awareness or acceptance of the use of high-powered mathematics in solving business problems. This, in turn, limits the use of large equipment in the related areas. I find this situation a difficult one to understand, since Operations Research, or "operational research" as it is called in England, was originally developed in that country during the last war.

What about electronic developments? Broadly speaking, they have been very slow, with acceptance substantially behind that found in this country. An exception is the computer used by Lyons, Ltd. I am sure you have heard about this machine, as it has been inaccurately described on numerous occasions in the United States as an electronic computer installed in a tea shop. To set the record straight, Lyons is a very large organization. It does, as a matter of fact, have a great many retail outlets which might be described as tea shops, but these stores might also be called bakery shops, as they sell all forms of bread and other baked goods. In addition to this, Lyons has a very substantial wholesale business and they supply food products to hotels, restaurants, and, I suppose, to the corner "pub."

It isn't the error in describing the company, however, which is important, but the fact that Lyons did not rent or buy the machine from any office machine or electronic manufacturer. Rather, they built the device themselves! Do you happen to know of any business organization in this country, schools excepted, which has built its own computer?

There is quite a lot of interest in England in the development of paper handling equipment and in the sensing of characters electronically. This is similar to the work which is being done in this country in the banking field and in the retail gasoline sales field.

As many of you may know, character recognition, which is the sensing of information from printed characters rather than from punched holes, has developed in this country primarily along the line of sensing impressions made with magnetic ink. In England there appears to be strong interest in reading printed characters photoelectrically. This is a point worth watching, as photoelectric reading was the first method proposed in this country. There are still some very stout exponents of this method here, but it has receded to second place because of the claim that magnetic reading is "more positive."

An important company working on this development in England is EMI, Electrical and Musical Industry. You probably know this company as the manufacturer of Angel Records.

If not in realization, electronic computers are at least in expectation. I was informed that IBM will shortly build a tape testing laboratory in England to supply magnetic tape for Europe. This laboratory will be much like the one which they have just outside Minneapolis, and through which every reel of tape which they sell must first pass. I gathered the impression that this English laboratory may be a joint operation of Minnesota Mining & Manufacturing Company and IBM.

This brings me to my closing point, a discussion of the future. The greatest single economic force which has or could affect the countries of Europe has just been placed in motion. I refer, of course, to the "common market," which should have a marked effect on the development of mechanization in Europe.

For centuries European countries have been independent states, both politically and economically. Just what the social effect would be if there were a unified political confederation, with representation covering Western Europe, is difficult to forecast. The effect of unification on an economic basis is more obvious.

Perhaps because it is so generally known, there is little stress laid on the fact that in our country there are no tariff or other economic barriers between the various states. This simple situation has contributed materially in providing the proper climate for our tremendous industrial expansion, our enormous productivity, and our long-term pattern of prosperity.

European business has not had the advantage of this type of free trade, with the result that the mass market for goods produced within any country has been limited to the country of manufacture. Couple this with an almost inherent tendency of the European businessman to be a small shopkeeper and what do you have? Small or, at best, modest-sized enterprises, for the most part. But if Western Europe were to operate as a single economic unit, the potential market in terms of population would be the equivalent of the population market in the United States.

Six countries have now decided to operate as a single economic unit. They are Germany, France, Belgium, Luxembourg, The Netherlands, and Italy. This is the "common market." As it is recognized that the effect of such a market may be explosive, it will be instituted on a gradual basis over a period of twelve years. There is little doubt that the other countries of Western Europe will be forced into joining this group as time passes.

England already recognizes the disadvantage of being external to this market and this has been the subject of parliamentary debate for many months. There is no doubt that England would like to become a party to this market, but "empire preference," the favorable and restrictive trade agreements she has with the crown colonies, throws a stumbling block in the way.

As the common market becomes a reality, the results will be inevitable. Trade will increase and productivity will be the cornerstone of success. Let me illustrate. In Europe today there are many major automobile manufacturers and literally hundreds of small custom companies. This in contrast to three major manufacturers in this country.

With a broad free market the marginal producers will find themselves in serious trouble; they will be forced to merge or go out of business. The premium will be on productivity, and competition will exact its price on all outmoded methods. Europe may end up with more than three large automobile manufacturers but the important point is that they will be limited in number and they will be large.

Growth, expansion, size involve many problems in finance, in organization, in management, and even in accounting and record keeping. Thus it seems inescapable that Europe will not continue to lag behind this country in accounting and accounting methods and procedures, but will be challenged by the results of its own economic manipulations to bridge the gap of twenty-five years in ten or possibly less.

This then is the picture of machine accounting in Europe as I see it, past, present, future. The past, uninspired, influenced by low wages, high tariffs, provincialism, and a small shopkeeper concept. The future, potential beyond description, influenced by free trade, dynamic growth, and an expanding economy.

The common market is no common thing. Today, to Western Europe it may seem to be the means to achieve prosperity and all that goes with it, including data processing machines. Tomorrow, the rest of the world may find that this uncommon market is the vital force which will re-establish the balance of economic power.

And the balance of power is the balance of peace.

Planning for profit— the total systems concept

Before the Data Processing Conference, University of Florida, Gainesville, April 26, 27 and 28, 1962

Introduction

As MOST OF YOU know, in the United States we are protected from the surprise of an enemy air attack by a vast and complex information system which is tied together by a super electronic computer. This protective network is known as the Sage system.

In essence, the operation of the Sage system consists of relating up-to-the-minute observations on flying objects to information which is stored within the system pertaining to aircraft which are supposed to be in the air at that specific time and in that particular area. To accomplish this, information on flight plans are filed by all commercial airlines, private planes, and military aircraft. These flight plans contain information such as the time of the flight, the route to be covered, the altitude of the flight, and so on. This information is stored within the Sage computer. In addition, other information such as current weather readings are also stored in the computer system, since the weather affects flying schedules, flying speeds, and routes. Of course, other basic information relating to our defense facilities is also stored permanently in the computer. This information includes the types of facilities, whether missiles or aircraft, their location, and the operating boundaries or ranges of the weapons.

Finally, current data is continually fed into the system from radar sites located in and around the North American continent. You have all heard of the Dew Line, and the Pine Tree Line which stretch across Canada. These outlying observation posts contain many such radar sites. Other radar information is picked up from land-based stations around this country, from aircraft equipped with powerful radar equipment, from ships, and from the Texas Towers in the Atlantic Ocean off our eastern coast.

The up-to-the-minute bearings from this far-flung radar network are compared with the information stored in the system to determine whether known aircraft are flying in the particular area. If any question exists as to the identity of a craft, it is kept under constant surveillance until positively identified.

Although the Sage system is certainly an interesting subject and has unquestioned importance to our continued safety and well-being, you are probably wondering at this point just how this impressive development is germane to our subject today. Actually, although the two subjects of business and defense against air attacks are unrelated in most respects, there is a definite parallel between them from the standpoint of the technical problems involved and the basic objectives to be accomplished. I will indicate this parallelism to you as we move more deeply into our discussion.

From a conceptual standpoint, the Sage system is designed and oriented toward one objective, making decisions. More specifically, the system is designed to point up those situations where a problem or a potential problem exists, and to do so at the earliest possible time. To accomplish this, it is necessary to relate what is happening to what was expected. In other words, to relate current activities to a plan. When the expected is, in fact, taking place, this information is retained only for reference purposes. However, when the unexpected, the deviation from plan, occurs, this fact is quickly pointed up and followed until a corrective action is taken. The system then continues to follow the situation in order to ascertain that the corrective action is effective, and to provide the opportunity to take further steps if the problem continues.

I am sure you would agree that it does not take too much imagination to substitute the operations of a business system for the principles involved in the defense oriented operations of the Sage system.

Broadly, we would replace the defense equipment facilities, the aircraft, missiles, etc. with the production and other facilities of a business organization. The flow of papers and data relating to orders, production, inventories, costs and external events, such as marketing and economic conditions, would replace the information fed into the system from the radar network. And finally, the budget and other operating plans of the business would be substituted for the information pertaining to commercial and military aircraft flight plans.

Without exaggeration, a Sage system, if installed in a complex business, would be the ultimate in automation! At first, this image may appear to be rather farfetched to you. However, at least in part, this is a picture of the not too distant future, the future in which all of us will live, and it is to this that we should address ourselves if we are to profit from the developments which we know will inevitably come.

Looking backward for a moment, we observe that automation in the office has been steadily increasing for the past thirty years. During this entire period the single most important consideration for the installation of mechanical-electrical and electronic equipment has been the desire to reduce operating expenses. The basic criterion for automation have been economic. Could the operations which were to be converted to machines provide sufficient savings in personnel and equipment to offset the cost of the newer forms of mechanization? As you know, the applications which could meet this criterion were called, aptly enough, "bread and butter" applications.

In looking to the future and viewing the ever-widening horizon of automation, I am sure we can expect that there still will be a heavy emphasis on cost reduction but, in addition, automation will become more and more inclusive and will be directed toward control and toward providing information for management decision-making. This means there will be an ever-widening horizon for those engaged in methods work and data processing, but it also means there will be a requirement for a better understanding of the total business process, of business problems, and of the new tools and techniques which are becoming more available everyday.

My purpose today is to discuss several of these newer areas of development with you, with the hope that your interest will be stimulated and that you will study them in depth.

In order to approach this very extensive subject in an organized manner, let us first enumerate the results which can be expected within the reasonably foreseeable future from automation. First, we can expect that there will be a more complete integration of the various areas of business as a result of better systems of communications. Second, there will be a more extended use of mechanization; information from the factory, field warehouses and outside sales offices will be captured and handled mechanically at the source. Third, systems and procedures will be developed which will be oriented toward providing management with the type and quality of information which is required to operate a business in the most efficient manner.

These are far-reaching and impressive accomplishments and they will be reached through the following means: First, more complete integration of the various areas of business will be achieved through the use of new and improved communication methods and techniques. Next, the extended use of mechanization will result from the development of new equipment and techniques which will be devised as stepping stones toward complete automation, or what has often been described as the "total systems concept." And finally, the overall system itself will be designed to provide management with operating data and, through the combined use of scientific methods and the electronic computer, with the information which is required by management to make decisions relating to operations.

This is an extensive field, and today we can only touch lightly on these three areas, but in the time available let us investigate some of the what's and how's of each of them.

Communications

While we think of data transmission as a new and important subject, actually its roots go back to antiquity. Recognition of the need for the ability to communicate information from one location to another dates almost as far back as the development of the first alphabetic system of writing. And in meeting this need, history shows that regular postal service was first established by King Cyrus of Persia five hundred years before the birth of Christ. Postal service was relatively slow then as now, and faster communications were needed to carry on affairs of state and wars, just as today. To accomplish this, techniques such as drums and smoke were used to convey messages through the mediums of sound and sight. As a matter of fact, these techniques are still in use today in some of the more primitive countries throughout the world.

Since the earlier civilizations, the field of communications has continued to grow and play an important part in the development of nations. As the United States grew and the west began to develop the necessity for establishing a reasonably fast communications link across the country was recognized. In one effort to accomplish this, the Pony Express was organized and operated for one year, 1860. But progress quickly brought an end to it, and its short life was due to the fact that a telegraph link from coast to coast was established the following year.

Toward the close of the century, in 1897, to be exact, an experiment was carried out by a man named Marconi. This resulted in the transmission of a wireless message from land to a ship at sea. Thus by 1900, wires and wireless were both available as basic techniques for rapid communication, and they still provide the basis for communications in the business world today.

These basic techniques have now been utilized in a tremendous number of ways to meet the many requirements of industry. For example:

1. Closed circuit television is being used for such functions as the monitoring of production processes.

2. Facsimile transmission is used to transmit complete printed pages, pictures, maps, and so on.

3. Telemetering is used to measure and transmit physical measurements and movements in operations such as the measure and recording of the amount of gas flowing through a pipeline, and in the measurement of the internal functions of a missile in flight.

And to some extent communications techniques are being used for the automatic transmission of the raw data and processed information needed in the operation of a business. It is this use of communications techniques, the transmission of business data, that we are particularly concerned with. For, as industry has grown and expanded, effective communications have become increasingly important to it. As a matter of fact, they have been essential to this growth.

The growth of industry has taken place in many different ways. Individual organizations have acquired other companies; they have expanded their own production facilities; they have established sales offices more conveniently located in the market areas covered by them; and they have built ware-houses better situated with respect to transportation facilities in order to reduce costs and better serve their customers. Of course, with every such step the magnitude of communications problems has increased.

This is obviously true in the large nation-wide company with the problem of providing communications between manufacturing plants and sales offices spread throughout the nation. But it is equally true for the smaller company with communications needs limited to a link between two locations within the same city. Despite difference in size, communications are equally important to both, and potential communications problems and the need for effective communications exist whenever a business is carried on in two or more locations.

In general, communications can be considered as that part of data processing which provides the link between the devices used in the original recording of data and the equipment which is used to carry out the actual processing, that is, the punched card or other electronic equipment.

Specifically, data communication depends on two closely related parts, the facilities and equipment through which the information is transmitted, and the equipment which reads the data at the transmitting terminal and records it at the receiving terminal.

Just as the overall data processing requirements of industry vary from one company to another, so do communications requirements. To meet these varying needs, many options are available with respect to both the facilities for transmitting data and the equipment at the terminals of the communication lines.

Let's look first at the transmission facilities offered by the common carriers, such as A.T.&T. and Western Union. One of the major variables in these facilities is concerned with the speed at which data can be transmitted over the lines.

In those situations where the workload is relatively low and rapid transmissions are not necessary, lower speed transmission facilities can be used. These low-speed facilities, or circuits as they are usually termed, operate at rates of 6 to 10 characters per second. They are frequently referred to as teletype grade circuits and this term stems from the fact that they have been utilized in teletype communication systems for a number of years and are in common use today.

In other cases where larger workloads and tighter time limits exist, higher speed transmission facilities are required. The higher speed facilities in general use in business today operate in the range of 60 to 150 characters per second. However, even higher rates than this can be obtained, and they are being used in certain applications in connection with electronic computer facilities. The important technical point to note here is that the transmission speeds obtainable are dependent upon the quality of the circuit. The higher the quality of the circuit, the higher the transmission speeds that can be obtained. And as you would expect, the cost of the facility is directly proportional to the quality of line used.

Actually a circuit consists of many parts: the wires, cables or radio equipment, and amplifiers at various points along the route to boost the power of the signal and switchboards. For illustrative purposes, however, a circuit may be considered as a wire. In its simplest form a circuit consists of a wire whose characteristics are such that it can carry one signal at a time, in one direction only, and at a slow speed. This would be comparable to a single lane country road, wide enough to permit only one car to proceed along it and at a slow speed because of the low quality of the road.

On the other hand, the characteristics of a high-quality circuit are such that it is capable of carrying many signals at the same time, and at higher speeds, each different signal traveling along a separate channel in the circuit. Thus a high-quality circuit is analogous to a wide expressway in which cars may proceed simultaneously in either direction, each in its own channel or lane. The high quality of the construction permits the traffic to flow at much greater speeds than on the bumpy country lane.

In actual practice, voice or sound transmission requires the use of high-quality circuits, since a single voice transmission requires the simultaneous use of many channels. Because of this, the term "voice grade circuit" has come to be associated with any high-quality circuit, whether or not it is used for voice or data transmission.

Irrespective of the type of transmission facilities or the rate of speed, the transmission of data as opposed to voice is accomplished through the use of signals or impulses. Similar to the code used in connection with magnetic tape input for computers, combinations of these signals and the absence of signals are used to form codes which represent the letters in the alphabet, numbers, and special characters.

Consider, for example, a code built around a six-position structure. In such a coding structure the letter A might be represented by one pulse or signal, an interval in which no signal is sent and then four more pulses; the letter B by one pulse, an interval, three more pulses, and then, one more interval, etc.

In practice the basic coding structure and the specific codes will vary with the type of transmitting and receiving equipment that is used. Actual coding structures consisting of five, six, seven, and eight positions are in common use today.

While the speed at which messages can be transmitted is an important consideration in planning a data communications system, it is only one of several factors which must be weighed. The carriers provide transmission facilities which perform at different speeds, and they also provide alternative plans under which the transmission circuits can be obtained. These plans provide different options covering the two basic elements of circuit use, time and distance. Time is the period during which the circuit is used, and distance is the geographic area covered by the circuit. It is possible, for example, to contract for service which permits communication at any time to any other point. This, of course, is exactly the type of service which is used in conventional long-distance telephone calls, and it represents one end of the wide range of services available.

Another basic plan which is widely used for data communications is the so-called private wire teletype service. In this type of service the user. has unlimited use of the channel or channels linking two or more points. A modification of this plan permits the use of a circuit linking two or more points for certain fixed periods of time such as from 8 A.M. to 6 P.M.

Another relatively new plan is known as WATS, for Wide Area Telephone Service. This service provides unlimited use of telephone facilities from one selected point to any and all other points which have telephone service within a predetermined area. For example, with this type of service, a subscriber in Chicago might have a set-up which would permit the placing of any number of calls to any other point in Iowa, Wisconsin, Indiana, and parts of Illinois and Michigan. Of course, this type of service could be arranged for any geographic set-up in any part of the country. While this service is known as Wide Area Telephone Service, it is equally applicable to data processing functions, since toll telephone facilities can usually be utilized effectively in digital or data transmission as well as in the transmission of sound.

So far, one aspect of the data transmission picture has been covered, the transmission facilities. As we have seen, the major variables concerned with the transmission facilities are speed, time and distance. The second aspect of data transmission concerns the terminal equipment.

I am using the term, terminal equipment, with reference to those devices which provide the link between data processing equipment and the transmission facilities of the public carriers. To put it another way, it is the equipment which translates the source media, such as cards or tapes, and produces the signal necessary for transmission. At the receiving end the terminal equipment then converts the signal back to the original media. This equipment is manufactured and marketed by both office equipment manufacturers and the public carriers. Because of the varied requirements of the communications field, a wide range of terminal equipment has been developed.

Where punched-card recording and data processing equipment is used, terminal devices are available which provide for transmission of data from a punched-card source and for a rerecording again in punched-card form at the receiving terminal. Punched-card transmission equipment ranges all the way from devices in which the cards are manually fed into the reader one at a time, to more conventional high-speed automatic card readers. Of course, transmission speeds with these devices are limited to the speed at which the cards are read, which would be in the range of a few characters per second to 8,000 per minute in the case of an automatic card reader.

In many systems source data is recorded in perforated paper tape and the tape is usable later as input media to either punched card or electronic equipment. Such systems would usually utilize paper tape terminal devices for both transmitting and receiving data. This equipment is obtainable with a wide range of characteristics; speedwise, for example, paper tape equipment operates from rates of 6 characters per second to about 150 characters per second.

In other systems which utilize electronic equipment, high-speed communications facilities are frequently required to match the speeds of data processing. This is obtained by the use of terminal equipment which reads and records on magnetic tape, the same medium used to feed the data into the computer. These devices operate at much faster speeds, ranging from 15,000 to more than 90,000 characters per second. In such situations high-quality transmission circuits would be essential to obtain this extremely high-speed operation.

It is possible also to obtain terminal facilities which provide direct communication between computers located at remote points. In such cases, data is actually transmitted from the memory of one computer to that of the other, just as if the two memories were built in the same computer.

Finally, terminal equipment is available to convert from one medium to another, either during the transmission process or as a separate step. For example, in many systems, data is recorded in punched cards at remote locations such as warehouses or sales offices. However, the processing of data is accomplished through electronic equipment in the general offices. Thus, a translation from punched card to magnetic tape is necessary at some step in the process. This could be accomplished by reading punched cards at the sending terminal and by recording the data on magnetic tape at the receiving terminal. In this case the translation would be accomplished during the transmission process. A variation of this would be to translate the data from punched cards to magnetic tape prior to the transmission step. Such an approach would be used in those situations where it is desirable to tie up the circuit for the shortest possible time. This would be accomplished, since magnetic tape terminal equipment provides faster transmission speed than that obtainable through punched-card equipment.

From the preceding discussions of transmission circuit characteristics, service plans, and terminal equipment it can be seen that these three elements of a communications system are so interdependent that they must be considered simultaneously in order to arrive at the most effective combination. However, to properly evaluate and relate these three elements requires a complete and thorough analysis of the particular job.

The potentially effective uses of data communication facilities are almost without limit. With the proper matching of communication equipment and facilities, sound applications exist even in small organizations with a relatively limited geographic spread in their operations. Recognition of this is important if the full potential of data communications is to be realized.

Look at this actual situation as an example of what is really a very simple system. A grocery distributor, whose offices and main warehouses are located near the center of a city, ships meat products from a second warehouse located more conveniently to their suppliers. This second warehouse is about thirty miles from the main offices in which the company's accounting and tabulating department is located.

As is common throughout the industry, this company followed the practice of pre-billing for regular grocery products. In this system bills were prepared on punched-card equipment located in the main office and they were then delivered with the food products which were shipped from the adjacent warehouse. However, this procedure was not possible with meat since the actual weights are not known until the meat is removed from the storage lockers and loaded on trucks. This is due to the fact that meat orders are not usually specified in terms of weight, but rather as a specific part of some animal, such as a side of beef. Therefore, with meat shipments the actual weights of products shipped were sent to the office by messenger after the delivery was made, and a post billing system was used.

Under the revised system with machine communications equipment, a tub file of prepunched cards containing product description and price is maintained at the meat warehouse. When orders are received, appropriate product cards are pulled from the file, and customer number, along with actual weight of meat loaded on trucks, is punched into cards. All cards for each order are then placed into a card reader for transmission to the tabulating department where they are received and recorded in punched cards. An extension of price times weight is made there, and product cards are then associated with matching customer name and address cards. The completed product cards and name and address cards are then transmitted back to the warehouse where they are printed on a teletype printer in an invoice format. All of the foregoing steps take place while the truck is being loaded, and it is now possible to prebill for meat products, as well as for groceries.

As a result of this simple change in operation, a uniform billing system and the elimination of messenger service was obtained. Of even more importance, prebilling brought about a reduction in receivables of approximately $25,000 through the resultant speed up in the billing process. A great deal was accomplished, yet monthly rental for terminal equipment and transmission facilities was less than $150.

At the other end of the scale, consider the case of a manufacturer of missiles, rocket engines and other similar products, which has installed a communications system that is as advanced as its products. As a part of this system, microwave equipment, which is leased from a public carrier, is used to link two EDP centers located about forty miles apart. In this system information is picked up from magnetic tape units, converted to signals compatible with the microwave equipment, and then transmitted to the receiving terminal, where it is rerecorded on magnetic tape for further processing on either computer or off-line equipment.

A peculiarity of microwave radio transmission is that, as a general rule, the distance of transmission is limited to the line of sight. That is, the transmission and receiving stations must be within sight of each other. In this case, although the company's two locations are only a relatively short distance apart, a low-lying mountain range is between them. The effect of the range is to make the two points out of sight of each other as far as the microwave system is concerned, since the mountain range blocks the signal.

To meet the problem, it was necessary to build a relay station on the top of the range in order to maintain the line of sight requirement. Messages pass through the relay station where they are automatically retransmitted to the receiving terminal. This relay process does not interfere with the extremely high-speed transmission of data that is possible with microwave radio equipment. However, it does point up one of the basic reasons for the high cost of microwave transmission systems, which has sharply limited the construction of privately-owned systems by industry.

Transmission speeds of 41,000 characters per second are attained through combination of magnetic tape and microwave equipment. With this speed, a tremendous volume of data can be transmitted, more, certainly, than the average organization requires. However, in the case we are discussing, the communications link ties together six large-scale electronic computers which are used for engineering, research, and business data processing. The workload, therefore, requires a high-capacity communications system.

In another part of the company's overall system, a private wire circuit is used to provide communications between the general offices and a manufacturing plant located in the central part of the United States. This circuit is used to transmit business and accounting material such as data related to payrolls, production, and inventory control. The requirements for volume, transmission speeds, and so on, in connection with this part of the system are such that extremely high-speed transmission is not necessary, and perforated paper tape equipment is used at the transmitting and receiving terminals. Thus, in a single company two different types of communications facilities are used, each tailored to fit the specifications of a particular function.

The contrast between this manufacturer of defense equipment and the wholesale grocery distributor is great, but it is representative of the vastly differing needs actually found in industry. It is representative, also, of the many potential uses of communications techniques as a tool for providing improved business systems.

Used in conjunction with electronic data processing equipment, communications equipment will contribute greatly to providing systems for better control over business operations. This will come about, for example, through more up-to-date information on which to base decisions, better coordination of production facilities with inventory needs, and better planning of inventory levels to meet customer demands. By speeding up the processes of data handling, transmission devices will contribute to reduced working capital requirements for maintaining inventories and accounts receivable balances, as in the case of the grocery distributor.

Data transmission techniques will make possible the development of more efficient systems. It will provide a direct link from remote points to data processing centers, thus tying the various points together as though located at a single point. It will permit the elimination of repetitive recording in those situations where, in the past, source data was typed at an outlying point, then mailed to the center for transcribing in machine language. Finally, when properly employed, recent developments in new transmission services and new equipment will permit substantial reduction in communications costs.

Because of these potential benefits, a tremendous growth in the use of data transmission facilities is anticipated over the coming years. To meet this expected load on communications facilities, many fascinating research projects are now being carried out by industry and by the government. As a result, communications networks of the future will be relying on such techniques as the use of satellites circling the globe to meet the demands for high-speed, high-capacity communications.

Data Collection

In the first section of our discussion we covered the basic principles relating to the various methods of data transmission and we pointed out the major variables which are involved, those of speed, time, and distance. Although the basic equipment (or hardware) for collecting the information which is used in data transmission was mentioned, you undoubtedly noticed that we did not probe this particular area in depth, since it appeared desirable to discuss this area of the subject separately.

Within any single plant or industrial complex, operations are taking place continually which initiate a chain reaction of processing. A man reports for work and this fact must be recorded to provide one small part of the data that must be transcribed, sent to the payroll department, and then used in the preparation of his paycheck. If he is a production worker, each job he performs during the day initiates additional transactions, which set up other processing chains. The job must be identified, along with the time spent doing the work and the number of parts produced. Such data is used in the preparation of cost accounting and other records. It may also be used in the preparation of the paycheck if some form of piece rate or production incentive system is in use. In addition, records of the individual's production are used in scheduling plant and equipment operations, in controlling production processes and in controlling inventories.

The initiation, recording, and collection of data such as this is the foundation of any data processing operation. At the same time, however (and this is most important), these steps are both costly and time consuming. As a matter of fact, I have seen many reviews for the possible installation of punched cards where the cost of the mechanized system would be greater than the manual system even though the application was well-suited to mechanization. In many cases, the primary reason for this uneconomical situation was directly attributable to the high cost of transcription, that is the cost of key punching and verification. It has not been unusual to find that the cost of transcription will amount to roughly one-half the total cost of the entire mechanized system.

As we all know, any type of manual transcription operation is subject to errors, and the detection and correction of these errors is, therefore, an integral part of the transcription process and, of course, is a part of its cost.

The objective of data collection equipment, then, is to reduce the possibility of error, to reduce costs, and to achieve better control over production processes through faster and more accurate reporting. To accomplish these objectives, in-plant data collection systems have been designed to carry out three basic functions, to sense required information automatically, to automatically transmit this data to a control point, and to record the data in machine processable media.

In a basic application of this equipment for payroll a number of the recording stations would be located throughout the plant, possibly at the timekeeping or dispatching stations. These stations provide the means for recording the source data and, in addition, transmit the data to a central collection point, usually the data processing center. Recording is usually accomplished through a combination of prepunched cards or tags and the manual insertion of variable data through a keyboard attached to the recorder.

In such systems, files of prepunched cards or tags would be maintained at each recording station. One such file would contain a card for each employee working out of the station, and this prepunched card would contain basic payroll data such as his clock number, job cassification, and rate schedule. The other file would consist of cards containing information concerning the different jobs assigned from the station. The cards in the second file would contain a job number, the department number in which the specific job is performed and the account number to which the job is charged.

Upon completion of a production job, the appropriate employee card would be selected from its file and placed in the recorder to obtain the appropriate data concerning the job just completed. Finally, the quantity of parts produced would be manually entered in the keyboard along with any other variable information. All of the data pertaining to the particular transaction, the fixed employee and job data and the variable data, would then be transmitted to the central collection point where it would be transcribed in the proper media for subsequent machine processing.

The data collecting and transcribing equipment serves to link many recording stations located throughout the plant. The specific number of stations which can be tied in to a single collector varies with the type of equipment. Irrespective of the actual number of recording stations to be linked, the function of this device is to transcribe the data entered at recording stations which are located throughout the plant and to transmit the data to the central location through a network of cables installed for this purpose. In some instances, the design of the equipment permits the use of telephone trunk lines already installed for telephone purposes.

So far as we have discussed the subject of data collection on a basic and somewhat theoretical basis. However, before we leave this section of our discussion I would like to describe an actual piece of this equipment so that you will have a better understanding of the developments which are being made in this field.

One particular piece of equipment which is presently on test throughout the United States is set up somewhat in the manner of a control tower at an airport. That is, instead of having a series of recorders located around the plant, all of the work stations throughout the plant are connected directly by wire to the control center. This means that full information with respect to the operation of each machine or of each working location (such as a welding department) is reported to the control center on a continuous basis. In addition, there is a paging and direct communication set-up included in the overall system. Let us take a closer look at this type of system.

Starting first on the production floor we find that each machine used in the manufacturing operation has a sensory device which determines the production count. This sensor transmits the count to the control center board.

Next to, or mounted on, the machine are two boxes. The first box has two lights, one red and one green. A steady green light on the signal box tells the worker that he is in contact with the control tower and thus his work is being recorded. A flashing green light indicates the end of a run. The worker

ceases operation and awaits a new assignment. How this works will be explained when we discuss the control tower equipment. Each worker understands that production counts are not made while his green light is off or the red (time down) light is on.

The control box sends an electric impulse to a panel in the control room every time the machine operates. Each impulse operates a related counter and thereby the production total is accumulated. There is a dial at the center called a page switch. It permits the employee to call for any type of assistance he may need. In other words, depending upon where the dial is turned, a recorded voice system pages the foreman, a crane operator, etc. Presuming now that something has broken down on the machine, the operator would page his foreman by turning the switch to the proper point.

The foreman, upon determining the problem, would insert a key into the downtime switch lock. When the key is turned, it turns on the red light at the signal box and also at the control room panel, and at the same time starts a count of downtime in the control room.

As you probably know, if a production worker is paid on an incentive basis it is necessary to have an arrangement whereby he is paid at an hourly rate, or on some other equitable basis, in the event that his machine breaks down, or the raw material which he processes does not reach him at a fast enough rate, or if there is any other type of interruption in the production process which is beyond his control.

In the operation being described, each foreman is furnished with a telephone handset, which is carried in a holster attached to his belt. When a problem arises he can plug into a phone jack on the machine and talk directly with control tower. He can explain a production problem or he can advise that a worker is being moved to another machine, etc.

Let us now discuss the control tower. Around the walls are panels, each unit of which is wired to a unit of productive equipment. There is a microphone on the control desk through which response is made to the telephone calls from the floor.

There is at least one panel for each productive machine, and each panel is wired to a control box. Among other things, the panels contain several counters. The first keeps count of the productive time, the next counter records the downtime, the third keeps a count of the units of production, and the fourth counter is a subtracting counter. Where specific production runs are planned, the exact quantity to be produced is initially set in the counter. As each piece is made one unit is subtracted. Thus, as you can see, this counter always shows the number of pieces yet to go on the planned run, and when it reaches zero it starts the green light flashing down on the production machine. As mentioned before, this signals the operator to stop production.

Each panel contains sockets for five jack plugs. The first jack is used to identify the employee. In other words, there is a separate plug available for each productive worker in the same manner as there was a punched card for each employee in our earlier example. Remembering that each of these panels is connected to a productive machine, it follows that the plug identifying the particular man is plugged into the panel corresponding to the particular machine where the individual is working. Naturally when a man moves from one machine to another, the plug is moved to the panel corresponding to the new machine.

The next two jacks and plugs are used for identification. Generally, this would mean the drawing number and the type of operation being performed. The fourth jack might be used for cost accounting identi-

fication or some other similar type of classification.

And finally the fifth jack is used for entering the pay rate for the operation being performed. There are two dials that are used in lieu of the plug for certain types of incentive pay situations. The exact use is not important. What you should appreciate is that the entire system is extremely flexible.

There is a read button on the panel which is used to read all of the information out of the panel into an IBM card. This button records all data present and automatically resets the dials and counts to zero.

In operation the individual in charge of the control room sets up the board in accordance with the men expected on the shift and the planned production schedule. At the end of the shift the controller throws a switch on the control device. This automatically starts a read-out of all information that has been recorded throughout the day, and simultaneously the information is recorded on tabulating cards. The automatic read-out takes place at 100 cards per minute but the reading mechanism is actually capable of reading-out at rates which would be equivalent to 10,000 cards per minute!

Within minutes after a shift is finished, information relating to payroll, costs, and the efficiency of the work performed during the shift is available for processing. Thus without undue haste in the data processing department this information can be summarized and reports prepared which will be available for management early the next working day. Without some system such as this it might take up to a week or longer before the information with respect to a day's production would be available for the operating management's use. Needless to say, data collection systems will continue to be an important development in the years ahead.

Before leaving the subject, I should probably make one more observation. Even though impressive results can be obtained from the machines and devices discussed, we still are working in an "open loop" operation. By this is meant that process information flows to the computer where it is compared with standards in memory. Then the computer calculates corrections and suggests action. However, in the open loop system operators monitor the computer and transmit action commands to make necessary adjustments and to open and close valves or switches.

Already in some industries, like oil refining and chemical production, there is a hint of the future, the closed loop control. Here again process information flows to the computer, it is compared against standards, corrections are calculated, and action commands are transmitted. In the closed loop situation, however, the valves and switches react to computer commands and the only evidence of the instructions are print outs for reference.

Here is the ultimate in automation and its extensive use is as certain as that the sun will rise in the morning. The closed loop of production control, coupled with the use of computers in the management decision-making area, will certainly minimize the use of manpower in many business areas.

Unquestionably, the most important requirement for the future will be a considerable amount of education in order to be able to adapt to the opportunities which will be available.

Footsteps toward professionalism

Before the Chicago Chapter of the
Data Processing Management Association,
October 21, 1963

Set your sights above the horizon, make the future more important than the present, let obstacles become mere challenges to your abilities, follow in the footsteps of those who have turned manual skills into technical arts and technical arts into professional attainments.

WHEN YOUR PROGRAM chairman first asked me to address you on the subject of professional development I readily agreed, because even though this was a subject on which I had not written or spoken previously, I knew there were few topics which would be of more interest to you than your own personal development and what you can do to improve your business status and, most important, your income.

I must confess that I thought this was going to be a relatively easy paper to prepare. I say relatively easy because the preparation of an article or address is never an easy chore. But when I sat down to go to work I found myself stopped before I even began. I discovered quickly that this presentation was not going to be as easy as I had thought.

"Footsteps Toward Professionalism" was my title. But just what is a profession? And what is a professional? I began to realize that here were two terms that have been heartily overworked during the past few years. "He's a pro," is an all too common accolade which is used in almost any situation which requires an uncertain compliment. But what is a profession? And when is a man or woman truly a professional?

Inescapably, I suppose, there crossed my mind that meaningful phrase, "the world's oldest profession," but after mentally conjuring up a picture of soft curves, long black stockings and high heels, I quickly backed away from this vision as definitely not being the professional concept I was to pursue with you this evening.

Equally unsatisfactory as a case in point for this discussion is the eminently honorable use of the term, professional, as used in sports. In this context, the term is used primarily to differentiate between the unpaid amateur who competes for recreation and honor and the top flight individual who participates for remuneration, usually of significant proportions.

After a quick check of a dictionary, which offered nothing useful insofar as my research was concerned, I knew that I had that proverbial bear by the tail, and I was going to have to do some original thinking if I was going to have anything substantive to say to you tonight.

Shortly after having reached this impasse I had dinner with one of our younger audit managers and I took this opportunity to delve into this matter again.

"Dave," I began, "do you consider yourself a professional man?" "Of course," he shot back without a moment's hesitation. "Why?" "Well, I believe you're a professional, too," I agreed. "But tell me," and I'm afraid I said this almost slyly, "just what is a professional man, Dave?"

My Socratic technique produced the expected result. Dave's jaw dropped and the ensuing silence was so loud you could feel it. Finally drawing himself together he concluded that a professional man was one who is highly educated, that he is an individual who is dedicated to his work, and that he is highly skilled in his particular field of endeavor. This was a start, and from this beginning I developed ten characteristics, which I believe describe an individual who carries the title of professional. You may wish to match your own identity against these ten characteristics to see what steps you have already taken and what steps are still ahead of you.

First, and in complete agreement with my friend Dave, a professional is a highly skilled person. Second, he is very well educated. To be more specific I should say that he is educated broadly. Essentially this means education and training in allied fields which adjoin or relate to the particular specialty in which the individual intends to practice.

This broader education, incidentally, is one of the significant factors which separate the professional from the highly trained technician. The X-ray technician, as contrasted with the medical doctor, is an example which typifies the distinction I am trying to make. Both men are highly trained, but the required breadth of education of one far exceeds that of the other.

Shortly, we will discuss the implications of this important element of broad education as it applies to your own future. But first let us continue with our definition of the genuine professional.

The third characteristic of the professional is that he holds, and cannot escape, the ultimate responsibility for his work. Here in a few words is one of the fundamental attributes which identifies the true professional from other important people. Let me repeat this characteristic again, the professional is one who holds and cannot escape the ultimate responsibility for his work

In the final analysis, it is the engineers who design the aircraft, and not the men who build it, who are responsible for the ability of the craft to carry its cargo of human lives in perfect safety from one point to another. Perhaps the next time you create a new system or design a new procedure, you will ask yourself if your efforts meet this standard.

The next and fourth hallmark of the professional is one that naturally follows the degree of responsibility which is attached to his work, and, logically, it is concerned with the personal character of the individual. He must be a person of unimpeachable integrity.

Now, before the obvious objection is raised in your mind let me hasten to add that this statement does not by any means imply that there is one standard of conduct expected from professional persons and that there is some lower standard of conduct which is acceptable from individuals who are not associated with a profession. Far from it! Rather the significance of this point stems from the fact that, in the practice of his profession, the professional is more likely to be placed in a position where the opportunity for some form of skulduggery is presented than is usually the case with other forms of employment. Further, this opportunity for improper gain is often available with a minimum of personal risk. The lawyer who might misuse the confidence of his client, or the doctor who might perform an unnecessary or illegal operation are extreme examples of the degree of exposure which the professional may face in the daily course of his work, and this accounts for what may appear to be undue emphasis on the high character of the individual aspiring to move into professional practice.

Directly related to and designed toward insuring the irreproachable character of the professional is the next distinctive feature which should be mentioned; he practices within the framework of a code of ethics which defines professional standards of conduct. And again I hasten to add that this concept of moral rectitude is not to be construed as being only of concern to the professional.

The type of work generally performed by a professional requires certain specific mental skills. And high in the order of these skills are analytical and creative capabilities. The typical routine of the professional requires him to analyze a problem or a situation and then develop a solution. As you know, in the practice of medicine this is called diagnosis and treatment.

Recognized professions involve broad bodies of knowledge and, what is perhaps more important, bodies of knowledge which continue to expand. Therefore it is incumbent upon the individual who calls himself a professional not only to develop a basic or original level of competence, but also to meet the challenge of evolution through a lifetime of self-improvement which involves diligent study and exhaustive research. In addition, there is an obligation to contribute to the furtherance of the profession through personal effort in pioneering new fields.

I believe that our profile of a profession and a professional is now beginning to take shape. We see that a profession itself is built around a boundless body of knowledge, that it is concerned with broad fields of endeavor, that it often deals in concepts and ideas rather than their implementation, and that in many respects it is almost inseparable from the individuals who practice in it.

In turn, the professional is also beginning to emerge. He is a broadly educated, highly skilled individual. He is a man of character, dedicated, resourceful, and fully able to carry the total responsibility for his efforts. He may deal in concepts, but he never neglects attention to detail. He sets his own high goals.

Once Michelangelo, painting frescoes in the Sistine Chapel, was lying on his back on a high scaffold, carefully outlining a figure in a corner of the ceiling. An observer asked him why he took such pains with a figure that was so far away from the viewer. "After all," the observer said, "who will know if it is perfect or not?" "I will," said the artist. Of such proportions are professionals made.

But we are not quite finished with our profile. There are still two other characteristics of the professional to be named to complete the ten which were promised.

The first of these is idealistic in nature and consequently is more easily demonstrated through actions than explained with words. You are all familiar with the free medical clinics and the availability of legal counsel for those requiring such assistance. Perhaps less well-known, but important in the context of our discussion, is the fact that these services are available from the physician and the lawyer because the individual practitioners have freely donated their time and effort. Even less well-known is the equally important contribution of professional men in donating their services on a regular basis to instruct in schools and clinics, and to otherwise participate in the training of the future generation of practitioners in their own profession.

Implied then, in this donation of time and service, is a degree of altruism not generally found in the commercial business world, and it is best characterized by saying that the professional is not solely motivated by monetary considerations. Rather, he is concerned with being of service to all who need his talents.

The final characteristic of the professional is that he is a member of a group which is banded together into a strong professional organization. The function of this organization is to establish standards for admittance to professional practice, to stimulate the individual member to advance the profession's body of knowledge, to provide for an exchange of experiences and to maintain the ethical standards set for the profession by a process of self-discipline imposed upon the individual members by the organization as a whole.

This then completes the picture of a profession and the professional. And from this description we can now identify four major steps which lead toward the ultimate goal of professionalism. These four steps are evaluation, determination, preparation, and dedication.

Let's spend a few moments and see how these points might apply to you. We start first with evaluation. And in this sense I mean evaluating your work. What is it? More precisely, what is your business? Before we answer that let me ask, "What is your company's business?"

Peter Drucker in his book, *The Practice of Management*, says:

"Nothing may seem simpler or more obvious than to answer what your company's business is. A steel mill makes steel, a railroad runs trains to carry freight and passengers, an insurance company underwrites fire risks. Indeed the question looms so simple that it is seldom raised, the answer so obvious, it is seldom given."

Actually "what is our business" is almost always a difficult question which can be answered only after hard thinking and studying. And the right answer is usually anything but obvious. American Telephone & Telegraph Company recognized early that their business was not telephones, it was communications, and the success of the company proves it.

On the other hand, the steady decline of the railroads' competitive position in the freight and passenger business indicates that management in decades past must have thought they were in the business of merely moving rolling stock from one point to another on rails.

A business is not determined by a producer but by the consumer. Thus the question of what is our business can only be answered by looking at a business from the outside, that is, from the point of view of the ultimate customer.

So with that little aside, again I ask, "What is your business?" It is not machines or tapes or cards or flow charts or programs or plug boards. You are not card pushers, tape handlers, programmers, machine operators or supervisors.

As I see it, you deal in information. You are, whether you know it or not, information specialists. And if you are going to build a career with substance and with a future, you had better build it on this foundation. With this statement I have, at least for some of you, identified the outlines of the first footstep to be taken.

The second step toward professionalism was identified as determination. This footstep is so obvious and so personal that it needs no further elaboration, and I do not intend to give it any here.

The third step is preparation. Here we get to the very heart of the subject, and also to the core of this discussion. Preparation involves education; it involves study; and it involves research. As was pointed out earlier, the scope of this study must extend considerably beyond mere technical details.

Looking just a little closer at this situation, we see that if your objective is to be a specialist in information, you are confronted with the problem of educating yourself along these lines. Information, like all intelligence if it is to be useful, must be communicated to others. Communication requires language and accordingly those subjects which relate to the language of business must be the framework around which you build your educational program.

The basic language of business is accounting, and an understanding of the underlying principles of this subject is certainly a first prerequisite to other more advanced areas of instruction. Accounting, as its name implies, is primarily a reporting of past performance, and as such it is of extreme importance to any business executive. Of perhaps greater importance to management is the future, and there is a growing use in business today of statistical and advanced mathematical techniques to assist in forecasting future trends.

Often when trends are identified and specific plans are laid down, the expected future results are expressed through the use of budgets. Budgets to the businessman are what road maps are to the motorist. They do not guarantee that you will not lose your way, but they are mighty useful in giving direction and they can be invaluable if you become lost.

The use of forecasts and budgets is still a relatively new technique, and many businesses still rely on the use of last year's results as the yardstick for this year's per-formance. This is rather close to driving an automobile while looking through the rear-view mirror. And while it is true that no one can forecast the future with absolute certainty, a look ahead, even if through a distorted windshield, is obviously the preferable practice.

When forecasts and budgets are used to develop a plan for the operation and control of a business, it is essential that the individuals responsible for overall direction receive reports periodically which match actual performance against the plan and indicate clearly and explicitly any deviations from the plan. I hardly need point out that the necessary mechanized procedures are directly related to the accounting and statistical concepts involved in the system, and as such play an integral part in providing management information in a meaningful manner and with sufficient speed to be truly useful.

The conception, development, and installation of a business control system can best be accomplished if it is handled by individuals having the broad level of competence which embraces the entire field. This is the person I visualize as the "information specialist" of the future and this is the role I am encouraging you to assume.

The surface has hardly been scratched in the development of business information systems which are responsive to the needs of the business manager, and consequently the potential for individuals who are geared mentally, educationally, and emotionally to be information specialists is beyond my power to describe.

The program which your organization has set up to become effective in 1965, which establishes standards and provides for the examination and certification of individuals meeting these standards, is in accordance with what I am suggesting and represents both the educational and certification requirements which were among the ten characteristics identifying the professional person.

97

I urge you to review the course outlined in the Data Processing Management Association bulletin and to consider the advantages of a formal program of study for yourself. I particularly commend to your attention the elective courses that are listed in the brochure. They are representative of the type and variety of subjects which might well comprise the background of an individual who would qualify as broadly educated. And this you will recall is another characteristic of the professional.

We have been discussing education as it relates to our third footstep toward professionalism, which as we have said is preparation. But personal development involves more than formal education. Education by its very nature is a process of internal absorption; it is a form of inward development. The process of becoming educated is, as must be obvious, essentially a struggle within one's self.

Equally important to the individual with high aspirations is what I might call his external development. Development, here, is the result of conflict and conquest of forces outside one's self. This is where leadership begins and this is where recognition starts. It involves active participation in business, professional and civic activities. It involves giving instead of getting.

You ask for particulars? The specifics are easy. As a member of Data Processing Management Association you can direct your attention toward raising the level of its operation. This does not suggest or even imply a criticism of its present form or direction. As a matter of fact, foresighted individuals have already laid the groundwork for the future. Whether or not this organization achieves the goals that have been set depends upon you.

Your field of endeavor, like those fields already recognized as professions, represents a constantly expanding body of knowledge. It is up to you, individually, as well as collectively, to press its boundaries back.

It is up to you to pass along the knowledge you possess. This means writing articles for your own and other periodicals, it means taking your place on this speakers' platform and not being heavily dependent upon outsiders. It means discussing subjects which are controversial and not just those topics on which everyone agrees. It means study; it means sacrifice.

And this leads directly to our fourth and last footstep, which is dedication.

None of the things which I have talked about can be accomplished without the development of those personal characteristics which, when molded together, create the individual who competes rather than collapses, who inspires rather than irritates, who leads rather than lags. Neither can these goals be reached without a sustained effort which is supported with unflagging energy.

The horse in the field, the falls in the river, the power within the atom, all must be harnessed if their energy is to serve a useful and productive purpose. So it is with your own energies. They must be directed, channeled and reinforced. This, perhaps, is the essence of dedicated purpose.

Set your sights above the horizon, make the future more important than the present, let obstacles become mere challenges to your abilities, follow in the footsteps of others who have turned manual skills into technical arts and technical arts into professional attainments.

Disgrace lies not in failure to attain such a high goal, but in failure to strive for it.

Controlling the computer system

Before the Eleventh Annual Electronics Seminar, American Gas Association— Edison Electric Institute, Chicago, November 19, 1963

No computer should be set up to control itself in its entirety. The overall accounting control, which confirms the accuracy of the total, should be independent of the mechanics of the operation itself.

ONE OF THE questions that I am asked most frequently by people who have read pseudo-scientific stories about the electronic machines of the future is whether or not I think that the day will ever come when man's life will be controlled by some form of super computer or machine. Needless to say, these questions are not asked in an argumentative manner nor have I had any reason to believe they are raised facetiously. Rather I have felt that they represented the outward manifestation of a certain sense of insecurity which many people are beginning to feel because of the tremendous inroads which automation has made since World War II in both the factory and in the office.

Under the circumstances my reply to this question, which varies in length according to the situation, is usually summed up by the comforting observation that as long as man can pull the plug out of the socket or throw the main line switch to "off," he has nothing to worry about no matter how intelligent or how powerful future machines may be.

This is usually a satisfactory answer, at least for the moment, but fundamentally I recognize that this is too much like taking a narcotic to soothe an agonizing pain, for in actual fact an ever-increasing number of social, economic, and scientific problems are raised by the rapid spread of automation, and these problems are not going to be answered by simply pulling a plug or throwing a switch. They must be faced soberly, thoughtfully and forthrightly by all of us who are associated with the fields of computers and automation.

I would have liked to have explored this highly important aspect of control with you today. However, I do not believe it was the intent of your program chairman that I discuss this side of the subject at this time. Instead, I think it was expected that I would devote my remarks to those aspects of control which relate to accounting rather than social problems, to business rather than science, and to the immediate present rather than the future.

As must be evident, control is not a concept which can be put into a few meaningful sentences nor can it be described with a limited number of simple or interesting examples. Actually, some aspect of control is found in one form or another in every segment of every business. To the executive it implies authority; to the engineer it involves restraint; to the lawyer it means regulation; and to the auditor it instinctively suggests internal controls and audit trails.

Whenever I hear the term "audit trail" I visualize a picture of deep forests with sunlight glancing through a tracery of leaves, and then I see a lone indian slipping silently and stealthily through the half darkness, stopping occasionally to carve a crude symbol on selected trees to identify his trail for later use.

Gradually this image dims and then I see a grey-suited auditor complete with white shirt, striped tie, felt hat, and leather brief case carefully making his way through a maze of electronic tape and piles of paper, tick-marking his way back to the source document.

This is indeed the audit trail, the thread of reference leading to the original documents and relating these documents to the figures in the financial statements. I hardly need tell you that here is an important element of control and one that is of serious concern in any computer system. However, this particular aspect of control has been written about so frequently and discussed so often that, having now mentioned it for completeness, I do not think it needs any further emphasis on my part today.

One of the essential thoughts which I wish to leave with you today is that control is not a unique abstraction. On the contrary, it is a dynamic and vital technique. It is a device which is diversified and variable and it is a useful procedure only to the extent that the proper type of control is applied in the proper proportion at exactly the proper time.

A close examination of the many controls incorporated into a computer system, from the time it is a gleam in someone's eye until that splendid moment when it finally reaches full operational status, completely confirms this observation. It will be found that for each specific stage of computer system development there is a particular type of control which seems to especially characterize the period. An inspection of the primary considerations during the evaluation stage of a computer system, which is obviously the first stage, will illustrate this relationship very well.

Broadly speaking, all management is oriented toward the objective of maximizing profits while using a minimum of capital. To achieve these objectives, administrative direction centers around increasing sales (or the use of the company's product or services), reducing working capital requirements, and minimizing operating costs. Computers are quite capable of assisting management in achieving all of these required objectives and ultimately they will do so. Up to the present time, however, the most important reason for installing electronic equipment has been reserved for the last named of these management goals, that of reducing cost.

It is true that there have been a few individuals who have publicly decried such a mundane motivation for mechanization, but during the past ten years it would have taken an extremely farsighted and optimistic management or an exceedingly imprudent one to pass up those miserably unsophisticated direct cost savings for some highly sophisticated but ill-defined application with a well-defined cost of $25,000 a month.

A form of cost control, then, is the primary and perhaps the only type of control which should be involved during the period of evaluation. At this point the problem is not how, but how much, and the proper answer to this question, which, incidentally, will also define the size and character of the equipment, will lay a solid foundation for the installation steps which follow.

The second step in the installation of a computer is the development of the system. This stage naturally divides itself into two segments: design and programming, and there is a unique type of control which must be given overriding consideration in each segment.

In the design stage the fundamental method for controlling the accuracy of the total operation is established or, to put it another way, this is the point where the overall accounting controls are formulated. Since this is an accounting meeting and you are all particularly knowledgeable of the requirements in this area, there would be little purpose served in restating what is to you elementary detail. Suffice it to say that it is mandatory to maintain some form of overall manual control which is completely independent of the machine which is handling the processing.

Since the computer is such a powerful computational device, there is always a tendency to assign the accounting control to the machine itself. Nevertheless, that first law of control, with which you are all familiar, is that there is no means of establishing and maintaining positive and effective control over an operation unless there is a clear separation of duties. This law has not been repealed, even in the presence of the awesome electronic computer.

All arguments to the contrary, no machine should ever be set up to control itself in its entirety. Internal controls in a computer system should be confined to operational controls. Such controls insure that the program is functioning properly and that the operators are performing the right sequence

of operations. But the overall accounting control, the control which confirms the accuracy of the total, should be independent of and completely removed from the mechanics of the operation itself.

This period of development might equally well be called the period of inescapable transition. The individuals who are assigned the responsibility for the new venture start to work with high hopes, great enthusiasm, and a vital interest. Initially they compete with each other for original ideas and unique procedures. But as the days, weeks, and months go by and the voluminous detail, which unfortunately is inherent in all complex systems, begins to mount, the bounce and buoyancy of the personnel gradually begins to disappear. And at moments, which become increasingly frequent, the development of the system seems like an albatross around the neck of all those involved.

At this point in time there is just one form of control which is of paramount importance and that is control of the project itself. This type of control serves one purpose, and one purpose only, to provide a means of formal direction which will help insure that the computer system is completed, tested, and ready to operate on the date originally scheduled.

In my experience, the primary reason for a breakdown in project control, which ultimately results in the system not being completed on time, is an excess of high-level supervision and not enough supervision at the detail level. The installation of a computer, like any complex and extended project which involves control based on a careful appraisal of percentage of completion, is always susceptible to the unfounded optimism of the individual performing the detail work. Programmers are notorious for anticipating the completion of a run "within a few days." Realistically, these few days are often weeks and at times months.

The individual responsible for maintaining the work schedule can only recognize this situation if he is participating in the work on a daily and detailed level. This is the essence of project control and this is the key to supervising any type of creative or developmental work.

The period of conversion, which takes place after nine to eighteen months, depending on the period of gestation, is that inescapable time when your brainchild stands revealed in all its naked glory. That it breathes at all is often a miracle; that it is sound and healthy is always unbelievable. Looking back over many conversions, both easy and hard, I would say that the type of control which is most important at this juncture between development and reality is the control of conversion data.

How many conversions have been halted temporarily to reconnoiter and to regain control. How many have not been halted when they should have been, resulting in master files which are missing important accounts, contain duplicate data and are replete with invalid codes, incorrect balances and every other type of miscellaneous erroneous information. It takes months and sometimes years to recover from such a faltering start.

My repeated admonition to anyone embarking on a conversion is to do everything possible to purify data prior to the cutover day, so that any errors detected at the time of conversion, and there always will be errors, are of a manageable number. Certainly here is one situation where, through proper preplanning and the use of effective control techniques, problems of major proportions can be avoided.

The dust raised by the impact of conversion is usually barely settled before the average computer installation is snatched from its gathering sense of complacency and is rudely thrust back into an atmosphere of tumult and turmoil. The system now must enter the period of expansion. This is the phase of development in which many of you are involved and this, of all the periods

we have touched upon, can be the most critical. This is the time when with little warning success may turn into failure, a profit may become a loss, a promotion may turn into a dismissal. This is the period when all of the well-defined and correctly installed system and operational controls, like snow before the sun on a warm afternoon, silently melt away.

Rather than try to define or describe this loss of control which I consider so serious, let me ask you a few questions which bear upon some of the specific weaknesses that I have observed. With this approach you can mentally review your own operation and by your conclusions evaluate your own organization. Has an air of casualness developed in your computer operation? Has that sense of urgency which carried you through the difficult days of conversion faded away? Has the feeling for the importance and cost of time been lost in your operation?

Remember when the computer was first installed and everyone was aware that the equipment rented for $5.00 a minute? Under this realization everyone worked to compress set-up time and usage time to a minimum. Unfortunately, even with computers familiarity breeds contempt and the symptom of our disease is that progressively it takes longer and longer to get the same job done. Enthusiasm, attention to detail, and an alert and conscientious working force are not easy to maintain, but the maintenance of this attitude toward the job is one of the computer supervisor's prime responsibilities and is an excellent measure of his administrative and directional ability.

Closely related to this diminution in emphasis on all effort which relates to the computer is the change in sentiment which has developed toward new trainees for the department. At the inception of the installation operating personnel were given extensive training. They were sent to programming school and given programming experience; they were provided with carefully supervised "hands on" computer experience during preinstallation and testing periods; they were given the full story on how the system was to operate, and they were given detailed explanations on the "why" and "wherefore" of each run. In substance, they were taught enough about the total system to handle almost any situation which might arise, and they developed a real proprietary interest in the overall program.

Now let me ask about your new trainees. Are they being handled as though they are going to be button pushers or are you laying a solid foundation for their future? Are you training tape jockeys or potential executives?

And what about your computer room? Is it the show place it was when you first started? There is a direct correlation between the number of unnecessary reruns experienced and the degree of confusion which exists in the vicinity of the equipment.

Do you get the impression that the mechanized operations are always just a little behind schedule? Is there the suggestion that the computer room is always struggling to get the work out on time? If the answer is yes, there is a second question. Is there anyone who is responsible for scheduling all operations everyday or is the daily schedule merely a memorandum on a scratch pad of things to be done?

And how about the downtime on your computer? Are you accepting the fallacious suggestion that because your equipment is getting a little older you should expect and accept more lost time? This is indeed insidious propaganda!

This period of expansion is the time when new and additional applications are undertaken. Regrettably, I must report that I have observed a far different attitude, atmosphere, and approach on the second round of development than was existent during the days of initial activity.

Perhaps the most startling difference noted is in the attention and weight given to economic evaluations. Few individuals who have ever been associated with an initial study will ever forget the degree of effort expended in determining the economic feasibility of the proposed installation. Compared to this careful and controlled evaluation, the approach so often taken on subsequent applications might almost be considered irresponsible. It is safe to say that had the original evaluations been prepared with so little substance, few if any managements would have approved the furtherance of the program.

The real significance of this decline in quality and standard of work is not that some immaterial or uneconomic use may be made of a computer, but rather that it is symptomatic of a growing trend toward the relinquishment of forceful direction in this area of a business. It is a direct manifestation of that ailment characterized as "loss of control."

That problems of this type are critical is obvious but fortunately the solution is easy. It is merely a matter of reestablishing administrative controls which are commensurate with the importance and magnitude of the problem.

Although we have moved with great rapidity through the various phases of computer installation, it should be evident that the control of such a system is not something which can be achieved through the application of a few prescribed rules. We have not even approached the point of exhausting the many different ramifications of this varied subject, nor is there time to do so.

There is, however, one other aspect of control which is somewhat less obvious than those I already mentioned and which should be covered before I close, particularly since it is related to the theme of this year's seminar, "Beginning a New Decade of Achievement." The ever-changing pattern in the morals, thought, politics and dress of our society is directly reflected in the pages of our daily newspapers and in the contents of our current household periodicals. Equally informative as to the current interests, thoughts, and problems of management are the pages of the more widely read business periodicals. During 1952, 1953, and 1954, such stalwart stuffings of the executive's brief case as *Fortune, Harvard Business Review, The Controller,* as well as the more specifically directed industry publications, discussed, argued, forecasted and generally kicked around the story of a great new device which was going to revolutionize all of the business practices and procedures that were then in current vogue.

I mean to make no comment on the obvious optimism of early writers. Rather, I call your attention to the same periodicals ten years later. True, there are occasional references and articles, now generally aimed at the broader field of automation, but for the most part, the executive's reading material correctly reflects the downward trend in what was one of his chief areas of attention a decade previously.

I am not proposing or even suggesting that the executive's interest in computers in 1963 should be anywhere near the peak it reached in 1953, but I do have a feeling that it has drifted to a new low at just about the time when some of the earlier premature dreams are reasonably possible of fulfillment.

Who is to blame? In part, but only in part, the executive, because he has permitted early realities to falsely convince him that once having made a policy decision regarding the computer, there was no further need for top level interest and direction in what was, in his mind, just a mechanical problem.

The remainder of the censure I place squarely upon the shoulders of the men and women who have been responsible in any way for installing, operating, and supervis-

ing all of the thousands of systems now in existence. The reason for this failure to come up to the mark is that, with rare exception, the members of this vast group haven't known their business.

What is your business? It is not machines or tapes or cards or flow charts or programs or plug boards. You are not card pushers, tape handlers, programmers, machine operators, departmental managers or supervisors. As I see it you specialize in information. You are, whether you know it or not, information specialists. And, if you are going to build a career with substance and with a future, and if you are going to influence the action and reaction of top management so that the whole field of management control is placed in proper perspective, you had better do it on this foundation.

There is no substitute for the human mind. There is no human force that can do so much, control so much, produce so much. There are many aids to the mind—education, experience, and, of course, machines. It is vital that those working in the field of automation be not overcome by the sheer wonder of invention. Systems, devices and machines can accomplish great things in the realm of information and analysis, but they must be directed, managed, and controlled. This must be the objective of all those working in this field. Too many individuals set their sights too low. They permit their job to control them when they should be controlling their jobs.

Collectively, through your organization you have proclaimed this the "Beginning of a New Decade of Achievement." In this spirit, I say to each of you, set your sights above the horizon. Make your future more important than the present. Let obstacles become mere challenges to your untapped abilities.

Let the next ten years truly be a new decade of personal progress.

The scope of administrative services

A report to the partners of
Arthur Andersen & Co.,
Chicago, May 19, 1965

Our administrative services work will trend toward embracing broad segments of an enterprise and will move away from the solving of problems on a departmental basis. It will become more and more the work of a group of men with a variety of talents rather than the work of an individual or team with about the same background.

IT WAS JUST over ten years ago that John Higgins and I held a series of meetings around the firm to explain the operations and implications of a device which we believed was going to have a dramatic impact upon the record-keeping and computational activities of our clients and which would, in turn, have an equally profound effect upon the development, the direction, and the growth of our administrative services practice.

In the decade which has passed, this device, which was, of course, the electronic computer, more than confirmed our most enthusiastic projections, and the automatic processing of data, or datamation, as it has since been called, has found broad acceptance in practically every size of company and in nearly every type of industry.

Today we again stand on the threshold of a new technical era, an era which will be as different from that which we have just passed through as the industrial age was different from the agricultural. And the impact of this new era will affect everything, everything from office and plant to society itself.

In discussions on this subject which I have had during the past several years, I have identified this new technology as a transition from datamation to automation. But I was more than aware that this was an extreme understatement, and at best was only descriptive of that segment of the future in which we within the firm were likely to be involved technically.

More precisely we are moving into a period of cybernation, a period of automatic control using mechanical, electrical, and electronic devices which are interconnected by a complex communication network.

In order that there may be no misunderstanding about my own position regarding this developing technology, let me state that I believe that this combination of productive machinery and logical electronic componentry has within itself all of the explosive ingredients of a hydrogen bomb, and the basic know-how for applying it to many practical operations is already available. Today automation, in its broadest sense, is not nearly so much a question of *how* as it is of *when*. And this *when* is certainly not beyond the foreseeable future.

What I would like to do this morning is to give you a modest introduction to the potential of cybernation and I propose to do this, not by presenting a lengthy and theoretical harangue covering its probable applications, but rather by showing you a situation which I have personally observed, a situation where productive equipment has actually been coupled to and used in combination with an electronic computer.

Let me be more explicit. While the example I will describe is not entirely representative of a fully automated system, it does illustrate many of the basic principles involved, and it should serve to identify the type and variety of developments which are currently underway. Your own imaginations can then fill in the broader picture. This, I believe, is a far better approach than for us to wander around in a forest of technical system considerations involving open loop systems, closed loop systems, and so on, which is an area far best left for our especially trained systems personnel.

Obviously beyond becoming informed on important innovations in the business world, each of us has a primary and deep-seated interest in relating any new technology to our overall practice and more specifically to our own responsibilities. For this reason, I believe it advisable to begin this discussion by briefly tracing the evolution of business and control equipment, so that the full import of this technology, par-ticularly as it relates to our own individual situations, can be properly highlighted.

The technical evolution which has taken place in this field during the past twenty-five years has occurred in three stages; the electro-mechanical era, the electronic computer era, and the cybernetic era.

In each of these three periods the character of the equipment, the primary usage and the desirable characteristics for individuals who will design and install the system varies sharply. But before identifying these significant factors I would like to call your attention to one very important point.

During the electro-mechanical period conventional punched-card equipment was used for routine accounting purposes and a different device known as the card calculator was designed for scientific and other non-office types of computation. Similarly, in period two, or what has been designated as the electronic computer era, the equipment manufacturers have supplied two distinct categories of equipment, one line of machines which was designed specifically for business applications and a separate series of devices designed to be used in engineering, scientific, and control applications.

In the current period, which I have designated as the cybernetic era, the picture has changed completely. The machines and devices now being built are not designed with a specific end-use in mind, and the same machine will be capable of being used for business, engineering, scientific, or control purposes interchangeably.

A term which you will hear with increasing frequency in the future is interface. This is the coupler which permits the connecting of the main frames of the computers between themselves, as well as to all types of external mechanisms. This is an important element in the technical evolution of the equipment.

This unitizing of the computer design characteristics is not only important to us because of the more obvious technical considerations, but it also has important competitive implications which cannot be overlooked.

In the past with the distinct division in equipment based upon end-use, our practice generally centered around the development of systems and the application and installation of equipment designed to be used in the office and accounting areas of business. On the other hand, most of the engineering consultants and many of the management engineering firms devoted the major part of their efforts to the plant and its operations, with the result that their practice centered around the development of systems and the application and installation of equipment designed for scientific and engineering purposes.

The dividing line or wall between the classes of equipment formed a protective screen which was for many years an effective shelter for us from competitive encroachment. In fact it has not been an uncommon experience in the past to have an engineering firm installing a specialized piece of equipment in the laboratory or in the plant of a client at the same time as we were installing an improved accounting and reporting system in the office. This protective screen is now gone and overlapping applications, applied to the same machine, will introduce a new element of competition we have not faced before.

I have stated that each of the three periods of technical development had certain identifiable factors of significance. These were the character of the equipment, the primary usage of the equipment, and the desirable characteristics for individuals who will design and install the system. Let us examine each of the areas briefly and take note of these factors.

Datamation came into its own in the office through the use of punched cards, and it was just twenty years ago that this method of data processing really began to make its

impact felt. The equipment was simple and unsophisticated and every operation in the sequence of operations had to be manually directed and manually controlled. The key unit in a punched-card installation was the tabulator and the only device which could be connected to it was a device of limited ability called a summary punch.

Although there were some scientific and research calculations performed on punched-card equipment the use of the machines in these fields was minimal, due primarily to the relatively slow processing speeds at which the calculating devices operated. It would be completely factual to say that business applications predominated during the punched-card era and that these were limited to the more routine operations such as payroll, inventory records, sales analysis, etc.

In reviewing this era it is of particular significance for us to observe the desirable characteristics which were looked for in an individual who was expected to specialize in this work. Our man should have an accounting background, he should be logical in his thinking and exhibit creativity, and he should have the ability to work with and direct other personnel. In short, he was and is the prototype of the man the firm is looking for wherever and whenever there is a recruitment program underway. And it followed that we were quite able to develop the competence we needed in this field by the training of our own men selected from within the firm.

The first electronic computer was installed in industry in 1954, and since that date some 22,000 others have been placed in use. You may recall that in early articles the first business computers were called general purpose machines and this name aptly described their ability to perform all of the functions which were previously performed separately by individual pieces of punched-card equipment. However, this term did not imply that those early computers were designed for engineering or process control functions or even for certain business functions which were beyond the abilities of punched-card machines. For these operations manufacturers supplied devices called special purpose machines.

The early computer's most unique feature was the storing within itself of the program which directs, on a step-by-step basis, all of the operations to be performed. This idea separated the computer from all prior forms of mechanization, and it also upgraded sharply the requirements for the personnel working with the equipment.

There is still another characteristic of this type of equipment which should be noted, since it foreshadowed the future. This was the possibility of connecting certain peripheral devices directly to the computer proper. This direct connection of a variety of input devices and a number of different types of output mechanisms was a long stride forward in the elimination of manual steps involved in the processing, and added materially to the developing concept of automation.

The uses for the computer and the personnel needed to develop the applications and handle the installation was naturally dependent upon the equipment and the situation involved. For business purposes the general purpose machine and personnel with business backgrounds were required. Scientific devices for solving engineering and research problems required mathematicians, engineers, physicists, and personnel with similar training and background.

The control of a process by electronic means naturally requires an intimate knowledge of the industry and the process, and it follows that engineers with this background handle most of this work. The cybernetic era, which we are now just entering, will see a further change in equipment, in usage, and in the personnel who will be involved. The equipment will do much more than merely compute and we will come back to this point in a moment.

The control and direction of the process will either be by internally stored programs or by manual direction or by a combination of both. And perhaps most important will be the ability to directly connect a large number of peripheral devices directly into the main systems processor.

The equipment now being produced will be a multifunction device but not multifunction in the limited sense of the present computers. Rather their abilities will embrace, in addition to data processing, the means to handle involved engineering and research problems. There will be the internal devices needed to handle complex communication switching and there will be the needed circuitry to direct and monitor many automated process control functions.

These internal capabilities within the central processor will be complemented externally by the many devices which can be connected either directly or through communication links. These will include, in addition to routine input and output devices, optical readers and all forms of sensory mechanisms and controls. There will also be many forms of interrogating devices with television screens for direct viewing and reading. These latter, incidentally, are already in use.

Computers will be tied to computers with master and slave operation, and massive files, possibly operating through lasser beams for maximum speed of reading, will all be part of the system configuration. This array of devices, together with highly sophisticated communication facilities, opens up many new fields, some of which are now being explored.

Perhaps some of you may have seen the article which appeared in the *Wall Street Journal* about two months ago. This article discussed the possibility of what was described as a computer utility, in which giant computer centers, capable of delivering service to thousands of customers, would operate in much the same way as a utility distributes electric power. Since the unit cost of electronic processing appears to be proportional to the size of the equipment, there should be economic justification for this type of enterprise.

With this background on the equipment and its uses it must already be clear to you that the personal qualifications for designing and installing advanced systems are unlikely to be found in a single individual. What will be required is a combination of abilities supplied by a group or team. Such a team would be composed of individuals with a variety of backgrounds, assembled in each case according to the needs of the particular situation.

From the standpoint of the firm it is significant that the day is past when we can rely solely upon our own internal and on-the-job training programs to produce the competence that is needed in this new cybernated era. We must face up to the fact that if we want to work in these new technical areas we must have individuals with the needed background and experience to carry us along.

Differing sharply from our experience in the past, few, if any, of these men are likely to come from within the firm. Where they should be obtained, how they should be integrated into our operation, and what training we should give them are all problems which must be met in the years ahead.

Two years ago a printers' strike against the *New York Times* and the *New York Daily News* resulted in a blackout of the city's daily press for a period of almost four months. The issue which caused the strike is still far from being resolved. The basic issue for both unions and management was not wages or salaries or fringe benefits; it was automation. And it was not solely a question of job elimination, although this was certainly no small matter. It was also a question of union jurisdiction. For the same systems which can control the typesetting process can also be applied to circulation, billing, and a host of other accounting tasks. And the multiplicity of possible applications cuts sharply across fixed lines of jurisdiction which have been rigorously maintained by various newspaper craft unions for more than a generation.

One need be no eagle-eyed prophet to pierce the veil of the future and foretell that beyond the many technical problems which will be involved in the installation of automated computer systems there will be painful labor relations problems to be resolved both in plant and office, and even the conventional lines of organization in the upper reaches of management will not escape the effect of this new technology. This type of automation is no respecter of persons.

Here is an outline of a system which relates to a newspaper and which involves both the production and accounting areas. The particular system to be described is in use at a newspaper publishing company and is concerned with the handling of the classified advertising function. This is just one of many areas which has been automated by this publisher.

Several factors have encouraged the installation of this particular automated system. The classified lineage and volume of the paper ranks as one of the largest in the country. The credit problem is acute, not only for the newspaper but for the entire community. And most significantly and fortuitously, the paper is essentially a nonunion operation.

This is a somewhat elementary system, since it was designed around equipment which has been available for the past two years. Needless to say, it can be made considerably more sophisticated by the installation of equipment which will be marketed soon. However, even though I characterize this as an elementary system, I do not mean that it is a simple one. In our discussion today I will touch on only the highlights of its operation.

As originally conceived, the primary objectives of the system were to develop routines such as typesetting the basic copy, scheduling the ads, controlling credit, generating complete accounts receivable, and preparing operating reports and statistics.

Ads are received by phone, by mail, over the counter, and by direct solicitation by outside salesmen. Irrespective of how they are received, they are handled within the system in the same way. Most ads are telephoned in and are typed up by an ad-taker. In addition to typing the text of the ad, she also types the advertiser's name and address, the telephone number (which becomes the account number), when to run the ad, etc.

Her typed copy is placed in a channel of a continuously running conveyor belt which carries it to a row of some thirty operators, known as TTS operators, an abbreviation for Tele-Type Setters. These people operate a teletype device with a typewriter keyboard that prepares simultaneously a typed copy and a perforated paper tape. Their function is to retype the ad from the original copy.

It is natural to question why the punched paper tape was not prepared as a by-product of the first typing operation by the ad-takers. This particular newspaper believes that the ad-takers are first and foremost sales personnel and they should not be tied down to being overly conscious of the operating functions. Other newspapers might combine these operations.

When the TTS operators finish an ad or series of ads, they clip the punched tape to the corresponding typed copy and toss it onto the conveyor belt which then takes the material to the computer read-in station.

As the information from the TTS tape is read into the computer, a program is called for which will calculate the proper line spacing, handle any hyphenating which may be necessary at the end of a line of type, and then transmit signals back to the output station where a fully justified and hyphenated output paper tape is punched and is ready for transferring to someone in the linecaster department for automatic preparation and setting of the type.

At the present time, it is a manual operation to feed the justified paper tape into the input devices of the numerous linecasting machines. A more advanced computer with terminals for switching could eliminate this manual step and the composition copy could be fed directly from the computer into the linecasters on a sequential basis.

At the same time as the computer was reading in the raw TTS copy and reading out the justified copy it was also storing certain information called the ad record in its memory. This ad record contains such information as the advertiser's name and address, the account number, the number of lines in the ad (which was counted during the justification process), the insertion schedule, expiration date, text of first line of ad, and any other information needed for billings, accounts receivable records, or sales statistics.

From this ad record additional information required in the production process can be generated, including skip ad maintenance, which is the control over ads on days they are not due to be run, and marking, which is the identification of expirations and cancellations, etc. In addition, this record is the source for credit control, billing, accounts receivable, and various types of sales and statistical reports.

I do not think there would be any value in following out all of the detailed processing which follows from this point. It is automatic and controlled by the computer. However, I think you would be interested in the credit check that is made. This procedure, while perhaps not earth shaking, is imaginative and has proven very successful.

The credit check is performed within the system on a step basis. First the advertiser's telephone number is checked against the current accounts receivable file, which is also maintained in telephone number order. If the account is current, the item is passed. If the advertiser has other ads running and the additional ad exceeds his allowable credit limit, the system will provide information to the credit department that the limit has been exceeded. If the account is delinquent, the system generates an item which will appear on a "potential kill" list. Each item includes the first line of the ad, phone number, name and address, amount of delinquency, date the delinquency was established, and other credit history information. The completed list is again furnished to a credit supervisor.

If there is no open accounts receivable record, the computer system then checks the advertiser's telephone number with a previously stored listing of telephone numbers to which credit will not be extended. Passing this test, a final check is made by testing the advertiser's telephone number against a list in the computer's memory of public pay phones and hotel and motel telephone numbers to determine to the extent possible that the advertisement came from a legitimate and billable source. If it passes this final test, the ad is printed. Accounts not passing these tests are added to the "potential kill" list.

Viewing the illustration which has been described as being representative of what exists in the present and considering the many improvements and advances in machines, devices, and communication facilities that will be available starting this year as indicative of the future, certain conclusions are evident:

1. Our work in the future will trend toward embracing broad segments of a business enterprise and will move away from the present practice of solving problems on a segmented or departmental basis.

2. New horizons involving such concepts as computer utilities serving hundreds of individual companies, broad ranging management information system incorporating not only internally generated data but including external factors as well, simulation studies, and other work of this type will, while enlarging our opportunities to be of service, place a tremendous strain upon the abilities of individuals working in these advanced fields. What I am trying to say here is that both our work and the tools we will be working with will become increasingly complex, and as a result will push to the limit the abilities and the brain power of our most capable personnel. Needless to say our clients and the equipment suppliers are not going to escape the problem either.

3. Administrative services work will more and more become the work of a group of men with a variety of talents rather than the efforts of an individual or a team with approximately the same background, and the handling and control of engagements will have to be altered accordingly.

4. The recruiting of personnel will expand to include an increasing number of men with backgrounds other than accounting. However, except for different technical competence, such candidates must have the same qualities as we look for when recruiting other personnel for the firm. And we must follow a sound program for integrating those men into the division and into the firm.

5. Competitive forces from which we have previously been reasonably well-insulated can be expected to make every effort to encroach upon our practice. We must react, not only within the firm by developing the competence to meet this problem, but also externally by keeping our clients fully aware of the areas and extent of our practice and our continuing desire to serve them in the expanding field. We should be certain, however, that we have the ability to handle an engagement before we proclaim our wares.

We are attempting to carve out a policy for the future and we need all the help we can get, not only from administrative services partners but from everyone in the firm.

The golden rope

Given in Chicago, July 23, 1965, at the conclusion of the basic training school for new staffmen of the Administrative Services Division of Arthur Andersen & Co.

Integrity is, perhaps, the most important of all personal qualities, the true golden strand, and irrespective of how well-educated you are, how confident you are of your abilities, or how high you set your goals, you will not realize your potentialities for success without simple, basic honesty.

I AM GLAD to be here today and to have the opportunity to congratulate you, not only for your successful completion of this particular school but also upon your good fortune in having taken this forward step in your career at a most exciting and opportune time.

Never before have the younger men in our firm faced a future so filled with opportunities for progress and success. And one of the things I want to do this afternoon is share with you certain observations that I have made over many years concerning those personal characteristics which, like strands of gold when woven together, have formed a golden rope. A golden rope which you, like other successful men before you, can use to pull yourself to whatever level of achievement you personally desire.

It was only four weeks ago, but it probably seems to you like four light-years ago, when on the opening day of this school Mr. Lawrence told you something about the history of our Administrative Services Division and its phenomenal growth. How in 20 years we have grown from 1 man to more than 400 men; from one manager and no partners to 179 managers and 48 partners; and from contributing less than nothing to the overall revenues of the firm to our present contribution of 15% of the total fees.

But like the school which you have now completed, all this is history. At this point it is your heritage from others, a solid foundation to build on but never to lean on. A milestone to mark progress, not a tombstone to record the end of it.

Some years ago on Charles F. Kettering's 73rd birthday, notables from across the nation gathered in Dayton, Ohio, to honor the distinguished inventor, executive, and humanitarian. During the course of the evening someone asked, "Mr. Kettering, looking back over 73 years, what do you feel was your greatest achievement?" The reply came without hesitation. "I'm not interested in the past at all. I am willing to spend the rest of my life being concerned with the future."

And we, too, can better ask, where are we going? What are the opportunities? How large is our future? More specifically, how large is your individual future?

In any business an important function in the administrative process is to anticipate and plan for the period ahead, and our administrative services practice is not excepted from this requirement. We in the Home Office are constantly updating data on our projected growth, giving consideration to such factors as the increasing use of professional assistance by business generally, to the number of new offices planned for the firm, which number continues to grow, and finally to the scope of our practice, which for many reasons continues to enlarge.

And so I can tell you that our most recent efforts have indicated that on a very conservative basis we should double in size in the next five to eight years. Let me express this opportunity for you in another way. If we are to continue to serve our clients in the future as well as we have in the past, and I will be tremendously dissatisfied if we do not serve them better, we must build a division of at least 700 men by 1970. But that is not the full measure of your opportunity, because, in order to adequately direct such an organization, we must have 35 more partners and at least 150 more managers.

Now I would suspect that your first reaction to hearing figures of this magnitude might well be that they sound a bit optimistic. True enough, you want me to be

optimistic but equally true, I know you don't want me to stand up here and exaggerate.

Well, as that famous New York politician in the brown derby hat, Al Smith, used to say, "Let's look at the record." First, you should know that the size of our Administrative Services Division has doubled during the past five years, that is since 1960. On the other hand, anticipating that we will have 700 men in the Administrative Services Division by 1970, we are projecting an increase of only 61% for the coming five years. This, I am sure you will agree, is hardly a wildly overoptimistic estimate.

More factually, and certainly more current, on July 1st of this year 42 seniors were promoted to managers in our division, and we needed them desperately.

And to conclude my case and confirm it, one more statistic. Last year our practice grew 20% over the prior year and so far this year we are again showing an increase of 20% over last year. To say the least, we are certainly moving.*

As many of you know, during the years 1953 and 1954, our firm had the opportunity to work with the General Electric Company in the installation of the first electronic computer ever to be used for a commercial or business application. I spent a substantial part of my time on this engagement and I was constantly aware of a small printed card which was conspicuously placed on the desk of nearly every G.E. executive. This card contained a quotation by Ralph Cordiner, who at that time was the president of the company. The statement on the card was brief but pointed. It said: "Not customers, not products, not plant, not money, but managers may be the limit of G.E.'s growth."

---

* Editor's note: Mr. Glickauf was not overoptimistic. Early in 1970 the division included 98 partners, 300 managers, and 756 staff. This is a total of 1,154, a great tribute to the leadership of Mr. Glickauf.

We could paraphrase that observation and apply it to our own situation, "Not clients, not services, not resources, not opportunities, but only competent personnel will limit the growth of our particular activity."

We need now, and will continue to need, men in the future who recognize and are driven by what Clark Dougherty, the 41-year old president of the Rockwell Manufacturing Company, recently identified as the three P's which lead to management success: Preparation, Perspiration, Participation. These attributes are not static units of accomplishment to be temporarily pursued, endured, and then forgotten. Rather they are continuing elements of action which are plainly evident in the daily activities of every outstanding individual.

When I first came with the firm there were no such things as transistors, power steering, detergents, electric blankets, electronic computers or even the Beatles. We hear a great deal about the population explosion in the world and this is an important subject. But we are in the midst of a more important explosion, a knowledge explosion, and this knowledge explosion is one of the factors which is creating the unlimited opportunities for you and any others who are prepared to take advantage of it.

Mr. Leonard F. McCullum, chairman of the board of the Continental Oil Company, stated this whole idea most succinctly. He said, "If it works it's obsolete." So with this school which is just concluding, you should consider it as nothing more than an island, an island already passed as you move along a stream of continuous education and preparation.

But education and preparation are not enough. A successful career demands important personal qualities which you must have and which you must develop. Earlier this year, Monroe J. Rathbone, the chairman of the board of Standard Oil of New Jersey, was addressing the advisory council of Pace College and he expressed this point particularly well. "No matter how good a business school is," Mr. Rathbone said, "it does not graduate business managers. The most it does is graduate people who have an understanding of the world of business so that they can proceed to become business managers if they have the necessary personal characteristics."

Obviously, there are many facets to a man's character and in the few minutes we have together here, there is not time to discuss all of them. But, I would like to touch upon five which I have already alluded to as strands in a rope of gold.

First, you must have confidence, confidence in yourself and in your ability to be successful. Confidence is a developed attribute, not an induced one. It starts with accomplishment and is built up day by day. I particularly caution you not to mistake brashness or cockiness for confidence. Confidence is a quiet thing. But it speaks for itself, and when you have it you will find a reflected response in the attitude of your associates and clients alike.

This confidence must be accompanied by another highly important quality, the desire to constantly improve your performance. It is a fortunate fact that with all of us our potential ability is always greater than our actual performance.

I remember when the four-minute mile was considered an impossibility. Then one dramatic day back in 1954, Roger Bannister suddenly broke through this assumed barrier. Not by much; his time was 3':59.4". But this physical achievement was also a mental one, and milers all over the world suddenly began to better the new record. Today a mile runner who can't beat four minutes would have little chance in a major race.

Our clients expect us to break through old barriers too. They look for us to do this every time we serve them, and the reason they expect it is because we have performed commendably in the past.

In addition to confidence and the constant desire to improve your performance, there is another important personal quality you must have and develop. This is the characteristic that is best described by the term, adaptability.

I know that throughout the school your instructors have constantly emphasized that there is seldom one absolute answer to a particular business situation or one system or form of technology which is right at all times and in all places. Our administrative services practice deals with change. Our necessity, then, is to have a flexible attitude in response, in planning, and in action.

A German general once commented: "No plan survives contact with the battle," and I would hasten to add, nowhere is there a greater need for this quality of adaptability than in the type of creative work in which we in our division are daily engaged.

At the same time, I want to say that this adaptability to which I refer does not mean flexibility or pliability in personal or business principles. Integrity is, perhaps, the most important of all personal qualities, the true golden strand, and irrespective of how well-educated you are, how confident you are of your abilities, or how high you set your goals, you will not realize your potentialities for success in business, at least in our business, without simple, basic honesty.

And now I come to the fifth and last of my golden strands. It is a fibre that is, in a sense, the very core of our rope, the one around which all the other strands are woven. And strangely enough, it is at variance with that very popular and well-accepted maxim: "A fair day's work for a fair day's pay." It is simply this: you have to put more into your work than you get out of it. This is true for an assistant, a manager or a partner. It is equally valid for stockboys, foremen or presidents.

Today each one of you is standing on the ground floor of unparalleled opportunity. And you are here because the firm believes you are capable of developing those personal characteristics which are so vital to a successful career.

You have before you what that old preacher referred to in one of his more oratorical moments as the "doctrine of election." "And what is the doctrine of election, Pastor?" one of his parishioners asked. The old preacher's eyes gleamed. "Well, it's this way", he said. "You know God has one vote and he is always for you. The Devil, he has one vote and he is always against you. You have the deciding vote."

As you return to your own individual offices, you carry with you my very best wishes and deepest interest in your future.

Cybernetics, the next step in automation

Before the Graduate School of
Business, University of Indiana,
Bloomington, March, 1966

*The term, cybernetics, is derived
from a Greek word meaning
helmsman. It is used to identify the
whole field of control and
communication as applied to any
self-adjusting or self-regulating
mechanism or system.*

I HAVE ALWAYS been fascinated by a letter Benjamin Franklin wrote in 1780 to a scientific friend in which he comments on the rapid progress then being made by science. In this letter Franklin speculates on what may be achieved in another thousand years and as one possibility he suggests in the formal language of his day, "We may even learn to deprive large masses of their gravity for the sake of easy transport." Franklin thought in terms of a thousand years but it only took 122 years for the Wright Brothers at Kitty Hawk to deprive large masses of their gravity, and only an additional 63 years for man to develop the technology needed to send close-up pictures back from the face of the moon and from the surface of the red planet, Mars.

Scientific progress and change are not new; only the rate of progress has altered. If in Franklin's day change was evolutionary, today it is revolutionary and to most of us it is often bewildering. It is hard to realize that it was only slightly over ten years ago that meetings such as this one were being held around the country to explain the implications of a device which it was believed would have a dramatic impact on record keeping and computational activities of larger business enterprises.

In the past ten years this device, which was, of course, the electronic computer, more than confirmed even the most optimistic projections, and the automatic processing of data, or datamation, as it has since been called, has found broad acceptance in practically every size of company and in nearly every type of industry.

Today we again stand on the threshold of a new technological era, an era as different from that which we have just passed through as the industrial age differs from the agricultural age, and the impact of this new era will affect not only the office and the plant, but society itself.

In discussions on this subject which I have had in the past few years, I have identified this new technology as a transition from datamation to automation. But I am more than aware that this is a serious understatement, and at best only descriptive of that segment of the future in which most of us are likely to be directly involved. Because, more precisely, we are moving into a period of cybernation, a period in which machine power is combined with machine skill, a period in which operating efficiency rises and operating labor almost disappears. A time when the artificial wall separating the corporate functions of production, marketing, and finance will be broken down, and the entire spectrum of a business operation will be considered and handled as a single unified entity.

The technique of cybernation, which is basically the combination of automated machinery and the electronic computer, is no inventor's dream, for there is already available the basic know-how for applying this technology to many practical operations. Today automation in its broadest sense is not a question of how but of when, and this when is not beyond the foreseeable future.

Obviously beyond becoming informed on important innovations, each of us has a deep-seated interest in relating new technology to our own responsibilities. For this reason a good place to start is by briefly tracing the evolution of control equipment. There have been three stages of its technical development during the last twenty-five years. They may be identified as the electromechanical era, the electronic computer era, and the cybernetic era.

During the electro-mechanical period conventional punched-card equipment was used for routine accounting, while a different device, a card calculator, was designed and used for scientific and nonoffice computation. Similarly during period two, the electronic computer era, equipment manufacturers supplied two distinct categories of machines, one line specifically for business applications and a separate series for engineering, scientific, and control applications. But now in the cybernetic era the picture is completely changed. Machines and devices now being built are not designed with the end use in mind. They are capable of use interchangeably in business and engineering and for scientific and control purposes.

Let us look briefly at certain of the characteristics and applications which identify each of these eras. Historically, datamation came into its own through the use of punched-card equipment and unbelievably it was only twenty years ago that this method of data processing made its impact really felt. In retrospect the equipment was simple and unsophisticated. Essentially, each piece of equipment performed a single function. The punch punched, the sorter sorted, the reproducer reproduced. Perhaps most important, every operation, in sequence, was manually directed and manually controlled. Although there were some scientific and research calculations performed on punched-card equipment, the use of machines in these fields was slight. It would be completely factual to say that business applications predominated during the punched-card era.

The year 1954 saw the installation of the first electronic computer in industry, and since that date some 25,000 have come into use. The first business computer was called a general purpose machine, and this name aptly described its ability to perform all functions previously performed by separate pieces of punched-card equipment. However this term was not intended to imply that those computers were designed to handle engineering design work or process control or certain other functions beyond the ability of punched-card machines. For these operations the manufacturers supplied special purpose equipment.

There is an important point to note with respect to the first computers. While these devices could perform various functions automatically, such as to read tape, sort, calculate, etc., and thus were truly multi-function machines, they performed these functions one at a time or serially and without any overlap. This method of processing was often very limiting.

There was still another characteristic of computers which should be noted in tracing this evolution. This was the fact that other pieces of equipment or peripheral devices could be connected directly to the main frame of the computer, proper. This direct connection of a variety of input devices and a number of different types of output mechanisms into a unified system configuration went a long way toward the elimination of the manual steps involved in processing, and added materially to the growing concept of automation.

The cybernetic era which is now just beginning will see further changes in equipment, in usage, and in the personnel who will be involved. However, before pursuing this point further it might be well to pause a moment in order to touch briefly on the basic principles involved in this developing science of cybernetics. Actually the principle of cybernetics is not new and there have been a number of American and international symposiums on the subject. The term is derived from a Greek word meaning helmsman. It was used in 1947 by the late Dr. Norbert Wiener, distinguished professor of mathematics at Massachusetts Institute of Technology, to identify the entire field of control and communication as applied to any self-adjusting or self-regulating mechanism or system.

One of the underlying principles of cybernetics is the concept of negative feedback. This is the idea of recognizing a change of state or energy in one part of a system to regulate and control a situation in another part of the system. The concept of the automatic reorder of an item of inventory when a particular transaction causes the stock to fall below a certain predetermined minimum is a good example of the feedback principle.

Dr. Wiener in his book on cybernetics says that the first significant paper on feedback mechanism was published back in 1869. This paper described the operation of a governor which served to regulate the velocity of steam engines under varying load conditions. You are all familiar with this purely mechanical feedback system. It consists of two balls with attached pendulum rods which swing on opposite sides of a rotating shaft. They are kept down by their own weight and swing upward from centrifugal action, dependent on the velocity of the shaft. Thus, the position they assume depends on the speed of rotation. Their position is transmitted by rods and shafts to an intake valve on the cylinder. When the engine slows, the balls drop and the valve opens. When the engine speeds up, the balls rise and close the valve. By this means the speed of the engine is controlled or limited.

Another familiar and somewhat more modern application of the feedback principle is the combination of a bimetal thermostat with some form of heating plant for the purpose of regulating the temperature. Here, incidentally, we have a three element configuration, which is the classical representation of cybernetic control, the selector, the sensor, and the effector. The variable setting on the thermostat is the selector mechanism. The bimetal element, which closes to complete the electric circuit and opens to break it, is the temperature controlled sensor. And the heating plant is the effector mechanism. Although not explicitly identified in this academic configuration, there is obviously a requirement of some means of communication to tie the whole system together. In the case of our temperature control system this is accomplished by electric wiring on the one hand and movement of air on the other.

These two examples used in defining the feedback principle are essentially mechanistic in concept and represent a technology well-known for many years. However, cybernetics, particularly as I am using the term in a business context, adds another element to that of feedback. This element is information, which in practice may take many forms. Time does not permit carrying this point further. However the resulting combination of communications, computation, and control is neither mechanization nor automation. It is cybernation, which perhaps might be defined as the science of guidance and control under information.

With this background let us now return to a discussion of cybernetics as it applies to business and industrial functions. The computer is now being manufactured for use in cybernetic applications. Although it is similar to prior models in that it is under the control of internally stored programs, it has a number of important characteristics which differentiate it. One significant advancement is the ability to handle many problems at once, in contrast to one at a time. Another improvement will permit the connection of a large variety of peripheral devices directly to the main processor. Internal devices will be needed to handle complex communication switching and circuitry and interfaces will be needed to direct and monitor automated functions.

As a result, a single processor can be used for data reduction, including situations involving complex and highly integrated information systems, engineering and research applications, communications and communication switching, and for monitoring many process control operations. These internal capabilities within the central processor will be complimented externally by devices connected to the processor, either directly or through communication links. These will include, in addition to routine input and output mechanisms, optical readers and visual interrogating devices. These interrogating devices will use a cathode ray or a television screen for direct viewing.

Computers will be tied to computers, with master and slave operation. Sensory devices of all types will measure, weigh, count, and test. And finally, massive files, possibly operating through laser beams, will also be part of the total equipment configuration. This array of devices, together with highly sophisticated communication facilities, opens up many new applications and new business possibilities.

Moving along, I now want to describe a relatively uncomplicated system which automatically collects data on production and which is tied in to a computer. This particular system is set up in the manner of an airport control tower. Each piece of production equipment on the plant floor is connected directly by wire to the control center, which is located on the floor above and which has a large glass bay overlooking the manufacturing area. Information with respect to the operation of each machine is reported to the control center on a continuous basis. In addition, a paging and a direct communication setup is included in the overall system. On the production floor, each machine has a sensory mechanism attached to it, and each sensor transmits production data to an individual control panel located in the control center.

In operation, the individual in charge of the control room sets up his board in accordance with the men assigned to the shift and the planned production schedule. At the end of the shift the controller throws a switch on the control panel. This starts an automatic readout of all information recorded throughout the shift.

With this system information relating to production, machine time, downtime, payroll, costs, efficiency, etc., is available for processing within minutes after the shift ends. It is easily summarized by the computer and reports are available no later than the next working day. Thus information for management is speeded up tremendously, for prior to the use of this system almost a week passed before the information on the production was available. And one of the most cumbersome operations, preparation of input data for the computer, has been almost eliminated.

This as I have said, is an uncomplicated system, uncomplicated in the sense that it eliminates paperwork and factory clerical work, rather than production personnel. Probably it can be characterized as an obsolete system, because in the future systems which collect data from sensory devices will read data directly into the computer memory, rather than accumulate it first in individual control panels as was done here. This example lays the groundwork for defining real time and nonreal time systems and clearly shows the distinction between them. As described it is a nonreal time system. Connect sensory devices directly to the computer and it becomes real time. In other words, a real time system is one in which the processing of data parallels the physical process and the results are immediately available for use. Going one step further, when a communication link is set up between the machine and the computer as it would be in a real time system, it becomes possible to transmit signals from the computer as well as to receive signals in it. Thus direct operational control of the tool becomes possible, another large step forward in the automation of the total production process.

Viewing the illustrations we have described as being representative of what can exist in the present, and considering the many improvements and advances in machines, devices, and communication facilities that will be available starting this year as indicative of the future, certain conclusions are evident. First, we can see the advent of a truly integrated data processing system, a system in which the basic element of data is entered at the earliest possible point (and only once), and thereafter retained, processed, summarized, and analyzed entirely within the framework of the computer complex. Little information will be printed out and most results will be obtained by interrogation. Second, automation will not be limited to the medium and large business enterprises but will embrace all but the very smallest activities, and perhaps even these will not be exempt.

One of the most important of recent developments is time sharing. Fundamentally, time sharing is a term used to describe a system where a number of different users are all connected to a single centralized computer system. Each user is served as if he were the only user, although, in fact, many may be served concurrently. It is entirely conceivable that in ten or fifteen years we may have a computer center the size of a local telephone exchange office. Such a center might have a computer which cost forty or fifty million dollars, but it could provide computing facilities equivalent to a medium-sized computer which today rents for, say, $10,000 to $12,000 a month. At a cost of perhaps $700 a month such a set-up would truly revolutionize the approach to business systems.

To get back to our third conclusion, the demand for personnel capable of working in this field will skyrocket and this situation may be the limiting factor in terms of time in achieving the goals discussed.

A foretaste of what is coming is well-illustrated by the following excerpt from a recent technical publication:

"Witness the recent omission of a mere hyphen in some mathematics which caused the $18.5 million failure of a spacecraft-launching toward Venus.

The spacecraft, Mariner 1, which veered off course about four minutes after launching at Cape Kennedy had to be blown up in the air. The hyphen was a symbol which should have been fed, along with a mass of other coded instructions, into a computer governing the first phase of the rocket flight by radio signals. These signals caused the craft to go off course. As a result, the Air Force range safety officer had no choice but to push the 'destruct' button."

And mind you, this was only a slight error, just a slip of a dash, in an obviously very complex computer coding problem.

An old parlor game called Truth or Consequences found new life some years ago as a popular television show involving public participation. We have a new game today and the name of the game is Change or Consequences. Every individual, whatever his position in the business world, is going to be affected by technological developments, and he must be constantly aware of these changes if he is not to suffer the consequences.

This, then, is the face of the future. I know it is important to me and it is important to each of you. After all, the future is the place where we are all going to spend the rest of our lives.

Cybernetics, its relation to management information systems

John A. Higgins Memorial Lecture,
at the University of Minnesota, Minneapolis,
October 5, 1967

In the past, machines and methods have limited systems to the reporting of unstructured facts. Now, through the use of more sophisticated mathematical techniques and improved computational equipment and communication devices, facts can be structured and measured, so that the information content is more immediately available for making decisions and taking constructive action.

TODAY OUR civilization is both figuratively and actually reaching for the stars, and the impact of the technologies related to the achieving of such distant and monumental goals have already been forcibly felt in more earthly matters. Nowhere is this more evident than in matters of business and management, where techniques and equipment which have been either evolved or advanced by space exploration programs are opening up new avenues of progress both in managerial and in operational control.

The theme of this present series of discussions, "The Management Information System," is itself a term, or perhaps better, a concept that is a product of the most recent innovations and inventions. In fact, this term is so new that while it is certainly broad in connotation, it is still essentially undefined and at best only partially reduced to practice.

It is self-evident that as long as there has been any form of mercantile operations and as long as there have been individuals who have in any way assumed a managerial function, there has had to exist some form of management system. And certainly in today's complex business environment with its highly competitive aspects and its extremely complicated legal and tax situations, managements must receive data that is extensive, penetrating, and informative.

What then is different about today's management information system, and what are the difficulties in coming to grips with the present concepts? I think most practitioners would agree that a management information system differs in concept from the more conventional accounting and reporting system in at least three important aspects.

First, in its ultimate form it is not one system but a series of interlocking systems which are involved with the interaction between all the functional areas of the business, including engineering, production, marketing, personnel, and finance.

Second, it is not only oriented toward performance reporting but it is aimed at optimizing the performance of the individual manager by providing him with the best information which can be made available for his particular position and for the specific decisions he is required to make. Depending upon the individual's responsibility, it would provide the information required for strategic, managerial or operational control.

It is perhaps pertinent at this point to indicate that this does not mean that it is the purpose of a management information system to provide the manager or the executive with *all* the facts. He doesn't want all the facts and generally he can't use them all. What the executive wants and needs are facts carefully selected to provide information and insight into his primary areas of interest, such as causes, effects, and trends. Certainly he is not interested in a blob of figures or a mass of statistics.

And thirdly, a management information system is a dynamic and not a static concept. This means that the system must be viable, that it must be responsive to new goals and to a changing environment, so that at all times it will communicate to the user the information appropriate to the existing circumstances.

Overall, a management information system is a cybernetic system. It is a system that is capable not only of acting upon its various inputs, but also of reacting to such inputs in a positive and controlled way. Such a system represents an emerging technology, a technology that is step-by-step being developed around and is dependent upon several interdependent and highly complex elements.

The first element includes the techniques for processing, storing, and transmitting large amounts of information automatically, and is represented physically by such components as the electronic computer, mass storage units, visual display devices, and an increasing number of communication facilities and units. The second part is concerned with advanced statistical and mathematical methods for problem solving, and is represented by techniques such as mathematical programming and other methods of Operations Research. And the third element, still very much in the embryonic stage, combines the first two, computers and mathematical methods, into mathematical models, a technique by means of which high-order thinking is simulated and the effects of vast numbers of alternative courses of action can be studied at speeds which both excite and exceed the imagination.

Together these elements are capable of producing a highly sophisticated system or, as I have indicated before, a series of interlocking systems. But the problem, and there is a problem, is one of putting these elements together into a useful, cohesive, and effective whole.

Perhaps most significant is the immediately apparent need for a team effort, a team composed of individuals with varied abilities representing multi-disciplinary educational backgrounds and experiences and yet capable of communicating with each other, a matter of no mean accomplishment. And then, of course, this same team must be able to communicate with personnel at all levels of the enterprise involved. Equally important is the requirement for a master plan, a plan that will insure that everything that is to be accomplished will fit together. And then there is the requirement to build slowly and often bit by bit so that, in the words of the English cybernetician, Stafford Beers, "We build a proper edifice and not a sprawling muddle that enshrines the past in a graveyard of expensive tombstones."

But this has been done and is being done, albeit, I suspect, too slowly for some. But progress is being made and at this point I would like to discuss with you a few selected examples of these bits and pieces that identify the progress and advantages I have just referred to, bits and pieces that highlight and define a blueprint for the future.

Before we take up some of these definitive situations, I believe it will be worthwhile to take a few moments to touch briefly on the background and on the meaning of the word, cybernetics. Cybernetics is a term used to identify the whole field of control and communication as applied to any self-regulating mechanism or system.

Now some people think cybernetics is just another name for automation, some that it is concerned with biological experiments on living animals or a new course in mathematics, and others that it is the application of computers in matters of legislation and government. This variety of concepts is easy to understand in view of the diverse uses of the word. For example, within the past year at least a dozen books on the subject have been published here and abroad. Their titles indicate such a variety as *Cybernetics and the Laws, Psycho-Cybernetics, Cybernetics and Biology, Cybernetics and its Relation to the Information Theory and Thinking. Cybernetics and the Law,* incidentally, deals with Soviet law and is the only one of at least eight recently published volumes on the general subject of cybernetics which was written by a Russian author.

In another direction we find the International Society of Cybernetic Medicine, whose name is reasonably self-explanatory, and the Institute for Cybercultural Research, whose name is more ambiguous. This latter is presumably concerned with present and anticipated social problems arising from technological changes.

Business is also involved; we have the Cybernetic Corporation in the Chicago metropolitan area, Cybertronics, Inc., in Washington, D.C. Cybernetics Ltd. located in Canada. And if this were not enough, my attention was called recently to a sermon on the ethical and religious implications of Cybernetics given by a chaplain at Massachusetts Institute of Technology.

Why all this diversity and apparent confusion? Essentially because cybernetics is concerned with certain broad principles in the field of communication and control. And the application of these principles has been found to be equally relevant, whether they are applied to a business system, to biology, to engineering, to government, or to space technology.

One underlying principle of cybernetics is the concept of control thru the use of "feedback." Now feedback is the term used to describe the sensing or recognizing of a change of state in one part of the system to control an operation in another part of the system. Stated another way, feedback is the property of being able to adjust future conduct based upon past performance.

Dr. Norbert Wiener, in his classic on the subject of cybernetics, points out that feedback may be as simple as a common reflex or it may be of a higher order in which past experience is used to regulate whole policies of behavior. In explaining the term, Dr. Wiener illustrates this feedback principle by using the very familiar mechanical cybernetic system found in the thermostatic control of temperature. Although this is an extremely simple use of feedback, it does serve to illustrate the three basic components found in any cybernetic system. These three basic elements are known as sensor, selector, and effector. In our example the bimetal element in the thermostat is the sensor, which detects changes in temperature. On the basis of this detection, the bimetal element sets a selector (usually a mercury switch) to either an on or off position. The selector, in turn, controls or instructs the furnace, which is the effector in this example. Obviously there is a need for some means of communication to tie the whole system together. In the case of our temperature control system this is accomplished by electric wiring on the one hand and the movement or feedback of air on the other.

From a simple mechanical mechanism to a highly complex electronic system can be a very long step. And it is indeed a wide gap that separates the simple heating system from the most advanced application of cybernetics as used in a system for guidance and control of a ballistic missile. Even so, the basic principles remain the same.

With a missile, as with all goal-directed devices, situations, and operations, the first thing that must be determined is the objective or target. In the military, this determination is the function of the top command. In business it would be the function of the executive management. Once this target or goal has been identified, a system for reaching and hitting this objective can then be developed and installed.

Although admittedly the control system of a missile represents a very highly specialized application of guidance and control, many of the basic principles are the same as those found in a modern computer-based business information system. Further, and more important for us here today, this example provides an excellent analogy, an analogy that is directly applicable to this discussion. In the business environment management identifies the target; that is, management sets the criteria. Then it becomes possible to plan, to design, and install the control system best suited to hit the mark. With this in mind let us consider certain segments of a few engagements which are representative of both the progress and the problems involved in the development and installation of a truly effective management information system.

Our first engagement example is Travelers Insurance Corporation, whose management kindly consented to our using this material. Travelers is one of the oldest and certainly one of the largest multiple line insurers in this country. Their headquarters are located at Tower Square, a landmark in Hartford, Connecticut. Down the road a few blocks is another complex of buildings, including a mammoth new data center built in 1964. It was in the rear of this building, just a few months ago that computers and communications quietly joined hands, and the first of Travelers' seventy-one field offices began processing information on-line to Hartford.

My particular reason for introducing this case, which I would characterize as a relatively simple example, is immediately identified when I tell you that this event was the culmination of 245 man-years of study and design work which began back in 1961.

Innovation was one of the prime factors in this project and it began in the design of the center itself. There is only one row of columns supporting the 120,000 square feet of ceiling. The entire computer room is enclosed in wire mesh to prevent any electrical phenomenon from accidentally destroying the vast store of important records, and the fluted walls of the building encase a column of air to help insulate the interior from outside temperature changes. Behind the main entrance are spacious work areas for the 170 persons now employed and there is room, of course, for more.

Immediately behind this entrance and centered in the middle of the building is the heart of the electronic side of the operation. Here is located the computer and all of the auxiliary equipment. In this case an important segment of the auxiliary equipment is represented by huge electronic files.

Very briefly, the objective of the system is to reduce to a minimum all clerical and decision-making activities at the field offices. This is done by removing from the local offices every vestige of policy records, files, and other information. The computer at Hartford holds all the answers and any location anywhere in the country can retrieve information in less than ninety seconds by initiating a teletyped request. Changes and claims are all handled without local records and the computer performs all pertinent premium calculations. As data flows back and forth it bills and monitors collections, issues renewals, and checks driver safety records. If you have too many moving violations, it advises against renewal, and it accumulates all actuarial and under-writing data which is of significance in determining future rates and services.

A vital link in the process is the communications network. It represents one of the first of its kind, and when complete it will grow to 26 circuits and will carry an average of 34,000 messages a day. The point-to-point communication, which is extremely complex, is under the automatic control of one of the electronic computers. You might be interested to know that all Medicare cases handled in the state of Minnesota are carried over these lines, as well as the company's regular business. Most of Travelers' one million automobile policies will be on the system within the year. However, the company has seven more years' work to convert all the casualty lines and to realize all of the estimated savings envisioned from this system.

Over the years experts in organizational theory, as well as individuals not so expert in this field, have argued at length as to whether a centralized or decentralized operation was more advantageous. The argument still goes on, but it is likely that developments at the company involved in our second example may help resolve (at least to some extent) certain aspects of this dispute.

Our subject is one of the largest textile manufacturers in this country. The enterprise is composed of forty mills located for the most part in North and South Carolina and Georgia. Until recently the operations of the company were decentralized, with each mill operating for all practical purposes as an autonomous unit. Then the management made the vital decision to radi-

cally change this long established pattern and in its place to set up a centralized management information center. This decision was based upon management's belief that recent technological advances in electronic computers and data communication made the centralized management information and control concept both practical and imperative.

It was a massive task to bodily lift all information processing operations covering all functional areas within the company and bring them into one center. Yet, in less than a year the management information center was constructed in Wilmington, top management had identified nine outstanding managers who were knowledgeable and experienced in the various functional areas of the business and had moved them into one building, practically all the mechanized data processing operations had been transferred to the center, and most of the manual operations had also been centralized.

This was a tremendous accomplishment, but it quickly revealed that it was going to be a herculean task to transform forty independent systems into one integrated operation. Yet, this had to be done if the company was to realize the anticipated benefits from the management information center concept.

This is how the job was organized. Each of the management information center managers, working under the director of the center, was given the responsibility for identifying management information requirements for his particular function. In other words, an interdepartmental team was given the responsibility for the project.

This approach had two very specific advantages. First, it made the management information system an entire company project, not just one organized by finance or administration. And second, it brought the right talent into the project, since the basic information requirements should be set by the users of the information. I would like to call your attention to the fact that there were representatives on the team from sales and production as well as from the service departments. This assured that all information users would have a voice in the systems development.

After the group was organized, each of the functional managers organized his own task force, which was then asked to work with other qualified individuals who had had previous experience in developing a management information system. Each group was given the objective of determining the information that would be required to meet the planning needs inherent in the particular responsibility of the manager and the information needed to properly measure performance, so that the manager could control his own particular operations most effectively.

I should mention that included in the various managers' task forces were individuals with competence in such fields as industrial engineering, operations research, accounting, etc. In addition, all of the teams were supported by computer specialists and other systems personnel, who were responsible for defining the best method to meet the overall systems requirements.

Earlier I expressed the viewpoint that effective, and perhaps I should have added, economical systems are generally built slowly and often bit-by-bit or phase-by-phase. At this point I would like to tell you just a little more about the first phase of this installation, which was directed at a very sensitive and critical area of the business, that of coordinating the areas of sales, sales service, and production.

Broadly, the program was broken down into four steps. One, complete the definition of the system and determine the economies of the program. (Management still likes to look at cost.) Two, prepare detailed equipment specifications. Three, develop a plan for implementation. And four, work out a project critical path system to be used to keep the installations on the track over a three-year period.

As might be expected, the key characteristics of this system are based on centralization and integration. Centralized, as a means of taking advantage of the economy and power of the most advanced large-scale computer system, while still providing a consistent quality of service to all of the company's locations in Georgia, North and South Carolina, New York, Pennsylvania, Maine, and New Hampshire; and integrated, to get maximum utilization of each required item of information handled within the system.

As I mentioned, in this project particular emphasis was centered around the vital areas of sales and customer service. For example, when a customer representative receives an inquiry regarding the status of a particular order, he enters the inquiry code and customer identification number on the keyboard of his electronic visual display unit. The response shows the customer's name and data regarding all applicable contracts and products. In this case 100,000 yards are late in shipment. In order to determine the prospects for recovering from this situation, the representative would next inquire regarding the status of the particular product involved. And when he does so, he sees that prospects are not too good, as there are two contracts with shipments late already and there won't be any cloth to make up the deficiency for eight weeks. With such current information available, the customer representative can make a prompt reply and take any further action that is needed.

In addition, a response to the customer's inquiry about the delivery of possible future orders is immediately available. This is a small illustration of one of the many ways this real-time information system will provide managers with the most up-to-date information possible.

For those of you who are interested in the technical picture, the equipment used in the system consists of two computers capable of communicating with and supporting each other. The smaller of the two is the communication controller. The larger is the main processor, which handles the bulk of the information processing load and the scientific calculations. Both processors share the same electronic memory files, which is the primary way they communicate with each other.

Today it is full speed ahead on this segment of the total system, and the installation of systems relating to additional functional areas of the business are well under way. But I can assure you that a number of years will still elapse before the completion of this extremely significant effort.

And now we come to the last example. The company concerned is a major utility providing energy in the form of gas to most households in a large Midwestern metropolitan area. In addition to supplying gas, the company also provides maintenance service for its customers' gas appliances. This is quite a business in itself, since there are about 400 servicemen employed in this work and they handle roughly 1,600 service calls a day. Obviously, it would seem that providing a high standard of customers' service is simply a matter of properly scheduling the men to the calls. This wouldn't appear to be too difficult, would it? How complex is the problem?

Everything starts with a customer calling for service. The particulars are given quickly enough; the customer explains the nature of the problem and gives the address. The first move is to locate the address within the 500 square miles of the service territory, and then locate a serviceman within the same area and send him to do the work.

This might be called a matching job. But matching the call to the serviceman is not the only problem. There are also difficulties arising from the service orders themselves. One such difficulty is duplicate orders. You all know the background of this trouble-

some little item. A husband leaving home in the morning tells his wife to report the trouble they have experienced. Actually, however, he doesn't really expect his wife to remember to call the company, so sometime during the morning he places what turns out to be a second call. Unfortunately, the present system is not capable of recognizing such duplicate orders.

Then again, sometimes one and one add up to three. Take the case where a customer moving out-of-town places a call to turn the service off. The person moving in also calls. Naturally he wants the gas turned on. So far, so good, unless the serviceman who is to turn on the service arrives first. He checks the meter, finds the gas already flowing and naturally does nothing because there is nothing for him to do. Shortly behind him comes serviceman number two. His orders say very explicitly "turn the gas off," and so he does what comes naturally. The gas is on so he turns the service off.

Sometime later the new occupant arrives and shortly thereafter attempts to use the gas to heat the baby's bottle. Well, you know the rest of this story. We could recite many variations on this theme, but let's go on.

Another service gremlin is failing to recognize a special situation. A properly qualified individual may have been sent on a call for service, but it was not recognized that this was an industrial customer where, because of the size of the installation, service is limited by union contract to a restricted group of men. Another problem arises from the restrictions placed by union contracts on the type or class of work an individual may perform. There is no need to expand on this.

Of course, the problems aren't all one-sided. In 25% to 35% of these calls the serviceman can't get in when he arrives. In many cases this is because the company is unable to tell the customer, within reasonable limits, when to expect their representative. Without going further, it seems logical that there must be a better way to handle this problem; and there is, and it has been found.

In brief, the basic ingredients used in the new system are real-time electronic equipment, operations research techniques, and performance standards applicable to the jobs involved. Without going into great detail, this is how the system operates. Periodically servicemen call the dispatcher and report on the status of orders they are working on. This information is entered in the computer system. As customers' orders are received, they too are entered into the system, and immediately a series of operations takes place.

First, the computer will identify the service address within a square mile or less. Next, a standard time for the job will be assigned and the class of serviceman required will be determined. Naturally, if it is an emergency, proper action will be taken. A check will be made to avoid duplication. And based on all these criteria the computer will then identify the proper serviceman to be assigned to the work.

This system has many other uses and advantages, but time does not permit covering them here. It is enough for me to say this afternoon that certainly here is a basic idea which should be applicable, not only to this type of service, but to a multitude of situations where large groups of outside sales, service, or engineering personnel are employed.

Before closing, there is one more point I want to emphasize. I am sure you have noticed that in all of these examples the element of communication has played a vital role. About a year ago, arrangements were made with the General Electric Company to give a demonstration in the Chicago office of my firm of an on-line time-sharing system, so that all of our professional personnel would have some knowledge of this developing area of electronic communication and computerization. The equipment used in the demonstration included two terminal devices, one of which was a visual display unit. These units were connected directly to General Electric computers located in Phoenix and in Oklahoma City. Regular long-distance telephone circuits completed the communications link. It is interesting to note, and very significant in terms of potential uses, that this entire equipment complex was installed and made ready for operation in less than three hours.

But of course this is not the end; it is hardly even the beginning. As Professor Adrian McDonough of the Wharton School, University of Pennsylvania has said, "Progress in any field is determined both by the opportunity and the desire for advancement," and the field of business systems is no exception to this rule. As in the past, the future growth in management systems will continue to be generated by the opportunities inherent in the increasing size and complexity of business, in the development of new concepts and new mechanisms, and in the never-ending desire of everyone concerned to improve on past performance.

The emerging pattern of change in the management systems field was, if not explicitly identified in all of the examples just given, at least implicitly suggested. In the past, this work has, for the most part, been concerned with the gathering and summarizing of data. In other words, machines and methods have, in the past, limited systems to the reporting of unstructured facts. Now, through the development and use of better methods of measurement, through the application of more sophisticated mathematical techniques, and through the use of improved computational equipment and communication devices, data or facts can be structured, can be matched, and can be measured, so that the information content is more immediately available, either for the making of a considered decision by executive management or for the taking of constructive action by supervisory personnel.

We are starting to close the loop in the business function. We are beginning to feed back dynamic information, rather than static data, to the location where it is needed most. In situations where the interval between the time something happens and the need for taking action is very brief, we have the means to match the requirement. When time is not a critical factor, and it often is not, more mature technologies will still be used.

But we have only started; there is still so much to do! For instance, there is an urgent need for better methods of identifying primary units of measurement, primary units against which results or progress can be properly matched. In fact, this is a particularly fertile field for research, experimentation, and accomplishment.

One example and I will close. Perhaps some of you are aware that in England hospital efficiency is measured by the average duration of a patient's stay. Needless to say, this can do nothing except put pressure on evacuating the beds as quickly as possible. As a matter of fact, if a patient dies within a day or two after arrival it raises the hospital's efficiency ratio.

Obviously, I am being facetious and the example is extreme. But let me ask you, is the measure of a police department's efficiency the number of murder cases solved or the number of burglars apprehended, or is there some better measure of its function and operation? Throughout the industrial operation the same type of problem remains to be solved.

Ours, then, is the problem of constantly trying to peer into the future, to imagine, to anticipate, to plan, and to work, so that we all can participate to the fullest in the opportunities of the cybernetic decade which lie in the years just ahead.

The electronic computer, its place in the decision-making process

Before The Texas A. & M. University Financial Management Conference, College Station, Texas, May 6, 1968

Now, through the use of the computer together with the techniques of modeling, it is possible to overcome the shortcomings of manual methods in solving a management problem.

On A SUMMER afternoon not too many years ago, Mr. Robert W. Nealy, checkers champion of the state of Connecticut, lost a game of checkers. This undoubtedly was something of a surprise for Mr. Nealy, since this was the first game of checkers he had lost in eight years. But except to Mr. Nealy this event was undoubtedly a matter of little note and minor importance.

Yet, it was an occurrence that may in years ahead be recalled with increasing frequency. For what was important on this occasion was not that Mr. Nealy lost a game of checkers, but rather that his opponent was a mass of wires, transistors, and whirling tapes, an electronic computer, to be specific. In fact, it was a computer of standard size and shape and one that has found general acceptance in many types and sizes of business organizations.

Lest there be any question about this phenomenon, let me quickly state that there was no trickery or fakery in connection with this exhibition, and the machine won the contest fairly and squarely, without help or assistance of any kind from the sidelines. Moreover it had learned to play the game as a human being would learn, from experience and observation, recognizing its own successes and mistakes and profiting from the former but not repeating the latter. In other words, here was a program that by some means or other analyzed its own performance, diagnosed its own failures, and of most importance, made changes to enhance its future effectiveness.

Perhaps the most remarkable fact of all was that the man who devised the routine, Dr. Arthur L. Samuel, was not a noted checker player and, as a practical matter, did not and could not have planned the moves and the strategy that defeated champion Nealy.

133

The computer, when Dr. Samuel first set it up to play the game, made only elementary moves. It was a raw beginner and even a child could beat it. But the machine was programmed to learn. And as it continued to play game after game its tactics continued to improve. Finally, after playing many games the machine began to defeat Dr. Samuel. Thus it can in all truth be said that in this instance, at least, a machine existed that outgrew the mental capacity of the man who instructed it.

Is the same thing happening in the business world? Are the electronic computers which today are so widely used in clerical areas of the business impinging upon the sacred precincts of the executive? Where do we now stand? And what is likely to be the case tomorrow?

Needless to say, the subject of computers and their use in management decision-making has attracted wide attention and, in fact, has become the subject of acrid disagreement and heated controversy. Already an astounding array of recognized academicians, brilliant scientists, and successful businessmen have expressed wide and varying opinions on the matter. And publications ranging from trade magazines through popular and scientific journals to the erudite *Harvard Business Review* have all carried articles which have supported countless differing views and positions on the subject. Why all this controversy and why all this difference of opinion?

There are, I believe, two very significant reasons. First, and perhaps the most forceful of the two, is that underlying the controversy stands the fact, so well expressed by Donald Fink, that of all man's natural endowments none is more highly prized or more fiercely defended than his gift of superior intelligence. Since tribal days man has always wanted to develop the means to transform geese into swans and to turn lead into gold. And yet since the invention of the first tool he has also had an abiding

concern lest he might be overcome by his own inventions. With each new device he has asked loudly and clearly, "What will this wonderful new invention do for me, for my business, for society?" Less loudly, and often unspoken but certainly not unthought, he has also questioned, "What can this awesome invention do *to* me, to my business, to society?" As we all so well know, with increased sophistication in science and invention such questions become more and more difficult to answer.

The second reason for the unusual degree of debate surrounding the subject of computers and management decision-making is to be found in the many different facets and factors which make up the subject itself, and in the failure to keep these facets distinct and separate when making evaluations and in reaching conclusions.

I have often been reminded, as I have listened to different discussions and read the many thoughtful and thought-provoking articles and essays on the subject, of that well-known poem by John Saxe describing the six blind men of Hindustan and the elephant. I am sure you all recall how each of the sightless men in attempting to visualize the physical appearance of the animal placed his hands carefully and searchingly upon the beast. Unfortunately, each of the blind men touched upon a different part. One happened upon the trunk, another, an ear, a third, the tail, and so on. And thus each of the six men drew a completely different mental image of the elephant. And of course each reached a different overall conclusion about the physical appearance and the temperamental characteristics of the animal.

Because there are so many prominent individuals who are vitally interested in and have expressed themselves so emphatically on the computer and its place in management decision-making, I am going to drop my blind men and the elephant analogy right here, since at all costs I want to avoid any possible indication that I, personally, attribute either the head or the tail to any particular advocate. However, let me state that in my opinion there is a distinct need to recognize and appraise each of the various segments of the subject before any attempt is made at a total evaluation. If this is not done, conclusions could be misleading if not downright erroneous. So with this in mind, what I would like to do during the remainder of my time this afternoon, is to share with you my thoughts on three of the more significant and interesting aspects of the subject.

As we have already made reference to the ability of a machine to learn and since this may, in fact, be the very core of much of the disagreement, let's start with that particular concept. You have heard it said on many an occasion that electronic computers do what they are told to do, no more, no less. I am sure you all agree with this. I certainly agree with it and, to the best of my knowledge, so do all of those who work in the design or use of electronic mechanisms.

Electronic computers do what they are told to do, no more, and no less. This is acknowledged but you can't stop there. What happens when the scientist tells the device to behave in a thinking mode? Scientists and engineers have been working for a number of years in an area they term "artificial intelligence." As a practical matter, when Dr. Samuel developed his now famous checker routine his purpose was far more profound than merely to pit a computer against a champion checker player. His objective was to demonstrate a method by which a machine could be made to learn from experience.

More specifically, Dr. Samuel's program did not, as I originally assumed, explore every possible path through a checker game. According to Dr. Samuel such a program would have involved perhaps 10 to the 40th power moves. Now, as I am sure you all know, 10 to the 40th power is a number so large that it is difficult to express in words. Let me put it this way. It would take a present day computer many centuries to explore every possible combination of play. Thus it can be stated unequivocally that Dr. Samuel did prove that in this small and admittedly controlled situation a computer could learn from experience.

Perhaps this is a good point at which to introduce a related and truly hard-core question, "Do machines think?" One of the unfortunate circumstances that occurred in the early days of computer technology was that the first digital computers were called giant brains. And starting from that point of literary license, early authors and particularly science fiction writers predicted, or at least hinted broadly at, the evolution of a mechanism that embodies not merely human attributes but clearly a machine endowed with superhuman qualities. Thus the birth of that highly intriguing question, "Do machines think?" A most positive answer of "no," or even a somewhat weaker reply, "it's questionable," is not inconsistent in any way with the direction of experimentation or the end results of developments which are presently underway in the area of artificial intelligence.

Let me explain, because this is unquestionably a significant distinction. It is more than that; it is, I would suggest, the key factor that all of us must keep in mind when contemplating how and where computers can be used and what they may accomplish in the years ahead. For example, man has always had the desire to fly, and one of the earliest stories of his quest to satisfy that desire is recounted in the adventures of the eleventh century Saracen who wished to show off before the emperor. At the moment the emperor was attending a sports meeting at the hippodrome in Constantinople. The Saracen dressed himself in a flowing cloak with rigid stiffeners to form a pair of wings. He then climbed a tower by the side of the arena and leapt off, flapping his wings wildly. But, it is reported, "the weight of his body having more power to drag him down than the wings to sustain him, he broke his bones and his evil plight was such that he did not long survive."

Many of you will recall that Leonardo da Vinci has left us pencil sketches of a similar experiment, and although unrecorded, we can be certain that the tests of his invention could only have concluded with the same result. Both Leonardo and the Saracen had made one mistake, the mistake of attempting to duplicate exactly the flight of a bird; and both failed. Subsequently, at Kitty Hawk the Wright Brothers succeeded. They succeeded because they did not try to duplicate the flight of a bird but only to simulate it.

I am told that linear programming was applied to refinery scheduling before a great deal was known or understood about how humans had scheduled refineries. And certainly, the automation of the electronics industry was not accomplished by building robots to duplicate hand wiring of electric and electronic circuits. Rather, it was accomplished through the invention of printed circuit boards which achieved the purpose of electrical linkage, but in no sense duplicated the process of connecting the circuits through the use of manual methods. So with computers and developments in the field of artificial intelligence.

Where or how far this type of program will be carried is unanswerable. It is somewhat comforting to know, however, that in any foreseeable future there is no current evidence of the machine becoming confused with its more human associate. But we can expect to see an increasing use of the computer as a sophisticated simulator and not just as a high-speed number factory. I shall return to this point shortly in somewhat more detail.

Another facet of the subject, which, like the area of artificial intelligence, has a tremendously intriguing appeal, is that of direct man-machine communication, partic-

ularly the use of voice input coupled with either audio or visual response. This is a significant extension of the command control concept so well typified by military operations and by a very few of our police departments.

When translated into the business office it would place the executive at an electronic desk surrounded by every kind of visual and audio terminal, and we would find him firing all types of questions at the computer, including those of an operative, tactical, and even of a strategic nature. All of these questions would then be answered without a moment's hesitation and with scarcely any probability of error. This sounds fanciful, but, like the concept which we have just mentioned of the computer in an humanoid role, this concept, too, contains elements of truth and embodies within it the seeds of potential future utility.

As Melvin Anshen has stated so succinctly, "The raw material for decision making is information." And today's commentaries provide distinct evidence that progress is being made in stuffing the computer with this raw material. Data base is the expression used to describe this initial development and management information system is the current phrase which identifies, in an embryonic way, the broader picture. However, most of the other elements required for direct audio man-machine communications are still in the experimental stage, although engineers already report some results.

One such development with which some of you may be acquainted is called DEACON, which is an acronym for Direct English Access and Control. Typical of so many new inventions today, including the computer itself, DEACON is a child of military necessity. The impetus for the DEACON project stemmed from problems which constantly face military commanders. When a crisis occurs in some part of the world, precisely how much military power can the commander dispatch to the trouble spot, how fast can he dispatch it, and can he sustain the effort by logistical support? Unless these questions can be answered accurately and quickly, the overall diplomatic and strategic decisions regarding possible intervention cannot be made properly, and must necessarily depend to some extent upon guesswork. To forestall this, many so-called contingency plans are prepared in full detail long in advance but they naturally cannot cover all possible eventualities. The unforeseen crisis in Lebanon, the trouble in the Dominican Republic, and the uprising in Hungary are examples that are representative of the basic problem. The goal of DEACON is to provide the commander with direct access to the data he needs and which is generally available somewhere, but (and this is the big but) without the need for machine programming.

At this point I can't tell you how much of this has been achieved; I just don't know. But I can give you some idea of the general direction of this work. The examples given are all couched in Naval terms, since the program was developed in the Navy. The question is asked in English of the computer: "Where is the Forrestal?" The reply comes back; "In Boston." Or again; "What ships are in Boston?" And the answer; "The Shark, the Forrestal, and the King." Or possibly the question might be: "What personnel of Task Force 60 are in X Port?" And the reply this time would be a list of personnel.

In essence the DEACON program consists of a data base, a grammar, and a vocabulary. The grammar has been programmed to analyze the sentences or questions posed, and it follows the rules of sentence diagramming or parsing as taught to children in school. This means that the development of DEACON has necessarily rested on an understanding of the syntactic structure of English.

Unfortunately, our language is far from simple and therein lies a major problem. In addition to the actual words that are used in a sentence, the structure and phrasing of the words are essential elements in conveying the meaning. For example, the statement, "Beacon Hill was at its highest point in the golden age of Boston," means one thing. But, "In its golden age Beacon Hill was at the highest point in Boston" uses nearly the same words but it has a markedly different meaning.

This is an extremely simple example of the difficulties involved in understanding the structure of English. I have been told that DEACON has generally succeeded in overcoming this type of difficulty. But this gives you some idea of the effort which must go into a project of this nature.

Undoubtedly, the successful use of direct English access to the computer by high-ranking military personnel will ultimately find its parallel in the direct use of the computer by top business executives, but this form of man-machine communication in the business world is still not visible, at least from my vantage point. Until such time as it is possible to converse with the computer without an intermediary or without becoming adept at using some machine-type language, it seems unlikely that the computer will find a very large place in day-to-day affairs of the typical top business manager.

Having made this point, let me now be sure that I am not leaving you with a wrong impression. In introducing this discussion I emphasized that there were many facets and segments of the subject of computers and their place in management decision-making and that, like the blind men and the elephant, it was important not to draw overall conclusions after having touched upon only one or two parts. We must be careful not to do so here. While the area of artificial intelligence is still in the laboratory, so to speak, and while the technical developments required for direct man-machine communications are still very much in the evolutionary state, this does not mean that computers have not and in the near future will not find a real place in the management decision-making process at the executive level. Within my own experience and that of my colleagues, I have personal knowledge of top management decisions which have been substantially influenced by results obtained through the use of electronic computers. And it is hard to believe that our experience has been unique.

So that you may fully appreciate what is taking place today and also to assist you in anticipating what to expect in the future, let me briefly illustrate with an actual case history or two. My first illustration relates to the experience of one of the major forest products producers of this country. This company, which has both plywood and lumber mills, also holds vast acres of timber which are capable of supplying the mills with a wide variety of species and grades of logs. About two years ago the executives of the company realized that their most immediate and pressing problem centered around the need for finding a better method for developing sound short- and long-range plans for timber management and for developing the related overall company marketing strategy, so that the operating organization, in turn, could develop tactical plans for increasing the effectiveness of the day-to-day operations of the company.

Without going into all of the background of the study which was required to identify all of the constraints which had to be considered in this particular situation, let me merely say that the end product of the study was a series of mathematical models programmed to be processed on an extremely large electronic computer. Today management has the information it needs, not only for better long-range planning in connection with its own timber holdings, but also for determining the desirability of the purchasing, selling, or trading of logs within the period immediately ahead. In addition it has the measures of profitability which it needs

to establish pricing policies and to set product sales goals.

By-products of the system are useful in evaluating the need and the value of adding additional machine capacity and in providing information to the operational personnel for many of their day-to-day operating decisions.

I could go on, but I do not want to get into detail here regarding the system itself. Rather, I want to place my emphasis on the fact that the use of a computer to assist in the decision-making process did not in this case and probably does not in any case require management to be in direct contact with the computer. But management does obtain guidance and benefits from various techniques which, in turn, depend for their practicality upon the computer.

It should be noted, however, that even though management is not directly involved with the computer itself, it is (and this is extremely important) very much involved in critically reviewing and approving all of the important assumptions that go into the individual calculations. Without this involvement top management would not be in a position to evaluate and take informed action on the results printed out by the computer.

The decision-making process of top management can usefully be described as a series of seven basic steps. These are:

1. Identification of the problem or opportunity.

2. Analysis of the situation to define the nature and priority of the proposition.

3. A determination of a course of action.

4. The evaluation of possible alternatives, identifying the advantages and disadvantages of each.

5. The selection of action to be taken.

6. The identification of the person to be responsible for taking the selected course of action.

7. The establishment of the method of feedback to test the effectiveness of the decision against actual results.

I think it would be interesting to review the example I have just described and see what parts of the decision process relate to computers. Identification of the problem or opportunity was our first point. And certainly in the case under consideration management was aware of an important and perplexing situation. Since the problem was industry-wide it hardly needed a computer to identify it, although the use of the computer in the preparation of sound accounting reports and statements would certainly have revealed the problem.

The second point relates to analysis of the situation and assignment of priority to the problem. This one goes to management all the way. Our third point relates to the determination of a course of action. Here again, management alone is involved.

Our fourth step involves identification of possible different courses of action and evaluation of the advantages and disadvantages of each. Since the possible courses of action in this situation could be defined quantitatively with reasonable accuracy and since the choices were multiple and complex, mathematical techniques in concert with the computer provided a practical answer. To the extent that qualitative factors, or perhaps better said, nonquantitative factors become involved, this particular method would become less practical. Our fifth point, the selection of the action to be taken, is, of course, the moment of truth, the point of decision, the time when someone and not something must take the responsibility for further action or inaction.

It is interesting that here again we can have what almost appears to be a play on words. If our situation or problem was one that resolved itself quantitatively into a single answer, in other words, if there was an optimal result, then obviously the facts would speak for themselves, and the decision would become a "fait accompli" as the computer turns out the answer. On the other hand, as Peter Drucker has enunciated so clearly, "A decision is usually a judgment." It is rarely a choice between right and wrong but, at best, a choice between almost right and probably wrong. But much more often, it is a choice between two courses of action, neither of which is provably more nearly right than the other. At this point the computer must necessarily await its master's voice.

Point six in our series of steps involves the identification of the person to be responsible for taking the selected course of action. A punched card may help identify a person with unusual or special skills, but I have the feeling that I am reaching here.

Finally, we need a method or a means to "feedback" the effectiveness of the decision. Feedback, by nature and definition, is generally a mechanizable function. Indeed, here is the very substance of the science of cybernetics, so here, again, the computer should be able to make a significant contribution.

Overall, then, it can be seen that the computer is, at best, only involved in a segment of the decision-making process. One point should be kept in mind, however. When the term, decision making, is used we generally think of the 5th stage or point, the item I previously identified as the moment of truth. In point of fact, much more management effort is allocated to the other six functions and it is among these that the computer can find deep involvement.

Let's look at another example. In this case the computer was used to assist management in connection with a substantial capital investment problem. The facts are, briefly, these. The management of a large beet sugar manufacturer planned to build a completely new refinery. This refinery was to be strategically located to take advantage of farming acreage which had recently been converted to the growing of sugar beets.

For you who are unfamiliar with this industry I should point out that after harvesting, sugar beets must be processed rather quickly. They don't keep well. Any inventory buildup must be in the finished product, bulk sugar.

The company's engineering department developed a full set of specifications for the factory, including operating capacities for each stage of the refining process and detailed specifications for the storage of the bulk sugar. The storage requirements had been estimated, based on certain averages and "guesstimates," and then a silo capacity somewhat in excess of the estimate had been specified.

Bulk sugar silos, incidentally, should not be confused, either on the basis of price or simplicity, with corn silos. In contrast, they are complex and expensive.

In reviewing the plans, top management recognized that they were faced with a complex set of intertwining problems, the economics of which would all be affected by silo capacity. There was, for example, the uncertainty of the size of the beet crop to be harvested each year, and it can vary tremendously. There was the complex problem of whether to allocate any of the harvest among the company's several other refineries. And there were a number of other complex and important considerations.

As in our previous example, management initiated a study to determine how all of these interrelated costs would be affected, particularly with respect to various levels of bulk storage capacity at the new factory facility. A computer simulation model was developed and, based on the results derived from operating this model, the return on investment was calculated for each of a wide range of possible silo capacities.

The final result was a decision to increase the capacity requirements to *twice* that originally specified, thereby making possible substantially lower annual unit costs of production and distribution. Again, there were other by-products of the study which were of great use in helping to solve operating problems, but this is outside the area of our immediate concern.

What I want to stress is that here, as in my previous example, the management of this company did not have any direct contact with the computer nor did it deal directly with the printed results generated by the computer. However, the computer did play an extremely important part in this top management decision.

Now basically, if you look beyond the details of what happened in this case, it can be seen that the process was essentially the same as that which occurred in the example of the plywood manufacturer. The management of the company was aware of a complex problem. It recognized the potential for a solution or a better answer through the use of a computer-based mathematical model. And the results obtained from this model entered directly into the decision to invest substantially more in a facility than would have been invested otherwise. In other words, the computer was a silent partner, working behind the scene. This has been the pattern of the past and it is, no doubt, the pattern we shall see repeated in the future.

I find it most interesting that over ten years ago Mr. Ralph Cordiner, then president of General Electric Company, recognized that the initial impact of the electronic computer on top management would be to force executives to make, and I am quoting, ". . . a far more penetrating study of the business in its entirety." Mr. Cordiner further expressed the opinion that computerized mathematical modeling appeared to hold the greatest promise for accomplishing this purpose.

In the intervening years since Mr. Cordiner made these prophetic remarks there has been steady progress along the lines he suggested and examples such as those I have described previously are persuasive evidence of this progress. Today we are seeing the true fruits of this earlier work in the emergence of substantially larger and far more sophisticated models.

These current models might be identified, for lack of a better name, as corporate models. And from my own observation and experience it appears that the utility industry is taking a leadership role in the development of this new technology. During the past year a number of utilities have placed their models in service, and an even larger number of companies have placed their models in the work-in-process stage.

What is a corporate model? There is no one answer to this question. In principle it is a series of mathematical expressions which may be used to simulate either a particular segment of business operation or the total business itself. It is essentially a planning tool and its purpose is to assist management in short- and long-range planning.

Management has traditionally faced three major problems which have limited the effectiveness of the planning function. First, manual projections of future company activities are extremely time consuming. I am sure every management has had its moments of exasperation waiting for the planning department to report the overall effect of a simple thing like, say, a recently revised wage agreement.

Second, and here we get closer to the heart of the subject, because of the extensive time required for manual projections only a minimum number of alternative plans can be considered. And quite typically, they do not consider all of the interrelationships. In fact, not too infrequently someone in the planning area may make a judgment as to which of the significant relationships will be considered.

And the third disadvantage of manual methods is that it is very difficult to consider in detail all of the reasonable alternatives. In view of the effort required to make even a single set of projections, management may, itself, screen out alternatives *before* projections are made and may do so without having the necessary facts at its disposal. But it is an expedient and expediency is frequently the name of the game with manual methods.

Now, however, through the use of the computer, with its great speed and capacity, together with the techniques of modeling, it is possible to overcome these shortcomings of manual methods. It is possible to work out in detail all of the important interrelationships; it is possible to consider all reasonable alternatives; it is possible to determine the full effect of each alternative; and it is possible to do all of this at computer speeds.

I am sure you can see that this is a subject which could easily occupy the entire afternoon. Obviously, this is out of the question. Let me close this point by saying that the corporate model when used with a computer represents a major breakthrough in the management planning function. It can be used in setting corporate goals and objectives and in translating these goals and objectives into targets for the functional areas of the business. Further, it provides a fast and reliable method of projecting on a fully integrated basis the future position of a company, based on a wide variety of possible alternative conditions. It is truly a mechanism for executive management. Here, certainly, the computer is used as a simulator and not merely as a large-scale number factory. This, then, is the situation as it stands today.

It is evident that human judgment is still the final arbiter in top level business decisions. The skill, insight, and experience of an outstanding man is still essential. Yet it is true that the computer is only about twelve years old and at best only a few halting steps have been taken. How far will computer progress go? To what extent will advances be made in artificial intelligence? How quickly will we see direct man-machine communications? How far will corporate models take us? No one can say precisely.

I tend to agree with an observation made by the late Norbert Wiener, one of the prime movers in the field of cybernetics. Mr. Wiener said, "The future offers little hope for those who expect our new mechanical slaves will offer us a world in which we will rest from thinking. The world of the future will be an even more demanding struggle against the limitations of our intelligence, not a comfortable hammock in which we can lie down and be waited upon by our robot slaves."

In the final analysis, with respect to the future each of you must reach your own conclusions. Certainly the past indicates that the future will be filled with great wonders. As to the specifics, ladies and gentlemen, I leave the answer up to you.

The corporate model, a tool for management

An article by Joseph S. Glickauf and
John M. Kohlmeier in *The Chronicle*,
September, 1969

*"One of the most far-reaching
computer techniques I know of is
the financial model. This is
management firepower only
dreamed of before."* Leonard Spacek

DURING THE PAST year, many individuals in top corporate management have become intensely interested in an exciting new business advancement which involves the use of computer-oriented techniques in the preparation of extensive and comprehensive financial projections. These executives foresee in this recent development the means to project, at electronic speed and with computer versatility, the effect of an almost unlimited variety of prospective assumptions on the future financial results of their complex corporate enterprises. We share the growing interest and enthusiasm in this new concept, because we believe that "Corporate Modeling," as this technique is now generally termed, will prove to be one of the most significant developments in business management in many years.

Advance planning necessary

The business executive today faces a world characterized by a rapidly quickening pace and continuing change. Furthermore, the business organizations which he directs have been growing larger, more diversified, and increasingly complex. Confronted by this environment, successful management cannot merely react to change; it must anticipate change. Advance planning is no longer a luxury for a few progressive companies; it has become a necessity to survive for all companies. Planning consists of defining objectives, then evaluating and choosing among alternative programs or strategies for achieving these objectives. It involves identifying future threats and opportunities and, more particularly, it requires exploring a wide range of "what if" questions.

The cornerstone of effective planning is financial projection, which is the process of calculating the financial results expected by a company from an assumed set of condi-

143

tions. Companies have been making financial projections for years, using manual methods; but because realistic financial projection requires the consideration of many factors and interrelationships often involving a large amount of detail, the process is time consuming and expensive. The slowness and expense of manual projection methods has usually resulted in limiting the number of alternatives to be evaluated, in curtailing the scope of the factors and interrelationships to be considered, and, in general, discouraging adequate financial projection. Yet, much of the process of making financial projections is repetitive. For this reason, the use of computers offers the potential to overcome many of the problems associated with manual projection methods.

A corporate model is a system for making financial projections of the expected results of operations for a company. The system is computer-based and, therefore, once developed, is capable of generating detailed financial projections quickly and inexpensively. A corporate model requires input data describing the current status of the company and the conditions expected to prevail in the future. The model itself is a representation of the company's operations. The outputs of the model are projections of the financial results of the company.

Modeling widely applicable

To illustrate what a corporate model might be like, consider the problem of projecting the financial results for an electric utility company. An electric company has been chosen for illustration because the utility industry has been one of the leading groups in the early development of corporate models. However, the applicability of corporate modeling is not limited to utilities; the need for financial projection exists in every company, regardless of industry. Experience has clearly demonstrated that the concepts of modeling are applicable to most, if not all, types of business enterprises. The details of the illustration would necessarily

be different for other companies in different industries, but the general principles would be the same. The objective is to project a set of financial statements: income statement, balance sheet and cash or fund statement for the particular company concerned.

In the case of the illustrative electric company, one approach to the design of a financial projection system might be to require the user to supply each item of revenue, expense, and ending balance as input data. For instance, the user would supply figures for revenue, cost of power, operations and maintenance, depreciation, taxes and interest, together with the closing balance sheet figures. The system would read the data, perhaps perform some summarization, and then print the statements. In essence, this concept requires the user to make the projections. Obviously, such a system is essentially a financial statement generator and represents the most simple type of model that might be constructed. Although this system offers some advantages over manual methods, this approach would not generally be recommended because it puts too heavy a burden on the user to make computations external to the system, and falls far short of fully utilizing the computer's innate abilities and capacity.

A better approach

An alternative approach to the design of a financial projection system would require the user to supply as input data the principal determinants of revenue, expense, and ending balances. For instance, instead of requiring the revenue figure as input data, the user would be required to supply the number of kilowatt hours sold and the average price per kilowatt hour. The system would then compute revenue by multiplying the number of kilowatt hours sold by the average price per kilowatt hour. The system could be further refined to recognize the fact that revenue per kilowatt hour varies substantially from one customer group to another, by requiring as input data both kilowatt hours sold and revenue per kilowatt hour for each of the customer classes, i.e., residential, commercial, industrial, etc. Going one step further, since utilities generally price electricity according to rate schedules where the price per kilowatt hour varies according to usage as well as by customer class, the system could be expanded to contain the actual rate schedules. The user would then only be required to supply data reflecting the kilowatt hours sold falling within each usage block of each rate schedule.

The motive behind these various steps in refinement is to improve the realism and accuracy of the projection by transferring the computational burden from the user to the system. As the examples have indicated, these refinements substitute relationships among basic underlying factors for figures which merely represent end-product results. The elaboration of the system, however, has advantages which go far beyond those which relate to the production of figures, important as this result may be. The expansion of the system permits the user to investigate the financial effect of various changes in both the assumed conditions and the company's operations. For instance, the inclusion of rate schedules and customer usage by block would permit investigation of the financial impact of alternate rate schedules, or variations in usage by customers in the different classes. This elaboration and refinement of projection methods in the model would proceed until the projections were realistic, and permitted the desired level of "what if" questions to be answered.

Since there are often no practical limits to the degree of complexity and sophistication which can be built into a model, it is generally desirable, in the initial stages of development, to establish time limits for the development of any single area. In maintaining a reasonable degree of simplicity, it is most important to distinguish those items and relationships which have a substantial impact on the financial results of the company from those with little or no impact. The important items are included; the unimportant excluded.

Elaboration of the model may increase the requirements for data input to the system, but this may be partially offset by making use of the computer's ability to generate data itself. For instance, the power demand in one time period may be related to the demand in previous or succeeding periods. Thus, the system could compute the demand in each of many time periods, by multiplying the demand of the immediately preceding period by a growth factor to arrive at demand in the next period, instead of requiring that each demand figure be supplied as input. Furthermore, once an appropriate data base has been developed, it can be maintained in magnetic form indefinitely, requiring as input only changes in the base data. To facilitate regular updating of the data base, a data collection system providing forms, instructions and due dates should be included in the development of the model.

After projecting revenue, the model of an electric company would then go on to determine the cash collection of receivables. In this segment of the program, the important time lag between the billing of revenue and the later collection of cash must be recognized and provision must also be made for the proper handling of uncollectible accounts. The model can be designed to account for these time lags on a routine basis, which significantly enhances the realism of the projection. It might be noted that this is an example of an item that adds substantially to the computational burden when manual projection methods are used.

The next step in the model of an electric company would be to compute the cost of power. Since kilowatt hour figures have been previously used for the projection of revenue, these same figures could be used to determine the electric generation requirements, and ultimately the cost of power, after appropriate recognition of line losses and the lag between the delivery of power and its subsequent billing. On the other hand, to produce a satisfactory projection of the cost of power, it might be necessary to use kilowatt hour figures in a different format in order to recognize the important influence of the peaks and valleys of demand on production costs. But, whatever figures are used, it is important that both the projected revenue and cost of power be based on the same underlying assumptions concerning the amount and timing of power sold. Assuring the internal consistency of assumptions is an important principle of succesful financial projection methods.

To continue the illustration, the model might be used to project the remaining items of expense and ending balances from appropriate underlying factors, providing for important interrelationships such as would exist between expected customer demand and construction budgets, while maintaining the internal consistency of the assumptions throughout. Once the financial statements have been projected, it would be a simple matter to compute rate of return, earnings per share, interest coverage, and other important ratios. Upon the completion of one set of statements and related statistics, the process could then be repeated for as many succeeding time periods as desired.

To facilitate the analysis of alternatives, the system could be designed to compare two or more sets of projections to determine both the absolute and percentage differences between projections and to identify exception cases, thereby further easing the clerical task of planning personnel, and freeing their time for the more creative aspects of planning.

A continuing effort

The approach to corporate modeling which has just been outlined, lends itself well to the evolutionary refinement and improvement of the model. Experience has shown that this process of improvement continues indefinitely. Thus, the development of a cor-porate model is not a one-time project, but must be undertaken with the understanding that, like all other areas of dynamic enterprise, it becomes a continuing effort.

During this discussion of making projections for an illustrative electric utility company, no reference has been made to higher mathematics or complicated relationships, because most of the relationships are arithmetic in nature. All of the projected results were developed from underlying factors and relationships, each of which would be familiar to the management of the company. The computations within the model parallel the calculations previously made manually during the planning process, but at greatly increased speed and at a much lower cost per projection.

The financial results projected by a corporate model are capable of being reconciled to the actual results of the company for a historical time period. This process of reconciliation between projected and actual results after the fact provides valuable feedback, and tends to focus attention on model accuracy instead of model elegance.

Key features

At this point some discussion of the key features of a corporate model would be appropriate. Like all models, a corporate model is a representation of something. A corporate model is much simpler, in most respects, than the company it represents; but this simplification must be carefully designed to capture the essential financial aspects of the company's operation. The question of whether the model is a suitable representation of the company for a particular purpose must be constantly reviewed. It can only be answered after a careful review of the assumptions embodied in the model and their relevance to the problem at hand.

The purpose of using a model is to facilitate experimentation. Management can test different assumptions about the future to investigate the effect of alternate courses of

146

action, and to answer a wide range of "what if" questions. To encourage this type of experimentation, a corporate model should be flexible, adaptable to change, and easy to use. Lest there be any misunderstanding, a corporate model itself cannot plan; only people can plan. The model is a tool which can greatly expand the effectiveness of business executives and their planning staff in studying and planning for the future.

The focus of a corporate model on an entire company; not just a division or a function, but the whole company. This feature encourages a global or overall viewpoint in the analysis of problems and enhances the likelihood of capturing the full financial impact of a proposed course of action. Planning in large companies tends to focus along departmental responsibilities and, as a result, plans sometimes lack overall coordination and the underlying assumptions may be inconsistent. A corporate model demands company-wide effort to take advantage of the knowledge and expertise in all departments of a company; it is a tool for executive management, not just the controller's department.

A corporate model emphasizes the financial dimension of a company's operations. The model may contain details concerning marketing, production, personnel or other factors, but the ultimate objective is the financial result yielded by these items. Nonfinancial factors may form an important part of a corporate model, but only because of their ultimate impact on the projected financial results.

Unlike financial reporting, the object of which is to disclose what has occurred in the past, financial projection and, correspondingly, corporate models are future oriented, projecting what is likely to occur in the future. Historical data provides useful insight into past relationships which, as a first approximation, may be trended into the future. Planning, of course, is concerned with the future.

A tool for evaluating change

Sometimes the argument is heard that the future is too uncertain to plan. Actually, the existence of uncertainty implies impending change and changed conditions require new strategies and revised programs which demand time to develop; consequently, there is a need for advanced planning. Conversely, the existence of a relatively certain environment implies stable conditions and a diminished need for new programs or revised strategies. A corporate model is an effective tool for evaluating the impact of changing conditions and new strategies on a timely basis, thereby coping with uncertain situations.

Historically, the term, "model," as used in business has been identified with work performed by specialists in operations research and usually in reference to an optimization type of model. A corporate model is not an optimization model, which means that the model does not contain a mechanism whereby it automatically and efficiently searches for the best solution to a business problem. However, an executive using a corporate model can successively evaluate the financial results of alternative courses of action. Based on his experience and judgment, and by using trial and error, he can usually reach a satisfactory solution which may approximate or even equal the best possible solution. Ultimately, corporate models may evolve into optimization type models but, as a practical matter, this development is a long way from achievement.

Unlike most models employed in business, a corporate model is usually not designed with a specific decision problem in mind. The purpose of a corporate model is to project the financial results of a company, based on an assumed set of conditions and strategies. Obviously, these projections provide valuable information useful for making a variety of decisions, but the exact nature of these decision problems is rarely known in advance. A corporate model is a research tool for studying a business in order to improve its operations. Like many research tools, it is difficult to predict in advance exactly how it will be used, or what findings may emerge.

Potential uses

The most obvious potential use of a corporate model is to assist in the development of long-range corporate plans. An appropriately designed corporate model is capable, in theory, of projecting the financial results of a company for an unlimited number of years. As a practical matter, the user will usually be restrained by his diminishing confidence in the correctness of assumed conditions in distant years. To develop a long-range plan, the executive should investigate a variety of alternative courses of action under different sets of assumed conditions, and then select the most appropriate as the corporate plan. Then, whenever new information causes the executive to change his assumptions or strategy, the corporate model can be used to evaluate the effect of a revised plan quickly and inexpensively. The executive can have at all times a detailed, up-to-the-minute, long-range plan. Contrast this with the situation of most companies using manual projection methods where a long-range plan is usually prepared once each year, based on an admittedly incomplete analysis of alternatives, because of the great clerical effort required to prepare a single projection. Unfortunately, this projection is frequently made obsolete by new developments even before it has been completed but, because of the effort required, revision waits until the following year. A corporate model provides a solution to this problem.

The use of a corporate model for long-range planning provides other benefits to the planner. The computer forces the planner to state explicitly his assumptions, and a printed list of assumed conditions can easily be made a regular part of the output of a corporate model. Use of the computer also results in the employment of precise, reproducible, documented methods. Discussion and analysis of the plans by the executive can then be based on an objective understanding of the underlying assumptions, conditions and projection methods, thereby eliminating misunderstandings arising from ambiguous assumptions and unclear programs.

A second use of a corporate model is for short-range planning. A corporate model can be designed to project results on a month-by-month or even week-by-week basis. The model can be used to evaluate plans for the current year, taking into consideration year-to-date actual figures and the conditions expected to prevail throughout the remainder of the year. Such use of a model would be particularly valuable for cash forecasting and the planning for cash management.

A third use of a corporate model is to make special studies which result from "what if" questions asked by top executives. The timing of the requests for these special studies is often unpredictable and, when handled manually, can result in a scheduling crisis for the planning staff. This problem is minimized when a computerized model is used.

Many "what if" questions arise from an unexpected change in the environment or a new insight on the part of management. For instance, several studies have been triggered by the many proposals for revision of the tax laws. Management typically wants to know what effect these proposed changes will have on earnings, cash flow, and future financing and capital expenditure plans. A corporate model can provide information for answering such questions by comparing the results projected using the existing tax regulations with those using various proposed regulations.

Another use of a corporate model is for training young executives. The development of such a model provides an ideal means for introducing the aspirant to the intricate details and involvements of the business. Further, once the model is completed it provides a vehicle for experimentation and learning without the potentially disastrous consequences which might result from experimenting with the company itself. The latter use and advantages of a model are, obviously, equally applicable to even the most mature executives.

The future of modeling

At this point in time, the development and use of the corporate model is still very much in its infancy. Looking ahead, there is an expanding horizon for models, and it can confidently be expected that corporate management's use of the computer for this purpose will soon be as fully accepted as it is today for payroll, customer billing, and other such data processing functions.

How far will this sophistication be carried? As in most fields, it is difficult to foresee with accuracy the changes to be wrought by the future. However, one trend has proved irreversible since the first mercantile operation was established. This has been a constant need to upgrade man's skills in operating and directing the enterprises which he creates and builds. The corporate model provides a means to fulfill this need.

The corporate model, a management system for the 70's

Given in Vancouver, B. C.,
on January 20, 1970

*The corporate model can be a most
effective tool for the strategic planner
and is, unquestionably, a development
of significant proportions.*

W<small>E ARE</small> certainly pleased to be with
you in Vancouver this afternoon, since it
affords us the opportunity to share with you
some thoughts and ideas which bear upon
a subject we are confident we will all be
hearing and reading a great deal more about
in the weeks and months ahead. This subject, the corporate model, is an exciting new
business advancement. It is an advancement,
like so many others we are experiencing
today, that is made possible by the spectacular developments which have taken place
almost overnight in the construction and in
the application of electronic computers.

As a matter of fact, being here today
reminds me of a similar occasion when I
made one of my early addresses on the
subject of electronic computers. This particular talk, and I well recall it, summarized
the results of a study undertaken by a group
of interested individuals who had critically
reappraised the use of the computer for
business purposes. The timing of these
studies was important, for they were undertaken at that particular segment of the computer's history which, from the standpoint
of management, could only be characterized
as the period of discontent.

Perhaps I should explain. I am sure you
all recall the tremendous excitement which
pervaded the entire business world as the
first announcements of the electronic computer were released. And then, even before
the first machine was installed, the blizzard
of articles and books which confidently proclaimed that here, at last, was a device which
would mightily enhance the executive's inherent abilities, immensely supplement his
natural skills, and would marvelously
broaden his technical proficiency. In short,
here was the final answer to the executive's
dream.

Unfortunately, it was still only a dream, for the waking reality of the facts were that after several hundred installations were completed (some excellent and some quite the opposite), it became clearly evident that the electronic computer, notwithstanding the fascination of flashing lights and whirling tapes, was finding no significant place in the affairs of the business executive; but, instead, was essentially being used to process the important but nonetheless the same routine functions that its lesser predecessors had previously processed, at a more leisurely pace.

In point of fact the computer, for all its power and speed, initially lacked the guidance it needed to move its abilities up the business ladder. In retrospect, this is probably just what should have been expected. For, like any other entity employed within the corporate structure, the computer had first to prove itself and pay for itself. This it has certainly now done. And, almost as if by plan, the computer is moving on many fronts into increasingly sophisticated areas of service, areas which do impinge upon and directly relate to the executive's field of responsibility.

Our purpose today is to share with you our thoughts regarding one of these new areas of service, an area in which the utility industry as a whole is taking the leadership role but one in which, I would confidently predict, companies in practically all fields of endeavor will be working with and using computers in the years immediately ahead.

Actually, this new concept has no official name. For purposes of this discussion, we have identified it as "The Corporate Model." It has been referred to by others as "The Planning Model," "The Financial Model," "The Computerized Corporate Model" and, even more elaborately, "The Computerized Corporate Planning Model." But whatever its name, it is first and foremost a viable tool for executives in the top echelon of corporate management. Let me tell you a bit

more about this most significant advancement.

As you all know so well, the major task of a telephone company executive, like that of all other executives, is dealing with change. And in order to successfully meet this challenge, the executive must carefully plan for the future. This "future" may be only next month, next quarter, or next year, or it may be five years or more away. But whatever the period, the corporate executive is looking ahead; he is projecting, he is planning, he is forecasting for this time to come.

Many techniques and tools have been developed to provide information and to assist management in this planning function. And the corporate model which is the subject of our discussion today is, by far, the most powerful means yet devised for this purpose. To be more specific, let us consider a question which might be posed to the management of a telephone company.

The company's economists have predicted a substantial growth in main telephone stations, together with a vastly increased volume of toll messages over the next several years. In addition, there is an indication that the data transmission requirements of businesses in the company's service area will increase rapidly. In order to meet this demand, the company has under construction several new central offices. In addition, it is planning the expansion and modernization of many of its existing facilities. A new policy has also been instituted. This policy involves the placement of all new cables underground.

"Now," asks the management, "what is the overall financial effect of these factors over the near term and over the long range?"

Of course, other factors facing a telephone company today might also have to be considered at this time. They include regulatory policies, high interest rates, inflation, and other items which, I am sure, must come to your mind.

Whatever the new development, however, the question for management remains the same. "What is the overall financial effect of these new developments over the next few years and for the long range?"

Now I know you are all familiar with the questions that must be answered in order to respond to inquiries such as this. But let us review a few of them, and try to show some of the interrelationships which are involved and which add so much to the complexity of the problem.

The starting point is, of course, the projected growth of customers and their telephone usage. This is a factor provided by the analysts after a thorough study of past trends and expected changes. Based on this projected growth in main stations, equivalent main stations and total telephones, a projection of local service revenue must be made. Of course, such factors as upgraded service, including shifts from multiparty service and those new services available from electronic switchboards, must be considered.

Next, projections must be made of toll messages and the revenue derived from toll service. Such factors as extended area service, special long-distance rates and intercompany settlements must be appropriately reflected.

The growth in customers and their telephone usage provides the basis for estimating central office requirements. Central office requirements, together with related trunk and cable requirements, are then translated into new construction plans. At this time it is also necessary to consider modernization such as the replacement of step equipment.

Obviously, new construction means changes in both book and tax depreciation. New construction will also affect the size and deployment of the labor force, together with its related labor costs. And, of course, once these facilities are completed they must be operated and maintained.

Next, interest and sinking fund requirements must be met, to service the debt. Then all of the tax consequences must be con-sidered. The changes in revenue, new construction, depreciation, labor costs and debt service will directly affect the amount of taxes to which the company will be subject, including not only Federal income taxes but also ad valorem, state and local taxes as well.

The interrelationships of these various factors become more apparent when we consider the effect of all these changes on available cash and the requirements for cash. Additional revenue will generate more cash, but these funds will be offset by expenditures incurred for construction, labor, debt service and taxes. This brings us to financing plans, which play such an important role in the economics of public utility growth. Logically, these plans are developed after giving consideration to all cash requirements and the amount of cash which will be generated internally to meet such needs.

And, finally, we reach the objective of all these interrelated calculations, which is the effect of the change in customer growth on net income, earnings per share, and rate of return. Unfortunately, even when all these calculations are completed, the job is not finished.

Throughout these calculations, assumptions had to be made, assumptions as to main station growth, tax rates, and toll message volume. Thus, it is necessary to again go through these calculations to develop alternate plans with different assumptions, and then to weigh these various plans against the corporate objectives, so that the best of the plans examined can be selected.

Questions about the future such as we have just illustrated, and many others, have been answered for years by planning departments, using well-developed forecasting methods. However (and this is the important distinction) they have, for the most part, been achieving their results by manual or, at best, semiautomatic means. When you consider all the complexities involved, both in the process and its implementation, you can only conclude that these planning departments have performed admirably. Unfortunately, manual methods of planning do have certain well-recognized limitations.

First, manual forecasting methods are, by their very nature, slow. Manual computation simply cannot compete with computer speed. Second, because of the cost involved, manual methods may not, and typically do not, consider all the significant interrelationships. Results may, therefore, be misleading. And, thirdly, with manual methods it is very difficult to consider in detail all the reasonable alternatives. The substantial effort required to make a single set of projections may tempt management to screen out alternatives before projections are made, and to do so without having all the necessary facts that might be obtained.

Now, however, through the use of the computer and the technique of modeling, the individuals responsible for corporate planning are in a position to overcome these shortcomings of manual forecasting methods.

With a corporate model, it is possible to work with all the significant interrelationships; it is possible to consider all the reasonable alternatives; it is possible to determine the financial effect of each alternative; and it is possible to do all of these at computer speeds. From this it must be evident that the corporate model can truly be a most effective tool for the strategic planner and is, unquestionably, a development of significant proportions. However, before elaborating further, it might be profitable to pause for a moment and examine the basic concept of a model itself.

What is a model? And how is it constructed? Now, some people think of a model as a mathematical equation; others regard it as a theory; while still others think of it as a physical thing. Actually, a model could take any of these forms, since it is a representation of something.

The purpose of constructing a model is to afford a means to study, test, experiment, or to perform manipulations in situations where it would be difficult, if not impossible, or where it would be too costly or dangerous to do so with the original. One interesting and perhaps important fact about a model is that it is not necessarily a miniature or a replica of the subject it represents. For instance, the models used by aircraft designers to study how full-scale planes will perform in actual flight may only approximate the appearance of the completed aircraft. Such items as doors, windows, landing gear, etc., are generally not part of a wind tunnel model.

A corporate model is a representation of a company, the results or output of which are expressed in financial terms. The structure of such a model includes all the important interrelationships which exist in the company's actual operation, and the medium used to represent the model is a computer program. This program is comprised of hundreds of statements or equations which are individually simple, but together represent the complex of interrelationships which is the company. Let me give you in a highly simplified form an example of some equations which might be contained in the expense section of such a model.

Total revenues, for instance, would be stated as being the sum of local service revenue plus toll revenue plus other revenue. Each of these revenue items would be computed from underlying factors. For example, local service revenue is equal to the sum of business revenue and residential revenue.

Business revenue is computed from main station revenue plus revenue from extensions and revenue from PBX trunks. Business main station revenue, in turn, would be computed from the number of equivalent business main stations and the revenue per equivalent business main station, etc., etc. The model, of course, contains many additional equations for the calculation of other operating results and, incidentally, I might mention that the results of any of these calculations can be displayed on a separate report for examination and study by management.

154

Ultimately, all of these calculations build up to the financial statements of the company, that is, to a projected income statement, balance sheet, and statement of cash flow.

Earlier we noted the complex interrelationship which exists between all of the underlying elements which support these reports. There is also another very important relationship which must be observed in building a corporate model. This is the chronological relationship of the various events involved. In the model, representations of events must be placed in the same sequence as they would actually happen.

Revenues and cash collection provide a good example of this particular point. Revenues recorded in February would be translated into cash collections not only for February, but for January, because of advanced billings, and also for March and a number of months that follow. To produce a proper cash flow picture, the model must not only take this timing of events into consideration, but must also provide for the eventual write-off of uncollectible accounts.

Other examples which require proper chronological consideration might include tax payments and dividend declarations which occur at specific times during the year. The building of facilities in advance of customer growth is another obvious and important timing sequence which must be recognized within the model. Incidentally, I might remind you that timing considerations are an example of an item that adds substantially to the computational burden when manual methods are used.

Now, how do you build a model? Building a model is primarily a matter of defining all the financial and operating relationships as they exist, placing them in the proper time framework, reducing these relationships to simple arithmetic and logical statements, and then programming them for a computer. These are the four steps involved in building a model. They are quickly and easily stated, but obviously they are not so quickly or easily executed.

During the process of building the model, it is essential that particular effort be made and that proper tests be incorporated into the program to assure that the model is a reasonable representation of the company. Unlike systems designed to process the more routine type of function, the output of a model is not and, from a practical standpoint, cannot be tied to predetermined controls. Thus, the need for very careful testing throughout the entire construction process.

It might be noted that the building and testing of a model is, in itself, a very valuable experience and affords excellent training and background for using the model when it is completed.

In operation the model must be fed current economic, operating and accounting data. But, given nothing more than current data, the model would be static. To use the model as a planning tool (which is its primary purpose) it must also be fed data about the future. This information about the future might include such items as anticipated changes in demand patterns, anticipated wage increases, possible changes in tax structures and rates, as well as possible changes in technological considerations, to name a few.

But whatever information it is given, the model will, based upon the rules and relationships established, determine the effect of these changes on the operating results of the company. It is in this manner that the model serves as a powerful means to evaluate the effect of possible changes which the executive foresees in the periods ahead.

As previously mentioned, the corporate model would produce a complete set of financial statements, income statement, balance sheet, and cash statement, together with the related operating statistics, and would produce a set of these statements for each of the years projected.

155

Now let us assume that shortly after the company has made a projection, some new information came to light which the management felt might affect the company's five-year plan. A new study has just been released which indicates that the population growth in the company's service area during the next five years is likely to be much greater than the company had previously anticipated, and much of this increase will be in the form of immigration. The study further suggests that several large new industries will be developed in the area during this time period, most of which will have substantial communications requirements.

The company has translated these factors into revised projections of main stations, total telephones, and toll message volumes. It is apparent that if these events come to pass, the company will require substantially more plant than previously anticipated.

Management is interested in the effect this new set of circumstances would have on revenue, costs, net income, investment, and rate of return. To answer these questions, the company would be required to consider all the factors we discussed previously. The company's corporate model, however, is designed to automatically reflect the interrelationships between these factors. Accordingly, we shall assume that the company, using the model, made several forecasts involving different assumptions about providing the expanded level of service. As you can appreciate, these projections would be analyzed in detail to determine the best alternative available to the company.

Throughout our discussion we have emphasized the use of a model to project the financial effect of various alternatives on long-range plans. But projecting long-range plans is only one use of a corporate model. A second use is to answer "what if" questions, a feature of great interest to many business executives.

For example, what if the volume of toll messages declines? What if additional con-struction is required? What if we issue preferred stock instead of debt? You could no doubt add many of your own questions to this list. The corporate model gives management a powerful tool to examine these "what if" questions and to determine the financial effect of each individually or of several in combination.

A third use of a corporate model is for making short-range projections. A corporate model projects results on a month-by-month basis. For long-range forecasts, these monthly figures are accumulated into annual statements. But the monthly results could be used as short-range projections such as forecasts of the current year, taking into consideration year-to-date actual figures and the conditions expected to prevail throughout the remainder of the period.

As you have observed, we have tried to demonstrate that the corporate model is an exciting new tool for management. You can no doubt envision other valuable uses of such a model, particularly as they might relate to your own company and to your own responsibilities, and this no doubt will lead you to the obvious question. What should be management's role in the corporate model? Let us discuss that subject for a few moments.

I cannot emphasize too strongly that a corporate model requires a very high degree of management participation and involvement. Like any tool, the value of a model is in its use, and only management can really use a corporate model; only management can act on the information provided by such a model; only management can assess the desirability of the results it projects. Obviously, management's use depends on its confidence in the model. Confidence comes from understanding its operations and underlying assumptions, experience in its use, and involvement with design and development.

Management's participation is a continuing requirement. A corporate model is not a static system. It must be responsive to changing conditions and modified assumptions. Old questions need to be reexamined and new ones posed. The value of a corporate model is directly related to its use and, ultimately, to management's degree of involvement. Lest there be any misunderstanding, management need not be concerned with the mechanics of the computer program. Technically qualified computer personnel will convert management's assumptions and policies into a computer-acceptable form.

What, then, can management do to develop a corporate model? As a first step, management should designate an administrator for the model project, which is probably a full-time responsibility. An ability to think logically and an understanding of the telephone business are more essential for this person than familiarity with computers. The administrator will need assistance, particularly during the construction of the model. He should have authority for full access to technical expertise in all departments of the company.

Second, management should define the objectives of the corporate model project. What problems are confronting management? What type of questions is management called upon to answer? What type of reports does management expect?

Finally, management should participate in the development of the model. It should review the major assumptions incorporated in the model and the results generated by it. During this process, management will develop confidence in the model, confidence that will assure its continuing use.

We see an expanding horizon for models, and we confidently expect that corporate management's use of the computer for this purpose will soon be as accepted as the computer's use is today for payroll, customer billing and other such data processing functions. How far will this sophistication be carried? As in most fields, it is difficult to foresee with accuracy the changes to be wrought by the future. However, one trend has proved irreversible since the first mercantile operation was established. This has been a constant need to upgrade man's skills in operating and directing the enterprises which he creates and builds. The corporate model provides one means to fulfill this need.

The corporate model, an overview of a new technique

Before the Association of
Business Administration
Graduates, Dublin, Ireland,
March 23, 1970

*The use of a corporate model in
financial planning makes it possible
to work with all significant
interrelationships, to consider all
reasonable alternatives, to determine
the effect of each alternative, and
to do all of this work at
computer speeds.*

Mr. CHAIRMAN, ladies and gentlemen, to be invited to speak outside one's own circle and particularly outside one's own country is an honor I deeply appreciate, and I want to thank each of you for the opportunity of being here.

My subject this afternoon is corporate financial models. At home, that is, in the United States, this concept is an exciting but very new business advancement. Certainly it is one of the most intriguing innovations which we have seen in the ever widening circle of electronic computer applications.

However, in order that there may be no misunderstanding concerning my remarks, I should tell you immediately that only a limited number of business enterprises have had any experience with this emerging technique.

This leaves me on somewhat shaky ground, since I am more than aware that one of today's most significant management techniques, operational research, was invented over here. And further, based upon my own observations as well as our firm's experience, it has found more ready acceptance and has been put to more extensive use in this part of the world than it has in the United States.

So it is equally possible that the corporate financial model may be more solidly rooted here than elsewhere. In any event I am sure it is still very much in its infancy and is a subject we will all be hearing and reading a great deal more about in the weeks and months immediately ahead.

With this in mind, then, what I would like to do this afternoon is to bring you an overview of the what, the how, and the why of the corporate financial model as I have viewed this development from my own particular vantage point.

Being here today reminds me of a similar occasion when I made one of my first public addresses on the subject of electronic computers not too many years ago. This talk summarized the results of a study undertaken by a group of interested individuals who had critically reappraised the use of the computer for business purposes. The timing of these studies is important, for they were undertaken at the particular moment in the computer's history which, from the standpoint of management, could only be characterized as a period of discontent.

A word or two of explanation is probably in order. I am sure you all recall the tremendous excitement which pervaded the entire business world as the first announcement of electronic computers was released. And then, even before the first machine was installed, the blizzard of articles and books which confidently proclaimed that here at last was a device which would mightily enhance the executive's inherent abilities, immensely supplement his natural skills, and marvelously broaden his technical proficiency. In short, here was the final answer to the executive's dream.

Unfortunately, it was only a dream. For the waking reality was that after several hundred installations had been completed, some excellent and some quite the opposite, it became clearly evident that the electronic computer, notwithstanding the fascination of flashing lights and whirling tapes, was finding no significant place in the affairs of the business executive. Instead it was essentially being used to process the same routine functions that its lesser predecessors had previously processed at a more leisurely pace. In point of fact the computer, for all its power and speed, initially lacked the guidance it needed to move its ability up the business ladder.

In retrospect, this is probably just what should have been expected. For like any other entity employed within the corporate structure, the computer had first to prove itself and then pay for itself. This it has now done. And almost as if by plan, the computer is moving on many fronts into increasingly sophisticated areas of service, areas which impinge upon and, directly relate to the executive's field of responsibility.

One of these areas is the corporate model. Actually this new concept has no official name. For purposes of this discussion it has been identified as "The Corporate Financial Model." It has been referred to by others as "The Financial Model," "The Computerized Corporate Model," and even more elaborately, "The Computerized Corporate Planning Model." But whatever its name it is, first and foremost, a viable tool for executives, an effective planning tool for those who are concerned with top corporate management.

If necessity is truly the mother of invention then the emergence of the corporate model concept at this particular time was almost inevitable. For as we all know the business executive today faces a world characterized by a rapidly quickening pace and by continuing change. This was well illustrated on the morning I started to prepare my final notes for this particular meeting. On that particular morning the *Wall Street Journal*, which is the most widely distributed daily financial and business newspaper in the United States, carried such feature articles as a report on President Nixon's order for a 75% slash in Federal construction budgets, a review of current economic developments, some rather lengthy comments on a commitment to land men on Mars, and finally a financial report on a record coupon rate covering a 50 million dollar bond offering by a major public utility. Confronted by this type of environment, successful management cannot merely react to change; it must anticipate it. It is a simple reality that advance planning is no longer a luxury; it is a necessity for survival.

Unfortunately, too many otherwise sophisticated business executives in the United States make the statement, "Our business is too uncertain to plan." At first this may appear to be a very comforting rationalization, but it can be a dangerous position to take. Uncertainty implies change, and if there is change there is a continuous requirement to rethink policies and revise strategies which have been previously planned.

Of course it is completely true that if you have a highly stable business and operations are based on well thought out plans and strategies, changes need not and should not be made as long as all assumptions remain valid. In practice, however, this situation is not likely to continue for a very long period of time, and consequently planning programs and methods become an absolute imperative.

It has been said before that citizens of our two countries are often separated by a common language. In an effort to avoid this problem, at least for the moment, let me define "planning." In the context of this discussion, planning is the process of establishing the overall goals and objectives of the enterprise and then evaluating and choosing among alternative programs the best ones for achieving these objectives. Planning involves identifying future threats and opportunities and requires the exploration of a wide range of "what if" questions. Finally, of course, it involves the development of programs and policies to implement the objectives.

Now as all of you in this audience know, the cornerstone of effective planning is financial projection. I say financial projection because in most cases the objectives are financial in nature, or at least are best expressed in financial terms. As a result, financial projection adds realism to planning.

It's fine to sit in an ivory tower or even in some less sumptuous office and develop concepts. We all do that, and indeed it is an absolutely necessary function that must be engaged in by all executives. From a purely practical standpoint, all overall planning must begin with one or more mental images or ideas. But it is when you start putting the numbers together to see what the actual results of your ideas are likely to be (and this means making identifiable and concrete assumptions) then and only then do you come face-to-face with the hard core realities of effective planning.

Put another way, the basis for effective planning is the calculation of projected results based upon an assumed set of conditions. Over the years many techniques and tools have been developed to provide information and to assist management in this segment of the planning function. And I might add that I hope when we have completed this discussion you will feel that the corporate financial model is one of the most powerful means yet devised for this particular purpose.

Volumes have been written about all the various areas and details of corporate planning and it is not my purpose at this time to pursue the subject in great detail. However, there is one aspect of this effort which is worthy of a few moments' review, since it lays the foundation for our overall discussion and perhaps even establishes the prime reason for the interest of executives in the corporate model.

To be more specific, let us consider a question which might be posed to the management of a manufacturing company. The company's marketing personnel have predicted a substantial increase in demand for its products. This, in turn, has triggered the need to consider plans for new plant facilities, the need for a sharply expanded labor force, and the need for the development of new and aggressive marketing programs.

Of course other factors will also have to be considered, such as revised tax regulations, possible changes in interest rates, wage rates, and other pertinent factors. The question which management must ask is, "What is the overall financial effect of these new developments over the next few years and for the long range?"

Now I know you are all familiar with the questions that must be answered in order to respond to inquiries such as this. But I want to illustrate a few of them because I want to remind you of some of the interrelationships which are involved, since it is these interrelationships which add so much to the complexity of the problem.

The prime difficulty faced by individuals responsible for the preparation of financial data designed to show the effect of anticipated changes in economic factors, operational plans, or strategies is that a change in even a single assumption results in a sequential series of changes in all succeeding figures, a phenomenon which is strongly reminiscent of the toppling dominoe principle. Interlocking items that form a veritable cobweb of interrelationships are the source of this particular difficulty. Furthermore, because of these interlocking relationships we may also have an amplification effect, which simply means that a modest change in an initial figure may and often does result in a substantial change in the final figure.

Our starting point is, of course, the projection of sales, services, or revenues, depending upon the particular business involved. This forecast is generally derived from a study of past trends, expected changes and knowledge of the market.

Based on the projected sales and other related data, a projection of the required labor force and its associated costs must next be made. This forecast obviously would, at this particular moment in time, reflect the sharp increase in labor rates which is taking place throughout the entire worldwide labor market.

The sales forecast also provides the basis for projecting raw material needs and the costs of these materials. The commitment strategy established for the purchase, delivery and payment of raw materials would probably be supplied to the model and would, of course, affect cash. I should probably also note that raw materials purchases must be responsive to any changes in the sales mix.

The cost of productive facilities, which is a term used here to include depreciation and all other burden costs, is next projected. The labor, material and burden costs are then combined and translated into cost of goods sold, after providing for anticipated changes in inventory levels.

Next, the expansion of existing plant and equipment facilities must be considered. Any new construction costs would be related to anticipated sales volumes and to future marketing strategies.

Selling, general, and administrative costs are now projected, based on marketing programs and administrative requirements. Interest and loan repayment requirements must be met to service the debt.

It is almost redundant to say that debt service is becoming a very significant cost as a result of the current high level of interest rates. Actually, what we are seeing in the United States is that the increasing cost of imbedded debt is resulting in many companies finding that their coverage of fixed charges is getting so narrow that their indenture restrictions prevent them from marketing further debt securities. But to go on, all of the tax consequences must be considered. The changes in sales, cost of goods sold, new construction, depreciation, selling, general and administrative expenses, and debt service directly affect the amount of taxes to which the company will be subject. At home this would include not only income taxes but state and local property taxes as well.

And at this point some of the complications of the interrelationships at work begin to make themselves felt. These interrelationships become more apparent when we consider the effect of all these changes on available cash and requirements for cash. Additional sales will generate more cash but these funds will be offset by expenditures incurred for labor costs, raw materials, new construction, selling, general and administrative costs, debt service, and taxes.

This brings us to financing, a problem which today has become unbelievably critical. Logically these plans are developed after giving consideration to all cash requirements, and the amount of cash which will be generated internally to meet such needs.

And finally we reach the objective of all these interrelated calculations, which is net income and earnings per share.

But even when all these calculations are completed the job is not finished. Throughout these calculations assumptions had to be made, assumptions as to sales levels, tax rates, labor costs, and many others. To get a full picture it is necessary to go through these calculations again and again to develop alternate plans based on different assumptions, and then to weigh these various plans against the corporate objectives so that the best of the plans examined can be selected.

Lest there be any suggestion here that this outline is biased toward a manufacturing enterprise, I would like to discuss briefly how it works out on an electric utility. In the utility industry the interrelationships are no less complex and are really not too different from those in the previous example for a manufacturing concern. In a utility model which has actually been built and is in operation we started with projected growth in customer usage, a factor provided by analysts after a thorough study of past trends and expected changes. Based upon this projected pattern of customer usage, together with a set of rate schedules, a projection of the company's revenue was made. Electric generation requirements were next forecasted and from these data the cost of fuel was determined. Next we considered the factors of new construction and depreciation expense, both extremely significant items in capital intensive industries. Labor for operations and maintenance followed, and finally we worked out the familiar items of debt service, taxes, and financing. Comparing this with the previous outline indicates quite clearly, I believe, the universality of the problem we are trying to illustrate.

In brief, financial projection is an assignment of multiple complexity. Viewing these two outlines and then considering all the other complications involved both in the planning process and its implementation, one can only conclude that over the years planning departments have performed admirably. However, and this is the important distinction, they have for the most part been achieving their results by manual or at best semiautomatic means, and from a purely practical standpoint, manual methods of planning have certain well recognized limitations.

First, manual forecasting methods are, by their very nature, slow. Manual computation simply cannot compete with computer speed. Second, because of the cost involved manual methods may not and typically do not consider all the significant relationships. Results, therefore, may be misleading. Third, and perhaps most important, with manual methods it is very difficult to consider in detail all of the reasonable alternatives. The substantial effort required to make a single set of projections may tempt management to screen out possible alternatives before projections are made, and to reach conclusions without having all the necessary facts that might have been obtained.

Now, however, through the use of the computer and the technique of modeling, the individuals responsible for corporate planning are in a position to overcome previous shortcomings. With a corporate model it is possible to work with all significant interrelationships, to consider all reasonable alternatives, to determine the financial effect of each alternative, and to do all of this work at computer speeds. It is for these reasons, among others, that the corporate model has already proven to be a most effective tool for strategic planning. It is, without question, a development of significant proportions.

Before elaborating further it might be profitable to pause for a moment and examine the basic concept of a model itself. What is a model and how is it constructed? Now some people think of a model as a mathematical equation. Others regard it as a theory, while still others think of it as a physical thing. Actually a model could take any of these forms, since it is a representation of something. The purpose of constructing a model is to afford a means to study, test, experiment, or to perform manipulations in situations where it would be difficult, costly, or dangerous to do so with the original.

One rather interesting and perhaps important fact about a model is that it is not necessarily a miniature or a replica of the subject it represents. For instance, a blueprint is in every sense a model and the models used by aircraft designers to study how full-scale planes will perform in actual flight may only approximate the appearance of the completed aircraft. Such items as doors, windows, landing gear, etc., are generally not part of a wind tunnel model. And incidentally, these models, unlike model planes built by hobbyists, won't fly.

A corporate model is a representation of a company, the results or output of which are expressed in financial terms. The structure of such a model includes all the important interrelationships which exist in the company's actual operation and the medium used to represent the model is a computer program. This program would normally be comprised of hundreds of statements or equations which are individually simple but which, taken together, represent the complex of interrelationships which is the company.

The input data to the corporate model specifies the current status of the company and the conditions expected to prevail in the future. The output of the model is a projection or a series of projections representing financial results, based upon the assumptions originally introduced as part of the input.

To give you a better picture of a corporate model let us briefly consider the possible variations, or perhaps I might better say the broad spectrum or range of the model system that might be developed to project the financial results for an illustrative company. There is no single program which can be called *the* model or *the* package.

One approach to the design of such a model might be to require the user to make a projection of sales and to enter this data as input into the system. Similarly the designer would make projections of cost of sales, general and administrative expenses, and taxes. Then the system would read the input data, perform some summarization, and print out various statements. In essence, this particular concept requires the user to do most of the work. Such a system is, essentially, a financial statement generator and represents the most simple type of model that might be constructed.

Simple as it is, this type of system, which I called a model "shell," can be very useful, since it offers distinct advantages over manual methods. But it puts a very heavy burden on the user to make computations external to the system and it falls far short of fully utilizing the computer's innate abilities and capacity. Nevertheless, a model shell might well be the place for some companies to start.

164

However, there is no need to stop here. The system can be refined to compute sales, cost of sales, and general and administrative expenses, based upon predetermined relationships, recognizing, of course, that the complexity of the model is increasing as each underlying detail is added. As must be evident, the purpose behind each of these increasingly sophisticated steps in the refinement of the model is to transfer the computational burden from the user to the system. As the examples have indicated, these refinements substitute basic underlying detail and related formulas for figures which merely represent end product results. In addition, with the expansion of the system the complex of interrelationships which we have previously identified is increasingly recognized within the total program. This means that a change of value in any one element or factor is mechanically, or perhaps I should say electronically, reflected in all subsequent related elements.

So far we have only considered an income statement and by inference, at least, a balance sheet and cash flow statement for a single period of time. Normally we would be interested in projecting a series of statements over a number of time periods. In addition we would want to be able to introduce numerous variables, by item and by year, so that we could ask a wide variety of "what if" questions, and could relate the effect of all the factors under consideration over a specific and extended period of time.

And at this point I am sure a question is formulated in your mind, the question being, "Won't the continued elaboration of the model substantially increase the requirements for data input to the system and thus reintroduce the problems inherent in manual efforts?" You may rightly ask, "Have we gone 360° round the circle?" This could be the case but I doubt that, in practice, the system would be so built. Rather, I would expect that this situation would be met, in part at least, by making use of the computer's ability to generate data itself.

Let us examine this point a little more closely and a little more specifically. Returning again to our previous example, assume we are making a five-year projection of sales. In this situation a simple solution might be to relate the sales units in our time period to the units sold in a previous period. Thus, instead of requiring that each sales figure be supplied as input, the system would compute the unit sales in each of many periods by multiplying units sold in the immediately preceding period by a growth factor, to arrive at sales for the next period. Obviously a comparable approach could be used for raw material, labor, and overhead. Further, this formula could be made variable as to periods or its complexity could be increased in other ways.

However, whatever the formula used, you recognize, I am sure, that this approach implies that, in connection with the development of a model program a data base is being built up within and as a part of the system. A data base, however, is not a static record; it must be updated in keeping with evolving changes. This means that to facilitate this operation a data management system providing forms and instructions must be included as part of the development of the model itself. This is not necessarily a difficult problem but it is certainly an important one, and one that cannot be ignored in the development of the overall system package. I will come back to this data base point again later in another context.

So far in this discussion we have tried to identify the purpose and need for corporate financial models. We have tried to point out the potentially broad spectrum of financial models which might be developed, starting with the simplest shell and continuing through to a model of considerable complexity and sophistication. We have tried to underscore the interrelationships which are such an essential part of their construction and operation. All of these essential factors we have looked at, basically, from the income standpoint. However, the executive and the financial analyst, as well as the investor, are not only interested in net income but also in cash flow. Consequently I would expect that the projection of cash would, in most cases, be a significant element to be considered in model construction.

Following this thought, I would like to comment on a very important relationship which must be observed in developing the overall system for a model. I refer to the chronological relationship of the various events involved. In the model representations of events must be placed in the same sequence as would actually happen. Revenues and cash collections provide one example of this particular point. Naturally the timing of cash collections will vary by industry. In some situations revenues recorded, say, in January would be translated into cash collections, not only for January, but for a number of months that follow. In still other situations the spread of cash collections may have little or no significance. However, there are probably some other items which would be important. In all these instances the model can be designed to account for these items on a routine basis, a feature that significantly enhances the realism of the projection.

And incidentally I might remind you that timing considerations constitute a factor that adds substantially to the computational burden when manual projection methods are used. For instance, tax payments and dividend declarations are items which require proper chronological consideration and which occur at specific times during the year. And the building of facilities in advance of customer or sales growth would be representative of a nonregular but significant occurrence.

Having reached this point in our overview of the corporate financial model, I am sure that many of you have observed great similarities between your budgeting activities and a model. There are no absolute specifics for defining either a budget system or a model, but I will point out certain factors which, I believe, do draw a distinction between these two important tools.

First, I would say that one of the primary purposes of a budget is for control. Responsibility is increasingly becoming a key factor in budgeting. And so-called responsibility accounting systems, which are designed to motivate, control, and appraise performance on the basis of defined responsibility, are now in very general use.

Then, too, the approach to budgeting tends to be from the bottom up. And this is certainly true of a responsibility accounting system, in which you start with the lowest organizational unit and build the flow of costs to the top. This bottom to top structuring is almost bound to reflect what various departmental supervisory personnel *expect* to happen. And this is generally in sharp contrast to an overall viewpoint which identifies what the chief executives of the company *want* to happen. Unfortunately it is all too human to set expectations sufficiently below potential achievement, particularly in situations where an individual has reason to think that his budget will be a target against which his performance will be judged. Let me conclude this part of the discussion on the completely factual point that a budget is routinized; that is, it is scheduled for preparation quarterly, semiannually, or annually, whatever is the appropriate period, and every effort is bent toward meeting this fixed schedule. On the other hand, a corporate financial model is designed for predictive purposes. It is a tool for planning. And, typically, responsibility is not built into the model, since one of the things management may wish to do is make changes in the organization.

Put another way, in a model the emphasis is on the "what" (what is to be accomplished), not on the "who." The "who" implementation comes later. Experimentation is a very important, if not the prime consideration in developing a model. Experimentation should be an aspect of good budgeting too, but I personally don't know of any company that uses its budget in an experimental way.

Perhaps the best way to sum up this whole idea is by simply saying that the name of the model game is "what if," and as a result, the approach to building a model tends to be from the top down.

Finally, the corporate financial model is used irregularly, as contrasted with the regularity of a budget. It is hard for me to imagine the scheduling of a model to be run on any particular day. Its use would normally be triggered by changing economic conditions or by imaginative possibilities arising in the mind of a creative and able executive.

Now, having reached this point, how do you go about building one of these paragons of virtue? Building a model is primarily a matter of defining all the financial and operating relationships as they exist, and placing them in the proper time framework, reducing these relationships to simple arithmetic and logical statements, and then programming them for a computer. These are the four basic steps involved in building a model. They are quickly and easily stated but obviously they are not so easily or quickly executed. Since my purpose is to give an overview, I will not elaborate on these points. Rather, I want to move on and touch upon the subject of design decisions.

In designing the model there are certain very basic decisions which must be made. First, "What is the basic time period?" This simple question embodies within it the need for making a decision that is of critical importance and one that will have tremendous impact on the complexity of the model. In every sense this is one of the key decisions, and it must be made before beginning the construction of the model itself. Are we going to project on a monthly, quarterly, or annual basis?

Today there are available on a prepackaged basis some relatively simple financial models which have limited computational ability and which project on an annual basis. We have several of these which we have developed within our firm. There are occasional inferences that these packages can be easily modified, that they can be used for short-range planning purposes, monthly, for instance. This may be possible. Some type of allocation or apportionment might be made of annual figures to derive the desired monthly data. This approach would probably be satisfactory provided both income and costs are incurred on a relatively uniform or on a predeterminable basis. Needless to say, this would then preclude the need for the built-in calendar within the model. However, if there are important seasonal variations in the business, or if some of the details of day-to-day operation have a substantial impact on the overall results, then it is more than likely that the model will have to be completely redesigned.

Second, "What is the horizon of the model?" In other words, how far out into the future should the model be capable of projecting? This decision is not too difficult to make. An appropriately designed corporate model is capable, in theory at least, of projecting the financial results of the company for an unlimited number of years. There can, of course, be limitations due to file size and other such factors. However, as a practical matter the user will usually be restrained by his diminishing confidence in the correctness of assumed conditions in distant years, and this factor alone will normally set horizon considerations.

It is probably appropriate to note here that a corporate model can be one of the most fantastic generators of paper man has ever developed, and if you are not careful you can actually be buried in paper projections.

The third design decision relates to boundary, and by this is meant what is included in the model and what is excluded. We have already identified this consideration in discussing the possible spectrum of models, starting with the shell and adding increasing sophistication by adding elements. I would again emphasize that all elements need not be in the first version of the model. However, this is only true as long as the design content is there. What I'm really saying here is that the corporate model lends itself well to the use of modular organization for the construction of the model itself. And since it is easy to go overboard in building a model, a slow and directed approach, module by module, is often advisable.

I should mention that the modular construction has another very distinct advantage in that it permits evolutionary refinements and improvements to be made. Experience has already shown that this process of improvement is a continuing one. Thus, the development of a corporate model cannot be considered a one-time project. It must be undertaken with the understanding that, like all other areas of a dynamic enterprise, it becomes a continuing and continuous effort. Without this commitment the development of a model could well be a waste of time and money.

No discussion of design decisions would be complete without some reference to the format of the system as it resides in the computer. Here again there are many avenues of approach. One format that has proved out well is composed of three basic segments: an executive routine, a series of computational modules, and a data base.

The computational modules referred to parallel the modules described earlier to illustrate the broad spectrum of possible models. Each of these modules contains all of the logical formulas required to compute and project the data relating to its own particular segment. In addition the module contains all of the programming required to develop any related statistics. The data base contains certain items called factors (which I will describe in a moment) as well as start-up data and projected results. The executive routine then validates the input, places the modules into the working area of the computer, maintains the files, and prints the output.

As an example of the items called factors, let us consider those which concern personnel. The first of such factors relates to the number of employees. This is followed by factors projecting increases in rates and providing for changes in the numbers of officers and employees. In a simplified form, average labor rates by plant and average manning by plant might be used. In a highly sophisticated form, manning by classification rates, by employee class, etc., might be in order. As I mentioned earlier, at this point in time I advocate simplicity. Perhaps the most important point to be made here is to note that with this format changes in factors, which means changes in the assumptions used in the model, can be made with great simplicity and no reprogramming is necessary.

Returning to design decisions, the fourth, depth of detail, involves another very important decision which must be made. In maintaining a reasonable degree of simplicity, it is most important to identify those items and relationships which have a substantial impact upon financial results and those with little or no impact. The important items are included; the less important are excluded. Here is a significant difference between a budget and a model, which can look at an operation on a very gross basis and still be useful.

The scope or, as it is sometimes expressed, the level of abstraction of the model is influenced by numerous considerations. However, I would like to make one point here. At this early stage in the history of the corporate model the substantial effort required to design and construct the model can end up as merely an exercise in ingenuity unless corporate management has the confidence to accept and use it.

There are many points which might be discussed under the subject of confidence builders and the level of abstraction is an important one. I say this because it is entirely possible that a high degree of abstraction, while representing a plus in the mechanics of building the model itself, may, from a practical standpoint, be completely self-defeating. It is well to remember that this particular technique can be a confidence destroyer to the extent that it raises questions of validity in the mind of the ultimate user. Consequently, in building a model it may be well to include certain detail which could and eventually may be eliminated.

To go on, since there are no practical limits to the degree of complexity and sophistication which can be built into a model, how, you may ask, do you control the efforts of the individuals who are designing the system? One very practical way is to establish time limits for the development of any single area. This may be a unique method of controlling the design of a system but the corporate financial model is a unique new tool.

Before closing these remarks on building a model, a word of warning is probably in order. During the process of building a model it is essential that particular effort be made and that proper tests be incorporated into the program to assure that the model is a reasonable representation of the company. The degree of abstraction will be an important element in determining the degree or extent of the testing and, obviously, this will vary by module. Unlike systems designed to process the more routine type of function such as payroll, the output of a model from a practical standpoint cannot be tied to exact and predetermined controls. Thus there is a need for very careful testing throughout the entire construction process.

Up to this point in our discussion the entire emphasis of our remarks has been directed toward what a corporate financial model is. A brief word on what a corporate financial model is not is certainly in order. Historically, the term model as used in business has been identified with work performed by specialists in the management sciences and in Operations Research and often in reference to an optimization type of model. Let me be most specific and very emphatic. A corporate model, in an overall sense, is *not* an optimization model. This means that the model, as a whole, does not contain a mechanism whereby it automatically and efficiently searches for the best solution to a business problem. However, an executive using a corporate model can evaluate the financial results of alternative courses of action. Then, based on his experience and judgment and by using trial and error, he can usually reach a satisfactory solution which may approximate or even equal the best possible solution.

I have stressed that corporate models may be built in segments or modules. I should make clear that certain of these segments could contain optimizing programs and others could include techniques for dealing with situations that are characterized by great uncertainty. Ultimately corporate models may completely evolve into optimization-type models, but at this time it appears that this development is some distance away from achievement.

Having generalized rather broadly on the concept of corporate models and having, to the extent possible in a presentation such as this, introduced some basic conditions involved in their construction, it seems appropriate to take the last few minutes of my time to identify for you the current status of model development in the United States as determined by what is believed to be the most recent survey, and then to close by summarizing the potential advantages and uses of the model. The survey was conducted several months ago by a professional society known as The Planning Executives Institute. The Institute received responses from over 300 companies, 102 of the respondents indicating that they have a corporate model, they are building one or intend to begin the development of one prior to the end of 1969.

My own experience has shown that there are a great many different opinions about what constitutes a corporate financial model. One company will use a time-sharing terminal and have ten pieces of data which go in to project one figure coming out, and they say they have a corporate model. Another company has a very elaborate system which projects financial statements by months for two years and then annually for many years thereafter, and they say they have a corporate model. Obviously these two systems are quite different.

The purist probably defines a corporate model as a comprehensive, coordinated, global representation of a company. At this stage of development, however, I'm not sure that this is significant. In the innovation of advanced business systems nomenclature, semantics, and exaggerated boundary definitions are often as great a stumbling block to discussion and consideration of a particular approach as are the underlying technical details. What is important at this juncture is the potential uses and advantages to be found in this embryonic technique. No matter what it is called or how performed, certainly the most obvious use is to assist management in the development of long-range corporate plans.

To develop such a plan the executive would, using the model, investigate a variety of alternative courses of action under dif-ferent sets of assumed conditions, and then select the most appropriate for the current and forecasted period. Then whenever new information causes the executive to change his assumptions or strategy the corporate model would be used to evaluate the effect of a revised plan, quickly and inexpensively. This means that the executive can have at all times a detailed up-to-the-minute long-range plan.

At this point in time I would emphasize that the development and use of the corporate model is still very much in its infancy. How far will the sophistication be carried? As in most fields, it is difficult to foresee with accuracy the changes to be wrought by the future. However, one trend has proved irreversible since the first mercantile operation was established. This has been the constant thrust to upgrade man's skills in operating and directing the enterprises which he creates and builds.

Melvin Anshen, the distinguished Professor of Business at Columbia University Graduate School, made an observation in a recent *Harvard Business Review* article, with which I heartily agree. Professor Anshen said, "New analytical techniques, largely quantitive and computer based, are presenting a management opportunity that is unique in at least two important ways. First, they provide an administrative capability without parallel in breadth, depth and speed. Second, for their full and efficient utilization, they press management to establish a unified command over the totality of a business, including the dynamic interface of external environment and internal activities."

The corporate financial model is certainly a new technique that falls within the purview of Professor Anshen's observations. Here is the opportunity. The question is "What will we do with it?" Only the future can answer this question.

Mr. Glickauf and the computer model he built and used for demonstration purposes.

Reflections on a quarter century in administrative services (1970)

Leadership is a commodity that is in exceedingly short supply in our world today.

IN line with the firm policy of relieving its personnel of administrative duties some years before their actual retirement, I have recently given up my responsibilities as head of the Administrative Services Division of the firm. In this connection, it seems appropriate to set down a brief summary of the development and activities of the division during the approximately twenty-five years of its existence, a period which parallels my own career with the firm.

Systems work was, of course, performed by individuals associated with the firm long before our division was formally organized and, in order to secure background information with respect to those early efforts, I thought it might be worthwhile if I were to refresh my memory by spending some time perusing the archives of the firm.

My research proved to be both an educational and enriching experience, and it revealed informative and interesting background material far beyond that which I can say, in all honesty, I had thought was in store for me.

I had no idea how deeply entrenched nor how far back the roots of our present practice penetrated.

I knew that we had handled certain engagements during the early 1940's, and I had heard of some scattered work during the 1930's, but I was surprised to find that as far back as 1918, in the very first decade of our firm's existence, we had a department whose functions were distinctly separate from our audit and tax practice.

I suppose I should be careful about making too close a comparison between our present and our pioneering work, for in those early days our efforts involved some areas that were far different and certainly far removed from those functions which fall within the constraints which we place around the current scope of our administrative services practice. The record shows that our pioneering unit was called the Industrial Engineering Department, and most of the engagements handled by this group were referred to as industrial and financial investigations. Many of these investigations were made at the request of investment banking firms which were considering the sale of bond or preferred stock issues for the companies involved.

The record for this period is necessarily dim, as almost half a century has passed since these early furrows were plowed in the systems field, but I gained the distinct impression that most of the work was directed toward the study of the past and possible future profitability of a business. This study involved an analysis and evaluation of, first, the equipment of the business, including the buildings and machinery, the personnel, and the products; second, the means for controlling and directing the use of the equipment, in short, management; and third, the conditions under which the equipment was used, including competition, markets, location, etc.

These industrial and financial investigations of the 1920's are discussed in detail by Arthur Andersen in the collection of his speeches and articles published by our firm in 1970 under the title, *Behind the Figures*.

The Industrial Engineering Department disappeared with the depression of the early thirties and the enactment of the Securities Acts, but it is interesting to note that in spite of the contrast with present practice, the changes in conditions, and the tremendous differences in technology, most of the basic fundamentals which we still follow today were, even at that early date, distinctly identified and clearly enunciated. For instance, in a summary of the department's operations dated in 1923, it was pointed out: that there was a need for the firm to provide formal as well as "on-the-job" training to staff personnel; (this we still do;) that the department must be an integral part of the firm, supported by the wholehearted interest of all the partners; (it still is;) that engagements should not be limited to reviews and consultation, but we should be ready and eager to assist in the actual installation and implementation and, finally, that all engagements should use client personnel to the extent possible, an imperative we still endorse.

One can only comment that, in spite of all the modern wonders of the world we live in, not everything under the sun is truly new.

Yet, in retrospect, I view those early efforts as the shadow of events to come; the substance of a firm foundation for the future.

Factually, it can be said that World War II laid the groundwork for our present systems division, for it was the almost unbelievable variety of mechanized data processing procedures used by every branch of the military that exposed thousands of present and prospective business executives to the potential that lay in an assortment of noisy machines and multi-colored cards, each of which contained a coded array of little punched holes. There are probably few today who recall that so extensive was the use of this new technique by the armed services that portable processing units, complete with key punch and machine operators and attended by highly competent maintenance technicians, were installed on enormous trailer units and shipped overseas to be used in the immediate battle zone.

An army may move on its stomach, but battles and wars are won because of superior intelligence and information. Above the sound of bugle, drum and cannonade, the business office was unknowingly being catapulted into a mechanized era. Many men and women were going to be swept along with it. I was among that group.

174

With the end of the war, two of my Navy associates, Walter Oliphant (who later became the managing partner of the firm) and John Higgins (who, before his untimely death, was Director of Administration) convinced me that I should join the firm of Arthur Andersen & Co. The fledgling systems department to which I was assigned had a total complement of about half a dozen, myself included. Parenthetically, the division had reached the 1150 mark by January, 1970.

This is probably an appropriate place to take note of the name of our division. Upon my arrival it was called the Administrative Accounting Department, and this title continued in use for a brief period. About two years later the name of the department was changed to Administrative Services, a name which we retain today.

I have already mentioned the impending era of mechanization in business. And it was truly the postwar acceptance of the use of punched cards for record keeping and accounting purposes, as distinct from their prewar use as a means for performing relatively simple statistical and analytical work, that provided the springboard for the first stage of development of our small but emerging systems practice.

Naturally, the transition to punched cards did not take place overnight, and this was due in part to the very real doubt by many an executive as to whether it was safe to commit his important records and carefully bound ledgers to the vagaries of an easily lost or mutilated piece of thin paper card. As a consequence of this widely held (and not completely unwarranted) mistrust, our first engagements were heavily slanted toward a concept of mechanized systems which left readily identifiable tracks and easily followed trails, and in explaining to the client just how their records could be reconstructed and replaced if a catastrophe actually took place. But confidence grew with experience and the field of business

mechanization continued to expand, and so did our little department.

If I were asked to pinpoint the one item which provided the greatest impetus to our early growth, I would unhesitatingly reply, the emphasis we gave to the development and recognition of a concept which subsequently became generally known as Responsibility Accounting.

The idea of controlling expenditures by relating the reporting of such expenditures to the individuals responsible for their control had been thought about and experimented with by numerous individuals over a great many years. But the problem of maintaining records that would provide data and produce reports for the multiple purpose of pricing inventories, developing product costs and, at the same time, provide the means for cost control on the basis of "who done it," represented a figure juggling operation on a manual basis of immense proportions.

With the advent of the punched card, however, it became possible to tailor a system to an organization so that costs were accumulated and reported by levels of responsibility within the organization, and then to reshuffle the deck of cards, so to speak, to arrive at product costs and the costs required for inventory pricing.

Public utilities were among the first to experiment with this concept and they found that it provided them with an entirely new dimension in operational control. I spent several years working with utilities in this area. Responsibility accounting effectively freed a utility from the constraints imposed by regulatory reporting while still permitting full compliance with all authoritative requirements. In this type of engagement the need for the dual skill of the accountant and the expert in the systems field was joined, possibly for the first time. Certainly it could be said that at this point the dimension and direction of the systems practice within the profession of public accounting began to take shape and identifiable form.

Around 1950 whispers began to circulate about the conversion for business purposes of a device of almost unbelievable speed and power which it was said, in its original design, had had tremendous significance in the scientific field. It was even suggested that this device was responsible for handling the mathematics required in developing the atom bomb. It was further hinted that two professors at the University of Pennsylvania were responsible for this transitional development.

It immediately became my objective to gain entrance to their laboratory. I was fortunate to find two close friends who were interested in this new development and who were in a position to make the necessary arrangements. Within a short time we were to see a prototype of the BIVAC, a formidable predecessor of the first electronic computer for business purposes.

If my mind is hazy about the exact date of the event, it is vividly clear with respect to the scenes in the laboratory and the events that transpired. I can still see in sharp detail the various components of the equipment as they were arranged in what appeared to be haphazard groupings in the laboratory workshop: input devices sitting on wooden sawhorses, a maze of wires sprawling around the floor like a zoo full of snakes, and twin towers of electronic gear looking not unlike the amateur radio transmitter I had constructed in my home many years previously.

The demonstration we were given was impressive, if brief. But it took no genius to see that we had before us a device that would outrun, outpower and outmode every device that preceded it. I left Philadelphia with a mission. It was to convince everyone I encountered, not only within the firm but also without, that this day I had indeed seen a vision of what would soon become a revolutionary reality.

If I erred in my enthusiasm, it was not an error of judgment, but only of timing. To me this electronic device which I had just seen was truly a wonder without compare. And because of my background and natural inclination, I then and there determined to build a model composed of all the principal units which would illustrate the operation and, in particular, the speed of this new device.

This I did. And this, I believe, was one of the most important efforts in my business career. This model computer was displayed across the country in offices and universities, and with its various identifiable components and flashing neon lights, it helped untold number of individuals to visualize what was most difficult to describe and certainly hard to believe.

Unquestionably the model had a tremendous impact within our firm, and it had a great deal to do with the support the partners gave to the development of a group of individuals who would be competent to work in this new systems area. As a consequence of all of this early preparation, a few years later the firm was entrusted with the installation of the first electronic computer to be used for business purposes, and I was given the supervisory responsibility.

The installation itself was, as would be expected, the combined responsibility of the client, the equipment manufacturer and ourselves. And even after all the years which have passed, it is difficult to place in proper perspective the enormous effort which was required to install this first business computer. However, one thing emerges clearly. Many of the difficulties that were overcome were not just solutions to the immediate problems of the moment, but were the seeds for numerous basic concepts which are today deeply rooted in the computer sciences field.

Let me say a bit more about those exciting and nerve-racking days. The client selected three functions to be computerized, the principal one being payroll. After many days and nights of what could only be described as Herculean efforts, the computer program was finally completed and the first payroll was ready to run. It was anticipated that the entire payroll would be run in a relatively short period of time. But after many hours of computer processing it became very evident that this first attempt was not going to successfully meet the rather limited time schedule which was a basic requirement of the client's system. As a result, the entire payroll program had to be completely redone.

One of the major reasons for the excessive time required to prepare the payroll was the frequent interruption to the processing operation due to a multitude of errors in the input data. It was evident that if you were going to have a high-speed operation in electronic data processing, you had to develop a system that was closely analogous to a high-speed transportation system. In short, runs had to be made without local stops. From this evolved the idea of validating data immediately upon its introduction into the computer system, a principle which is quite common today.

The analysis that was performed in preparation for reworking the payroll brought to light many items which, in the light of current sophistication, appear simple and self-evident. For instance, having completed the first go around, it was recognized that some items were the same in every computer run. These similarities included such functions as reading a record, checking the label, grouping and ungrouping records, writing the records out, etc. In order to capitalize on this feature of commonality, mimeographed flow charts were prepared for all items that would be similar in various runs. Next, mimeographed sheets containing the related coding were prepared. And, finally, the idea emerged of developing a shell which would embrace all of these functions on a preprogrammed basis. The programmers then fitted the detailed steps of their processing routines into this shell.

In a sense, this was the moment of conception of what has grown into the gigantic industry of software. But, of course, at that time no one foresaw this future. Rather, all of these ideas were devised simply to place the computer in an operational status. Fortunately, they were successful and the first hurdles were cleared.

However, even after the installation was finally completed and was running in reasonably routine fashion, all was not beer and skittles. My most vivid recollection of this whole period is of what occurred toward the end of the engagement. The client was just getting ready to run the plant payroll and the computer maintenance technician was completing his preventive maintenance check, when the screwdriver he was holding slipped from his fingers and fell across a high voltage bus bar and the line carrying current to the filaments of at least half the vacuum tubes in the computer. I suppose that the only event that I could compare with this catastrophe would be the blackout on the east coast several years ago. Our computer wasn't just down, it was out!

In this connection, it must be remembered that while those first generation computers used many vacuum tubes which, by number and type, were identical with those used in electronic devices for home entertainment, you just couldn't go down to the corner radio store for replacements. First, of course, a retailer wouldn't normally carry the necessary quantity in stock but, more importantly, tubes for those first generation computers had to be especially selected and matched.

Our replacement tubes would be many days in coming from the manufacturer, and the payroll couldn't wait. So personnel, tapes, and all the other paraphernalia required in the payroll processing operation were hastily assembled and loaded aboard a plane for a flight back to the factory, the only place where there was another machine available.

177

In the end, everything turned out well, and the payroll checks were completed and available on time. While no doubt a number of hairs turned gray over the incident, an increased degree of confidence was established and the acceptance of electronic data processing took a long step forward.

The early use of the electronic computer in business was limited, for the most part, to the performance of routine accounting functions, which it was able to do effectively because of its tremendous speed. But as time went on, there was a change from the emphasis on historical reporting to one of reporting in terms of the future and providing data for forming reliable management judgments and effective management controls. The use of the computer in assisting management to plan for future operations will be discussed later on.

Almost concurrently with the early development of the computer, another new development began to appear on the American business scene. This was called Operations Research, a term which probably was more of a hindrance than a help as far as its acceptance by the American businessman was concerned. Interestingly enough, Operations Research was developed in Britain during World War II. Since that time this highly sophisticated mathematical technique has found increasing use in helping to solve complex problems of business and government.

Even as steel bars reinforce concrete and make the whole structure stronger, so individuals grounded in this new discipline brought to our division a new dimension in systems work, enlarged our perspective on problems and their solutions and, in a very real sense, added materially to our total overall competence. In more recent years, we have brought into our division individuals, both men and women, with a wide variety of educational backgrounds and everything I have said about those individuals whose expertise lay in the field of

quantitative methods certainly applies to these other men and women as well.

During the decade of the 1950's, under the leadership of Leonard Spacek, the firm adopted the policy of rapidly expanding the number of its offices outside of the United States. Administrative services work, if it achieves its proper purpose of service to clients, has a significant effect in building a firm's reputation and growth. It is not strange, then, that the decision was quickly reached to push the development of our systems practice overseas, starting in Europe.

Our policy for developing an administrative services practice overseas was the same as that for the development of an audit and a tax practice, namely to build upon the nationals of the various countries. It was, of course, necessary to provide initial supervision and training from the United States, but this was only a temporary expedient. Building from within a country may be the slow way, but without question it makes good business sense. Today in most international offices administrative services has acquired sufficient maturity to enable the foreign nationals to take over on their own, and the development of these practices is gaining momentum rapidly.

There were, of course, many unusual problems which were encountered in the development of overseas systems practices, and these problems varied from country to country, as illustrated in a previous chapter covering my April, 1962, address on Machine Accounting in Europe. But in spite of these problems, the overseas practices have continued to develop and expand. In fact, several of the largest Administrative Services Divisions in the firm are now located outside the United States, and the contribution of the international divisions as a whole is increasing in importance every year.

To return to our discussion of the electronic computer, during the first ten years of its use in industry it was principally devoted to the processing of data, or datamation, as it has since been called. The mid-1960's saw the development of a change in emphasis from datamation to automation and the cybernetic era was getting under way. The term "cybernetics" is derived from a Greek word meaning helmsman and it is now being used to identify the entire field of control and communication as applied to any self-adjusting or self-regulating mechanism or system. From the standpoint of the business office, the term may be defined as the science of guidance and control based on information.

With the techniques of cybernation, which are described in more detail in previous chapters, it became possible to install systems which would automatically control production processes and report the accounting data required for bookkeeping purposes. The installation of such systems was a highly complicated matter and required the efforts of a team composed of individuals with varied abilities, educational backgrounds, and experience. It particularly required that the team have the ability to communicate with each other and with client personnel at all levels. Equally important was the requirement of a master plan which would ensure that everything that was to be accomplished would fit together. The installation of such systems (some of which are described in previous addresses) represented a large step forward in the development of our administrative services practice.

During the latter half of the 1960's the use of the computer, aided by advanced mathematical techniques, began to be extended beyond the processing of routine accounting and bookkeeping functions. For the first time, the future so long forecast for this exciting device started to be realized. At long last, the computer began to touch upon areas related to the executive's field of responsibility. One of these areas is that of long-range planning. Here, through the use of a technique called Corporate Model-

ing, the computer can be of tremendous assistance to top management in the planning function. Planning and forecasting techniques have, of course, been in use for many years with manual projections being made of assumed future company activities. However, such projections have been extremely time consuming, only a minimum of alternative plans could be considered, and it was not possible to consider all of the significant interrelationships of the various assumptions which were made. By the time the manual forecast had been completed, conditions had often changed to such an extent that the forecast had to be adjusted by strong-arm methods and the result was apt to be unreliable, to say the least.

Most of the difficulties encountered in making financial projections by manual methods have been overcome through the use of the computer and the model. Now it is possible for management to consider all reasonable alternatives and interrelationships, to test different assumptions about the future, and investigate the effect of various courses of action. As Leonard Spacek has remarked, "This is management firepower never dreamed of before."

This, then, is the history of the past twenty-five years.

The past, I have always felt, is something to learn from and then to forget. What is important is today and tomorrow.

In spite of the emphasis which I may have appeared to have given to the means and the methods used in our practice, it is vital to remember that our business is not computers or communication devices, not manufacturing controls or sophisticated mathematical techniques. Our business is to provide leadership; this is the service our clients need and want. Leadership is a commodity that is in exceedingly short supply in our world today. There is a crying need for leadership in all phases of government, in social service activities, and certainly in business.

If we provide this commodity, then in truth we will have only scratched the surface in the area of administrative services. We will have only taken the first step toward the future, and we can know with complete conviction that the opportunities for tomorrow will far exceed those of yesterday.